# India's Fiscal Policy

Fiscal policy has gained salience amid the challenges policymakers are facing in a post-crisis world. This book seeks to balance normative prescriptions on fiscal policy with its practical aspects in context of the Indian scenario. In doing so, it brings together views of leading experts from academic and policy spheres. It seeks to highlight the specificities of Indian fiscal policy and studies current issues like the impact of development expenditures, the GST, the challenge of reducing subsidies, and different aspects of political economy.

*India's Fiscal Policy* discusses rapid developments in the field following the fiscal stimulus of 2008, subsequent attempts at fiscal consolidation, and the formation of the NDA government. It focuses on policy and political considerations and adopts a wider approach for the analysis of fiscal policy by taking into consideration aspects such as the effectiveness and targeting of social expenditures, which are essential for a critical analysis of the Indian policy matrix.

**Supriyo De** is Senior Economist at the World Bank, Washington D.C. Prior to this he was Officer on Special Duty to the Chief Economic Adviser of India. He has a PhD in Economics from the University of Sydney and was a recipient of the Endeavour International Postgraduate Research Scholarship. His research interests include analysis of sovereign credit ratings, macroeconomic impacts of remittances, fiscal policy in developing economies, endogenous growth theory, technology policy and intangible capital.

# India's Fiscal Policy
## Prescriptions, Pragmatics and Practice

*Edited by*
Supriyo De

CAMBRIDGE
UNIVERSITY PRESS

CAMBRIDGE
UNIVERSITY PRESS

University Printing House, Cambridge CB2 8BS, United Kingdom
One Liberty Plaza, 20th Floor, New York, NY 10006, USA
477 Williamstown Road, Port Melbourne, vic 3207, Australia
314–321, 3rd Floor, Plot 3, Splendor Forum, Jasola District Centre,
New Delhi – 110025, India
79 Anson Road, #06–04/06, Singapore 079906

Cambridge University Press is part of the University of Cambridge.

It furthers the University's mission by disseminating knowledge in the pursuit of education, learning and research at the highest international levels of excellence.

www.cambridge.org
Information on this title: www.cambridge.org/9781107152632



First published 2017
Reprint 2020

Printed in India by Thomson Press India Ltd.

*A catalogue record for this publication is available from the British Library*

*Library of Congress Cataloging-in-Publication Data*

Names: De, Supriyo, editor.
Title: India's fiscal policy : prescriptions, pragmatics and practice / edited by Supriyo De.
Description: New York : Cambridge University Press, 2016. | Includes bibliographical references and index.
Identifiers: LCCN 2016030024 | ISBN 9781107152632 (hardback)
Subjects: LCSH: Fiscal policy—India. | Finance, Public—India.
Classification: LCC HJ1335 .I53 2016 | DDC 339.5/20954—dc23 LC record available at https://lccn.loc.gov/2016030024

ISBN 978-1-107-15263-2 Hardback

# Contents


| | | |
|---|---|---|
| *Foreword* | | *vii* |
| *Acknowledgements* | | *ix* |
| *Disclaimer* | | *x* |
| *Introduction: Contours of the Indian Fiscal Policy Debate* | | *xi* |
| 1. | Fiscal Policy in India: Trends and Trajectory<br>*Supriyo De* | 1 |
| 2. | Decentralization, Indirect Tax Reform and Fiscal Federalism in India<br>*Raghbendra Jha* | 35 |
| 3. | Fiscal Implications of Energy Subsidies<br>*S. Narayan* | 87 |
| 4. | Fiscal Implications of Food Security in India: A Critical Review<br>*N. R. Bhanumurthy and Ruth Kattumuri* | 111 |
| 5. | Land and Food Acts: Trading Economic Pragmatism for Political Gain<br>*Amitendu Palit* | 138 |
| 6. | A Separate Debt Management Office in India<br>*Charan Singh* | 155 |
| 7. | Show Me the Cash: Direct Benefits Transfer in India<br>*Rajesh Chakrabarti* | 182 |
| 8. | India's Education Challenges: Expenditure Effectiveness Issues<br>*Anu Rammohan and Itismita Mohanty* | 211 |
| *List of Contributors* | | 227 |
| *Index* | | 229 |

# Foreword

Fiscal policy is one of those unusual subjects on which there are more people who hold an opinion than know what it means. More worryingly, political leaders get to shape it often with the most rudimentary notion of what it implies for the economy. Yet the importance of fiscal policy is immense. Wrongly done, it can stall growth, increase bureaucratic costs, fuel inflation, and cause income distribution to deteriorate. And, by the obverse, it can contribute to enhancing our well-being on all those dimensions if it is designed right.

I am especially sensitive to the importance of this subject because I learnt what I did by fire, when I joined the Ministry of Finance in New Delhi, in 2009, as Chief Economic Adviser to the government. Fiscal policy was my major concern during those nearly-three years that I spent in government, by virtue of the fact that a large part of the work in the Ministry of Finance is related to the Union Budget. I had acutely felt the need for more research and better books that connect the tomes of work on the theory of fiscal policy done in universities and specialized research institutes to the challenges faced by India. And the challenges were, and are, many. India's tax revenue collection is too small compared to its GDP. If this can be enhanced by another 50 per cent, which is entirely within the realm of the possible, the country can have vastly better infrastructure – ports, railway, roads, power – and it could do much more to promote health, nutrition, education, among the poor, thereby closing some of the earnings gap and also promoting overall growth. India has systems of distributing food grain, health services and education to the poor but the organization is complex and plagued by fiscal leakages.

I am delighted to have in my hand a book which begins to deliver on precisely this need. *India's Fiscal Policy: Prescriptions, Pragmatics and Practice* edited by Supriyo De stands out for its effort to bring together the best of theoretical knowledge and ground realities of India between the covers of one book. It is also surprisingly topical. The book discusses at length the importance of the Goods and Services Tax (GST), and how it can be implemented well. The passing of the GST Bill by the Indian parliament earlier in 2016 was a landmark. If this is implemented well it can boost GDP not just by making the tax system more rational but by cutting down the transactions cost of paying taxes, which imposes a major bureaucratic cost on business enterprises in India, especially ones that operate across the states. The GST can be a major nudge towards a single market.

The book also analyzes food security, land acquisition, the panoply of taxes and subsidies that the energy sector has to deal with, and many other important and topical subjects. Apart from having major distributional impact, these taxes and subsidies also have important implications for the environment and for pollution control, topics of great urgency for India. Over and above all this, the book begins with a primer on fiscal policy which can be extremely handy for not just economics students but those thrust into high office without sufficient advance notice.

My only complaint about the book is that I did not have it when I worked as Chief Economic Adviser in India.

Kaushik Basu
*C. Marks Professor and Professor of Economics*
*Cornell University, New York*
*Former Chief Economist, The World Bank*

# Acknowledgements

At the outset I would like to thank Professor Kaushik Basu who encouraged me to write the Ministry of Finance working paper around which this book evolved. The mentoring I received from Professor Raghuram Rajan greatly increased my understanding of India's fiscal policy. Thanks are also due to the Ministry of Finance for granting leave and the Australia India Institute, University of Melbourne for the Emerging Leader's Fellowship during which the initial idea behind this endeavour germinated. In that respect, I also acknowledge the role played by Professor Amitabh Mattoo and others at the Australia India Institute who rekindled my research interests in this area. I am also indebted to many colleagues in the Indian Ministry of Finance, the Income Tax Department and the National Institute of Public Finance and Policy who shaped my appreciation of the intricacies of India's complex fiscal architecture.

Thanks are due to the authors who contributed to this book. The diligent and detailed comments of several anonymous reviewers helped improve and fine-tune the chapters greatly. The comments and suggestions of Sanjay Banerji, Rudrani Bhattacharya, Sacchidananda Mukherjee and Nirvikar Singh were extremely valuable.

My wife Monica gave enduring inspiration and helped in drafting and revising large parts of the book. Finally, this book would not have reached completion without the perseverance and dedication of the managing editor and others at Cambridge University Press.

# Disclaimer

# Introduction: Contours of the Indian Fiscal Policy Debate

Fiscal policy has gained salience amidst the challenges facing policymakers in the post-crisis world. As the title suggests, this book seeks to balance normative prescriptions on fiscal policy with its practical aspects in the context of the Indian scenario. In doing so, it brings together views of leading experts from academic and policy spheres. This book seeks to highlight the specificities of Indian fiscal policy (which are often not covered by conventional 'text book' approaches) to provide readers with a conceptual base as also bring them abreast with the most recent developments. Current issues like the impact of development expenditures, the challenge of reducing subsidies and political economy aspects are focussed upon. Considering rapid developments in the field, especially following the fiscal stimulus of 2008, subsequent attempts at fiscal consolidation and the formation of the NDA government, a fresh look into India's fiscal policy is warranted.

This book is different from others on the subject in terms of its focus on policy and political considerations, which have gained increasing importance in the Indian context. This is driven by the very obvious observation that divergences between prescribed fiscal policy options and actual practices, quite evident in most countries, are even more prolific in the Indian context. For instance, professional economists unanimously endorse a nation-wide goods and services tax (GST) and the need to curb subsidies. Yet, India's GST legislation process dragged on for many years while energy subsidies persist and food subsidy commitments were enhanced recently. These aspects are discussed threadbare in some of the chapters (Chapters 2–4). In debatable policy issues such as the separation of debt management from central banking, agreement and action seem to evade us forever (Chapter 6). It also adopts a wider approach for the analysis of fiscal policy by taking into consideration aspects such as political motivations and, the effectiveness and targeting of social expenditures, which are essential for a critical analysis of the Indian policy matrix (discussed in Chapters 5, 7 and 8).

This book proposes to cater to a large but often neglected readership – those who may not have a strong formal background in economics but need to grasp the essentials and complexities of India's fiscal policy; students of professionally oriented programmes such as Master of Business Administration or Public Policy/Administration, corporate executives including those in multinationals, staff at multilateral institutions and government officials.[1] It could also be used as a primer or supplementary material for undergraduate students of economics for public finance or macroeconomics courses.[2] This book, therefore, adopts a style that is bereft of jargon and explains the basic concepts required for an understanding of the subject. For the academic or industry economist, its utility would lie in its description of facts that are often not found collected in one place and also a focus on the most recent policy debates and dilemmas.

With purchasing power parity gross domestic product (GDP) of over $7 trillion (constant 2011 international $), India is the fourth largest economy in the world and home to around 1.3 billion people. India's per capita income (PPP-adjusted) at just over $5,500 makes it a lower middle-income country as per the World Bank classification. Since liberalization of the economy in 1991, the country has witnessed phenomenal growth. On the eve of the Global Financial Crisis in 2007, India was growing at a scorching pace of over 8 per cent. The Indian economy weathered the crisis rather well with the growth rate slowing to only around 4 per cent in 2008 when the high-income economies were nearly stagnant. India's growth bounced back to just over 8 per cent in 2009 even as high-income countries shrank by over 3 per cent.[3] The crisis and subsequent developments saw India become part of the G20, the group of large developed and developing economies that plays a key role in global economic governance. After a brief slowdown, it is projected to grow at around 7.6 per cent in 2015 and accelerate to 7.7 per cent in 2017.[4] This gives India a salient place among global economies in terms of growth momentum.

Yet, vast challenges remain. India accounts for one third of the world's poor, a whopping 400 million people. Social and economic inequality abounds and is heightened by factors such as gender and caste. Regional divergences in terms of income and growth are also abundant. The poorest state Bihar has a per capita net state domestic product that is around one eighth of that of the rich states such as Goa and Delhi.[5] Illiteracy, poor educational outcomes and slim employment opportunities threaten to derail a demographic dividend.

These dichotomies, rapid growth and persistent poverty, burgeoning opportunities available to the privileged few, great wealth amidst backbreaking poverty, shape the fiscal policy debate in India. The first manifestation of this is the tension between taxation and redistributive expenditures and subsidies. Furthermore, the underlying systems require substantial overhaul to cope with emerging challenges. Finally, the way the political debate is shaped tends to gravitate towards fairly irreversible outcomes that erode fiscal balances.

In its entirety, four main messages arise from this book. The first is the need to enhance revenues and refine the tax system, especially through the GST. Second, there is need for overhauling the architecture of some aspects of the fiscal landscape, such as fiscal federal relations and the debt management system. Third, effectiveness of allocated expenditures should to be enhanced through better targeting using devices such as direct cash transfers or improving outcomes in social sectors. Last but not the least, the political system has to evolve a mechanism through which redistributive urges are balanced against fiscal discipline considerations.

This book commences with this introductory essay followed by a chapter examining the trajectory of India's fiscal policy. The former places the Indian fiscal policy debate within the larger context of India's dynamic economy. The latter focusses on historical trends, fiscal discipline frameworks, responses to the global financial crisis and recent budgets. This part also deals with basic concepts in an approachable manner and prepares the reader for the more complicated arguments that follow.

The second chapter discusses the federal structure and evaluates the case for the GST. Indirect tax reform, the chapter avers, has been shackled by Constitutional provisions due to which neither the central nor state governments have the authority to levy taxes on a comprehensive base of all goods and services across all stages of production and supply. It finds that there is a case for the GST highlighting the cascading and frictional impacts of the current system. Furthermore, it argues that the federal transfer formula must cushion the fiscal implications of such a move on the states. The chapter also posits that there is an urgent need to review the totality of transfers from the central to state governments and local bodies.

The third chapter seeks to examine the vexing issue of the impact of energy subsidies on India's public finances. Political economy constraints that contribute to their persistence are discussed. It highlights that while in the oil sector, the aim is to protect consumers from the full impact of market-determined prices, in the power sector, the politically important rural consumers drive the demand for subsidies. The renewable energy sector, on the other hand, has price distortions due to input capital subsidies. Consequently, this cocktail of subsidies impacts the fiscal balance at the state as well as the central level. It also makes the system complex, fairly opaque and prone to inefficiencies.

The contentious National Food Security Act, which is the largest welfare programme in the world to alleviate hunger and malnutrition, and its fiscal implications, is the focus of the fourth chapter.

Continuing with the theme of politically oriented economic policies in India, the fifth chapter highlights the nuanced shift towards rights-based legislations during the tenure of the Congress-led UPA government. The chapter argues that while the new Land Acquisition Act, 2013, and the National Food Security Act, 2013, were vanguards of the rights-oriented focus by legally empowering individuals and households to higher economic entitlements, the two legislations, were not bereft of political motives. The possible fiscal impacts of these developments are analysed. It reiterates the disturbing possibility that if the current land acquisition law makes cost of land-intensive development excessively high, it might actually lead to greater demand for fiscal incentives from industry for undertaking new projects. Furthermore, slowdown in real-estate transactions may hurt sub-national tax collections such as property taxes and stamp duties.

Practical aspects of debt management are the focus of the sixth chapter. It states that the main objective of debt management is to minimize the cost of borrowings over the medium to long run, consistent with a prudent degree of risk. The chapter reveals the arguments for a separate debt management office as well as the post-crisis rethinking of the issue of separation of monetary policy, fiscal policy and debt management. In balance, it finds that separation of debt management will help establish transparency, and assign specific responsibility and accountability on the debt manager.

Continuing with implementation aspects, the seventh chapter on direct cash transfers examines the possible benefits and risks of this attempt at better targeting of social expenditures. It posits that the main debate has been between direct cash transfers and in-kind transfers. It states that the deficiencies of the old in-kind food distribution system have been recognized for decades. Direct cash transfers can tackle leakages by removing 'duplicates' and 'ghosts'. This would reduce the fiscal bill, bring transparency and help in financial inclusion.

The final chapter continues with the analysis of public expenditures, this time in the context of the education sector. It traces trends in India's public educational expenditure, its effectiveness and implications. India compares poorly to other Brazil, Russia, India and China (BRIC) countries in terms of secondary school participation and youth literacy rates. The empirical literature on the socio-economic and demographic factors that influence household level decisions on education in India is discussed. The chapter finds that India's expenditure on social sectors such as education suffers from both inadequate allocation of budgetary resources and ineffective implementation on the ground.

Supriyo De

## Notes

1 Across my career, I realized that this was a considerable chunk of decision makers. For instance, directly recruited generalists dominate the Indian civil services.

2 Indeed, I have received requests from academics teaching such courses to allow use of my Ministry of Finance working paper (on which the early part of this book is based) as part of their course material.

3 Data from World Bank World Development Indicators database.

4 "Global Economic Prospects: June 2016", The World Bank, Washington, D.C.

5 Data from Ministry of Statistics and Programme Implementation, India.

1

# Fiscal Policy in India

## Trends and Trajectory

**Supriyo De**

## Introduction

Fiscal policy deals with the taxation and expenditure decisions of government. Monetary policy deals with the supply of money in the economy and the rate of interest. These are the main policy approaches used by economic managers to steer the economy. In most modern economies, the government deals with fiscal policy while the central bank is responsible for monetary policy. Fiscal policy is composed of several parts. These include tax policy, expenditure policy, investment or disinvestment strategies, and debt or surplus management. Fiscal policy is an important constituent of the overall economic framework of a country and is intimately linked with its general economic strategy.

Fiscal policy also feeds into economic trends and influences monetary policy. When the government receives more than it spends, it has a surplus. If the government spends more than it receives, it runs a deficit. To meet the additional expenditures, it needs to borrow from domestic or foreign sources, draw upon its foreign exchange reserves or print an equivalent amount of money.[1] This tends to influence other economic variables. On a broad generalization, excessive printing of money leads to inflation. If the government borrows too much from abroad, an external shock (such as an exchange rate depreciation or inability to roll over the debt due to perceived lack of ability to repay) may lead to a debt crisis. If it draws down on its foreign exchange reserves, a balance of payments (BoPs) crisis may arise. Excessive domestic borrowing by the government may lead to higher real interest rates and the domestic private sector being unable to access funds resulting in the 'crowding out' of private investment. Sometimes a combination of these can occur. In any case, the impact of a large deficit on long-run growth and economic well-being is negative. Therefore, there is broad agreement that it is not prudent for a government to run an unduly large deficit. However, in case of developing countries, where the need for infrastructure and social investments may be substantial, it is sometimes argued that running surpluses at the cost of long-term growth might also not be wise (Fischer and Easterly, 1990). The challenge then for governments in most developing countries is to meet infrastructure and social needs, while managing the government's finances in a way that the deficit or the accumulating debt burden is not too great. It is difficult to theoretically or empirically characterize an optimal level of public debt in terms of welfare or social criteria. This would depend on the priorities and concerns of government and the society. In the circumstances, policymakers and researchers largely focus on the sustainability of public finances and management of public debt.

This chapter examines the trajectory of India's fiscal policy with particular focus on historical trends, the development of fiscal discipline frameworks, recent experience of fiscal response to the global financial crisis (GFC) and subsequent return to a fiscal consolidation path. The analysis focusses on the sustainability and cyclical response of fiscal policy and consequent macroeconomic impact. The initial years of India's planned development strategy were characterized by a conservative fiscal policy whereby deficits were kept under control. The tax system was geared to transfer resources from the private sector to fund the large public sector–driven industrialization process and also cover social welfare schemes. Indirect taxes were a larger source of revenue than direct taxes. However, growth was anaemic and the system was prone to inefficiencies. In the 1980s, attempts were made to reform particular sectors and make some changes in the tax system. But the public debt increased, as did the fiscal deficit. Triggered by higher oil prices and political uncertainties, the BoPs crisis of 1991 led to economic liberalization. The reform of the tax system commenced with direct taxes increasing their share in comparison to indirect taxes. The fiscal deficit was brought under control. When the deficit and debt situation again threatened to go out of control in the early 2000s, fiscal discipline legalizations were instituted at the central level and in most states. The deficit was brought under control and by 2007–2008 a benign macro-fiscal situation with high growth and moderate inflation prevailed. The GFC tested the fiscal policy framework and it responded with counter-cyclical measures including tax cuts and increases in expenditures. The post-crisis recovery of the Indian economy is witnessing a correction of the fiscal policy path towards a regime of prudence. Manufacturing industries, rebalancing centre–state relations, focussing on economic needs of the middle class, improving financial inclusion and governance are the priorities for the National Democratic Alliance (NDA) regime. In the future, the focus would probably be on bringing in new tax reforms and better targeting of social expenditures.

This chapter is organized into seven sections. Section 'Introduction' is introductory in nature, section 'Basic concepts and analytical framework' clarifies certain basic concepts, and section 'India's fiscal policy architecture' outlines India's fiscal policy architecture. Section 'Evolution of Indian fiscal policy till 1991' delineates the fiscal policy developments from the period of planned development in the 1950s to the eve of the country's BoPs crisis in 1991. Section 'Liberalization, growth, inclusion and fiscal consolidation (1991–2008)' describes developments following economic liberalization and the move towards fiscal consolidation till the GFC in 2008. Section 'Crisis and return to fiscal consolidation: The maturing of Indian fiscal policy' traces the role of fiscal policy during the crisis and post-crisis recovery of the Indian economy. Finally, conclusions are presented in last section.

## Basic concepts and analytical framework

At the outset, it is important to clarify certain basic concepts. The most elementary is perhaps the difference between revenue and capital flows, be they receipts or expenditures. While there are various complex legal and formal definitions for these ideas, presenting some simplified and stylized conceptual clarifications is deemed appropriate. A spending item is a capital expenditure if it relates to the creation of an asset that is likely to last for a considerable period of time and includes loan disbursements. Such expenditures are generally not routine in nature. By the same logic, a capital receipt arises from the liquidation of an asset, including the sale of government shares in public sector companies (disinvestments), the return of funds given on loan or the receipt of a loan. This again usually arises from a comparatively irregular event and is not routine. In contrast, revenue expenditures are fairly regular and generally intended to meet certain routine requirements such as salaries, pensions, subsidies, interest payments and so on. Revenue receipts represent regular 'earnings', for instance tax receipts and non-tax revenues including from sale of telecom spectrums.

The analytical framework to be pursued would assess India's fiscal policy based on its macroeconomic impact in terms of sustainability and cyclical characteristics.

***Fiscal sustainability:*** There are various ways to represent and interpret a government's deficit. The simplest is the revenue deficit, which is just the difference between revenue receipts and revenue expenditures.

Revenue deficit = revenue expenditure – revenue receipts
(that is tax + non-tax revenue)

A more comprehensive indicator of the government's deficit is the fiscal deficit.[2] This is the sum of revenue and capital expenditure less all revenue and capital receipts other than loans taken. This gives a more holistic view of the government's funding situation since it gives the difference between all receipts and expenditures other than loans taken to meet such expenditures.

Fiscal deficit = total expenditure (that is revenue expenditure + capital expenditure) – (revenue receipts + recoveries of loans + other capital receipts (that is all revenue and capital receipts other than loans taken))

To grasp the concept of fiscal sustainability, it is necessary to understand government's borrowing and deficits or surpluses in the context of government's budget constraint (see Burnside, 2005 for a detailed derivation). For a given time period, total expenditure has to be financed by some combination of total receipts (other than new loans), new loans and the printing of money (seigniorage):

Total receipts (excluding new loans taken) + seigniorage + new borrowing = total expenditure

Rearranging the terms:

New borrowing + seigniorage = total expenditure – total receipts (excluding new loans taken)

The term on the right side is the fiscal deficit. The fiscal deficit is an important measure of the government's fiscal policy since it encapsulates the impact in terms of the taking of new loans and the printing of money. Government need not necessarily have a fiscal deficit. If total non-loan receipts exceed total expenditures, there is a surplus. The surpluses can then be deployed by government for higher returns.[3] However, interest usually lies in analysing deficits since this is the more problematic and prevalent situation. Assume government takes and pays off loans for each period:

New borrowing = repayment of previous loan + interest expenditure on previous loan + expenditure (excluding repayment of previous loan and interest) – total receipts (excluding new loans taken) – seigniorage

But government need not take and repay loans each period. Repayment amounts simply need to be taken into account. The receipts (excluding new loans taken) less expenditure (excluding repayment of previous loan and interest) is referred to as the primary balance. If expenditure exceeds receipts, it is the primary deficit.

In an open economy, the country can also lend and borrow from the rest of the world. In such a situation, the country's budget constraint is determined by the current account balance (CAB). This, in turn, can be linked to the fiscal deficit since the government also has recourse to using foreign exchange reserves and foreign borrowing:

Total receipts (excluding new loans taken) + seigniorage + domestic borrowing + (foreign reserve use + foreign borrowing) = total expenditure

Rearranging the terms:

Domestic borrowing + (foreign reserve use + foreign borrowing) + seigniorage = total expenditure – total receipts (excluding new loans taken)

The fiscal deficit (expressed on the right-hand side) then impacts the external debt balance as well as the foreign exchange reserves.

At a broader level, this relates to overall macroeconomic variables. To derive this, consider first the country's overall domestic output or gross domestic product (GDP).[4] This is a sum of private and government consumption ($C$), investment ($I$) and net exports ($X – M$, exports less imports):[5]

$$\text{GDP} = C + I + X - M$$

Taking into account, net foreign factor income ($Y_f$) (returns on capital and labour income of nationals residing abroad less similar returns of foreigners derived from the domestic economy) and net transfers from abroad ($Y_{tran}$) gives the gross national income ($Y$):

$$Y = C + I + X - M + Y_f + Y_{tran}$$

The CAB is the sum of net exports, net foreign factor income and net transfers from abroad (such as remittances):

$$X - M + Y_f + Y_{tran} = \text{CAB}$$

Substituting above:

$$Y = C + I + \text{CAB}$$

Since income ($Y$) less consumption ($C$) is savings, rewriting the above in terms of private savings ($S_p$) and government savings ($S_g$) gives:

$$Y - C - I = S_p + S_g - I = \text{CAB}$$

If the government runs a deficit, $S_g$ is negative and the CAB is lower. Also part of the domestic private savings would be used to finance the government debt and investment may be lower unless financed by foreigners. The current account may also be negative in which case the country has a current account deficit (CAD). This has to be financed by net foreign borrowing through debt, non-debt capital flows such as FDI and portfolio investment or drawing down on foreign exchange reserves. If $S_g$ is negative:

$$\text{Fiscal deficit} = (\text{private saving} - \text{private investment}) + (\text{CAD})$$

Taking into account the above framework, the impact of various ways of financing deficits are discussed:

1. *Seigniorage:* If the printing of money by government is greater than the public's demand for cash balances, the public's attempt to reduce excess cash holdings would tend to increase the price level as more money chases a limited supply of goods. This leads to inflation. The relationship is not straightforward. In the short-run, government can increase revenue by printing money. But if inflation persists, the demand for real balances for a given inflation rate decreases (since holding cash during high inflation that fetches no interest erodes its value rapidly). The public loses faith in

the domestic currency and circumvents its usage through foreign currency or other means like barter. In that case, government cannot gain further revenue by printing money.

2. *Foreign exchange reserves:* Drawing down on foreign exchange reserves does not have inflationary effects. However, excessive reserve use leads to fears that the reserves may be depleted. This is usually accompanied by a rapid devaluation of currency. In turn, this makes repaying foreign debt more costly.
3. *Foreign borrowing:* This tends to appreciate the exchange rate and make exports less competitive. It also makes the repayment of the public debt subject to fluctuations of the exchange rate. Rapid depreciation of the domestic currency due to external shocks can make the debt difficult or impossible to repay leading to a debt crisis. Of course, government could follow a policy of fixed exchange rates. This requires government to buy and sell foreign exchange using the foreign exchange reserves. If the demand for domestic currency is less, foreign exchange reserves are used to buy up the domestic currency and maintain its exchange rate. This may open the currency to attack by speculators if foreign exchange reserves are perceived to be insufficient. They bet on a future depreciation of the domestic currency and rapidly sell it to a point where government no longer has sufficient reserves to intervene.
4. *Domestic borrowing:* This reduces availability of credit to the domestic private sector. Private investment is reduced and this phenomenon is referred to as crowding out. The private sector may borrow from abroad. This, however, increases the country's external debt and leads to dilemmas not unlike those resulting from foreign borrowing by government (see Fischer and Easterly, 1990).

***Cyclicality of fiscal policy:*** To grasp the concept of cyclical stance, it is important to distinguish the movement of any macroeconomic variable across time between a trend and a cyclical component.[6] Cyclical stance refers to the response of government to changes in the business cycle, which is the cyclical component of GDP. Fiscal policy is said to be counter-cyclical if government spending is higher and tax rates lower in bad times, or in good times: government spending is lower and tax rates higher. That is, government expenditure has a negative relation with the cyclical component of GDP while the tax rate has a positive relation. It is pro-cyclical if government spending is lower in bad times while tax rates are higher, or in good times government spending is higher and tax rates lower. That is, government expenditure has a positive relation with the cyclical component of GDP while the tax rate has a negative relation. By the same logic, fiscal policy is acyclical if government spending and tax rates do not change systematically across the ups and downs of the business cycle.

Counter-cyclicality is, in theory, a desirable stance of fiscal policy since it can smooth the amplitude of the business cycle in the short-run. This, in effect, means a less pronounced slowdown in GDP and consumption growth in bad times and a less accentuated jump during good times. However, Kaminsky, Reinhart and Vegh (2005) among others establish that in most developing countries fiscal policy tends to be pro-cyclical, that is, it behaves in a way that in all likelihood exacerbates the business cycle. On the other hand, most developed countries display counter-cyclical fiscal policy. In light of this result, and its importance in ascertaining fiscal policy's impact on short-run macroeconomic dynamics, a detailed examination of the cyclical properties of Indian fiscal policy is warranted.

To analyse the cyclical properties of fiscal policy, several candidate indicators may be considered. Of these, government expenditure unambiguously provides a clear guide (Table 1.1). Tax revenues are a product of the tax rate and the tax base. Since effective tax rates are not easily available or quantifiable for the economy as a whole and the tax base itself would increase during good times and decrease in bad times, the impact is ambiguous. Only if the relationship between cyclical components of GDP and tax revenues is negative or zero, there is unambiguous indication of pro-cyclicality. It would indicate

**TABLE 1.1 Relations between fiscal indicators and the business cycle**

| | Government Expenditure | Tax Revenue | Primary Balance | Tax Revenues/ GDP | Primary Balance/ GDP |
|---|---|---|---|---|---|
| Counter-cyclical | – | + | + | –/0/+ | –/0/+ |
| Pro-cyclical | + | –/0/+ | –/0/+ | –/0/+ | –/0/+ |
| Acyclical | 0 | + | + | –/0/+ | –/0/+ |

*Source*: Based on Kaminsky, Reinhart and Vegh (2005).

that in bad times the rise in tax rates is so great that it dominates the fall in tax base, or in good times rates fall significantly and dominate the increase in tax base. Similarly, the cyclical primary balance provides a guide only if it has zero or negative correlation with cyclical GDP. This shows that in good times, government spending increases so as to match or surpass increases in tax revenues or a fall in tax revenues in good times further strengthens higher government spending, indicating pro-cyclicality. The ratios of GDP to tax revenues or the primary balance do not provide clear guidance since the changes in GDP (the denominator) across the cycle makes it difficult to come to a clear conclusion.

## India's fiscal policy architecture

The Indian Constitution provides the overarching framework for the country's fiscal policy. India has a federal form of government with taxing powers and spending responsibilities being divided between the central and the state governments according to the Constitution. There is also a third tier of government at the local level. Since the taxing abilities of the states are not necessarily commensurate with their spending responsibilities, some of the centre's revenues need to be assigned to the state governments. The Constitution provides for the formation of a Finance Commission (FC) every five years to provide recommendations for the assignment of taxes and give medium term guidance on fiscal matters. Based on the report of the FC, the central taxes are devolved to the state governments. The Constitution also provides that for every financial year, the government shall place before the legislature a statement of its proposed taxing and spending provisions for legislative debate and approval. This is referred to as the budget. The central and the state governments have their own budgets. Formally, the budget is usually referred to as the Finance Bill of the particular calendar year and is passed by the Parliament as the Finance Act.

The central government is responsible for issues that usually concern the country as a whole like national defence, foreign policy, railways, national highways, shipping, airways, post and telegraphs, foreign trade and banking. The state governments are responsible for other items including law and order, agriculture, fisheries, water supply and irrigation, and public health. Some items for which responsibility vests in both the centre and the states include forests, economic and social planning, education, trade unions and industrial disputes, price control and electricity. There is now increasing devolution of some powers to local governments at the city, town and village levels. The taxing powers of the central government encompass taxes on income (except agricultural income), excise on goods produced (other than alcohol), customs duties and inter-state sale of goods. The state governments are vested with the power to tax agricultural income, land and buildings, sale of goods (other than inter-state) and excise on alcohol.

Besides the annual budgetary process, since 1950, India followed a system of five-year plans for ensuring long-term economic objectives. This process was steered by the Planning Commission for which there was no specific provision in the Constitution. The main fiscal impact of the planning process is the division of expenditures into plan and non-plan components. The plan components relate to items dealing with long-term socio-economic goals as determined by the ongoing plan process. They often relate to specific schemes and projects. Furthermore, they are usually routed through central ministries to state governments for achieving certain desired objectives. These funds are generally in addition to the assignment of central taxes as determined by the FCs. In some cases, the state governments also contribute their own funds to the schemes. Non-plan expenditures broadly relate to routine expenditures of the government for administration, salaries and so on. During his first Independence Day speech, Prime Minister Narendra Modi indicated that the government would replace the Planning Commission with an alternative body. The era of strong central planning in the Indian economy is probably a thing of the past. The budgetary distinction between plan and non-plan expenditure was sought to be removed from the budget process of 2016–17 as was the separation of the railway and main budgets (Subbarao, 2016).

The new regime has focussed on rebalancing the federal fiscal architecture with greater stress on cooperative federalism. In this direction, the new NITI Aayog has been established. The aim is to replace the top-down approach with one in which states build upon their strengths and build their own development strategy. The report of the 14th FC has also recommended greater devolution of taxes to the states. This includes a sharp increase of states' share of taxes from 32 to 42 per cent of the gross tax revenue divisible pool. Consequently, the centre–state funding pattern is being modified. Henceforth, the revenue expenditure on some schemes and programmes is to be borne by the states.

Other programmes would be discontinued as centrally sponsored schemes, but states could continue funding them given their increased allocation from the FC recommendations.

While these institutional arrangements initially appeared adequate for driving the development agenda, the sharp deterioration of the fiscal situation in the 1980s resulted in the BoPs crisis of 1991, which would be discussed later. Following economic liberalization in 1991, when the fiscal deficit and debt situation again seemed to head towards unsustainable levels around 2000, a new fiscal discipline framework was instituted. At the central level, this framework was initiated in 2003 when the Parliament passed the Fiscal Responsibility and Budget Management Act (FRBMA).

Taxes are the main source of government revenues. Direct taxes are so named since they are charged upon and collected directly from the person or organization that ultimately pays the tax (in a legal sense).[7] Taxes on personal and corporate incomes, personal wealth and professions are direct taxes. In India, the main direct taxes at the central level are the personal and corporate income tax. Both are till date levied through the same piece of legislation, the Income Tax Act of 1961. Income taxes are levied on various heads of income, namely, incomes from business and professions, salaries, house property, capital gains and other sources (like interest and dividends).[8] Other direct taxes include the recently removed wealth tax and the securities transactions tax.[9]

Indirect taxes are charged and collected from persons other than those who finally end up paying the tax (again in a legal sense). For instance, the seller collects a tax on sale of goods from the buyer. The legal responsibility of paying the tax to government lies with the seller, but the buyer pays the tax. The current central indirect taxes are the central excise (a tax on manufactured goods), the service tax, the customs duty (a tax on imports) and the central sales tax on inter-state sale of goods. The main indirect tax levied by the states is the sales tax. This tax levied on post-manufacturing transaction of goods (that is wholesale and retail levels) is now largely a value-added tax with intra-state tax credit. The complications and economic inefficiencies of this multiple cascading taxation across the economic value chain (necessitated by the constitutional assignment of taxing powers) are discussed later in the context of the proposed Goods and Services Tax (GST).

## Evolution of Indian fiscal policy till 1991

India commenced on the path of planned development with the setting up of the Planning Commission in 1950. That was also the year when the country adopted a federal Constitution with strong unitary features giving the central government primacy in terms of planning for economic development (Singh and Srinivasan, 2004). The subsequent planning process laid emphasis on strengthening public sector enterprises as a means to achieve economic growth and industrial development. The resulting economic framework imposed administrative controls on various industries and a system of licensing and quotas for private industries. Consequently, the main role of fiscal policy was to transfer private savings to cater to the growing consumption and investment needs of the public sector. Other goals included the reduction of income and wealth inequalities through taxes and transfers, encouraging balanced regional development, fostering small-scale industries and sometimes influencing the trends in economic activities towards desired goals (Rao and Rao, 2006).

In terms of tax policy, this meant that both direct and indirect taxes were focussed on extracting revenues from the private sector to fund the public sector and achieve redistributive goals. The combined centre and state tax revenues to GDP ratio increased from 6.3 per cent in 1950–1951 to 16.1 per cent in 1987–1988.[10] For the central government, this ratio was 4.1 per cent of GDP in 1950–1951 with the larger share coming from indirect taxes at 2.3 per cent of GDP and direct taxes at 1.8 per cent of GDP. Given their low direct tax levers, the states had 0.6 per cent of GDP as direct taxes and 1.7 per cent of GDP as indirect taxes in 1950–1951 (Rao and Rao, 2006).

The government authorized a comprehensive review of the tax system culminating in the Taxation Enquiry Commission Report of 1953. However, the government then invited the British economist Nicholas Kaldor to examine the possibility of reforming the tax system. Due to the narrow tax base and inadequate reporting of property income and taxation, Kaldor believed that the tax system was inefficient and inequitable. He also found the maximum marginal income tax rate at 92 per cent to be too high and suggested it should be reduced to 45 per cent. In view of his recommendations, the government revived capital gains taxation, brought in a gift tax, a wealth tax and an expenditure tax (which was not continued due to administrative complexities) (Herd and Leibfritz, 2008).

Despite Kaldor's recommendations, income and corporate taxes at the highest marginal rate continued to be extraordinarily high. In 1973–1974, the maximum rate taking into account the surcharge was 97.5 per cent for personal income above Rs. 0.2 million. The system was also complex with as many as eleven tax brackets. The corporate income tax was differential for widely held and closely held companies with the tax rate varying from 45 to 65 per cent for some widely held companies. Though the statutory tax rates were high, given a large number of special allowances and depreciation, effective tax rates were much lower. The Direct Taxes Enquiry Committee of 1971 found that the high tax rates encouraged tax evasion. Following its recommendations in 1974–1975, the personal income tax rate was brought down to 77 per cent but the wealth tax rate was increased. The next major simplification was in 1985–1986 when the number of tax brackets was reduced from eight to four and the highest income tax rate was brought down to 50 per cent (Rao and Rao, 2006).

In indirect taxes, a major component was the central excise duty. This was initially used to tax raw materials and intermediate goods and not final consumer goods. But by 1975–1976, it was extended to cover all manufactured goods. The excise duty structure at this time was complicated and tended to distort economic decisions. Some commodities had specific duties while others had ad valorem rates.[11] The tax also had a major 'cascading effect' since it was imposed not just on final consumer goods but also on inputs and capital goods. In effect, the tax on the input was again taxed at the next point of manufacture resulting in double taxation of the input. Considering that the states were separately imposing sales tax at the post-manufacturing wholesale and retail levels, this cascading impact was considerable. The system was also cumbersome to comply with and probably prone to significant tax evasion. Since input credits were not allowed, there was no incentive for maintaining proper accounts making verification and enforcement costly. The Indirect Tax Enquiry Report of 1977 recommended introduction of input tax credits to convert the cascading manufacturing tax into a manufacturing value-added tax (MANVAT). Instead, the modified value-added tax (MODVAT) was introduced in a phased manner from 1986 covering only selected commodities (Rao and Rao, 2006).

The other main central indirect tax is the customs duty. Given that imports into India were restricted, this was not a very large source of revenue. The tariffs were high and differentiated. Items at later stages of production like finished goods were taxed at higher rates than those at earlier stages, like raw materials. Rates also differed on the basis of perceived income elasticities with necessities taxed at lower rates than luxury goods. In 1985–1986, the government presented its long-term fiscal policy stressing on the need to reduce tariffs, have fewer rates and eventually remove quantitative limits on imports. Some reforms were attempted but due to revenue raising considerations, the tariffs in terms of the weighted average rate increased from 38 per cent in 1980–1981 to 87 per cent in 1989–1990. By 1990–1991, the tariff structure had a range of 0–400 per cent with over 10 per cent of imports subjected to tariffs of 120 per cent or more. Further complications arose from exemptions granted outside the budgetary process (Rao and Rao, 2006).

In 1970–1971, direct taxes contributed to around 16 per cent of the central government's revenues, indirect taxes about 58 per cent and the remaining 26 per cent came from non-tax revenues (Figure 1.1). By 1990–1991, the share of indirect taxes had increased to 65 per cent, direct taxes shrank to 13 per cent and non-tax revenues were at 22 per cent (Figure 1.1).

India's expenditure norms remained conservative till the 1980s (Figure 1.2). From 1973–1974 to 1978–1979, the central government continuously ran

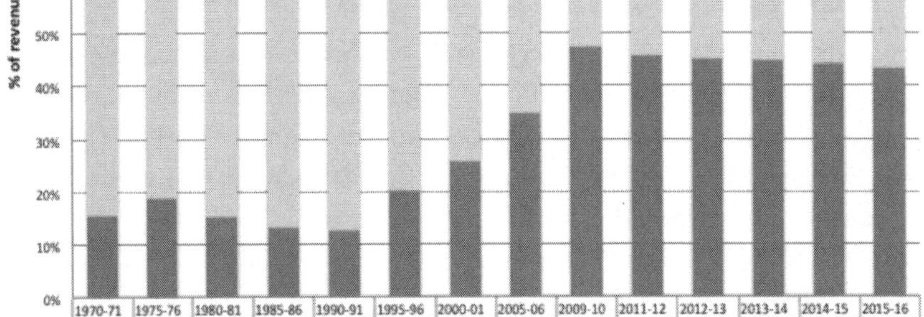


| | 1970-71 | 1975-76 | 1980-81 | 1985-86 | 1990-91 | 1995-96 | 2000-01 | 2005-06 | 2009-10 | 2011-12 | 2012-13 | 2013-14 | 2014-15 | 2015-16 |
|---|---|---|---|---|---|---|---|---|---|---|---|---|---|---|
| Non-tax revenue | 25.6 | 23.6 | 24.4 | 24.6 | 21.8 | 25.6 | 29.0 | 22.1 | 20.3 | 16.2 | 15.6 | 19.6 | 19.3 | 19.4 |
| Indirect tax | 58.9 | 57.6 | 60.3 | 62.2 | 65.6 | 54.2 | 45.2 | 43.1 | 32.3 | 38.1 | 39.3 | 35.5 | 36.3 | 37.2 |
| Direct tax | 15.5 | 18.8 | 15.3 | 13.2 | 12.6 | 20.2 | 25.8 | 34.8 | 47.4 | 45.7 | 45.1 | 44.9 | 44.3 | 43.4 |

**FIGURE 1.1 Composition of central government revenues.**

*Source*: Database on the Indian Economy, http://dbie.rbi.org.in (Reserve Bank of India, 2016).

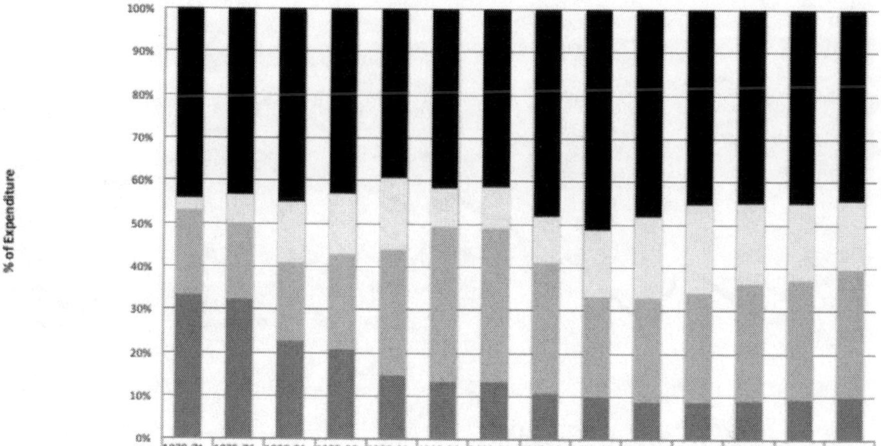


| | 1970-71 | 1975-76 | 1980-81 | 1985-86 | 1990-91 | 1995-96 | 2000-01 | 2005-06 | 2009-10 | 2011-12 | 2012-13 | 2013-14 | 2014-15 | 2015-16 |
|---|---|---|---|---|---|---|---|---|---|---|---|---|---|---|
| Other Revenue Expenditure | 44.0 | 43.4 | 45.1 | 43.0 | 39.4 | 41.7 | 41.2 | 48.0 | 51.2 | 48.1 | 45.2 | 45.1 | 45.0 | 44.5 |
| Subsidies | 3.0 | 6.7 | 14.1 | 14.1 | 16.5 | 9.1 | 9.7 | 10.8 | 15.5 | 19.0 | 20.7 | 18.6 | 17.9 | 15.9 |
| Interest | 19.4 | 17.6 | 18.1 | 22.1 | 29.2 | 35.8 | 35.7 | 30.2 | 23.4 | 23.8 | 25.2 | 27.3 | 27.6 | 29.7 |
| Defence | 33.6 | 32.3 | 22.7 | 20.7 | 14.8 | 13.5 | 13.4 | 11.0 | 9.9 | 9.0 | 8.9 | 9.1 | 9.4 | 9.9 |

**FIGURE 1.2 Composition of central government revenue expenditures.**

*Source*: Database on the Indian Economy, http://dbie.rbi.org.in (Reserve Bank of India, 2016).

revenue surpluses. Its gross fiscal deficit (GFD) also showed a slow growth with certain episodes of downward movements (Figure 1.3). The state governments also ran revenue surpluses from 1974–1975 to 1986–1987, barring only 1984–1985 (Figure 1.4). Thereafter, limited reforms in specific areas including trade liberalization, export promotion and investment in modern technologies were accompanied by increased expenditures financed by domestic and foreign borrowing sources (Singh and Srinivasan, 2004). The central revenue deficit climbed from 1.4 per cent of GDP in 1980–1981 to 2.44 per cent of GDP by 1989–1990. Across the same period, the centre's GFD climbed from 5.71 to 7.31 per cent of GDP. Though the external liabilities of the centre fell from 7.16 per cent of GDP in 1982–1983 to 5.53 per cent of GDP by 1990–1991, in absolute terms the liabilities were large. Across the same period, the total liabilities of the centre and the states increased from 51.43 per cent of GDP to 64.75 per cent of GDP.

This came at the cost of social and capital expenditures. The interest component of aggregate central and state government disbursements reflects this quite clearly. The capital disbursements decreased from around 30 per cent in 1980–1981 to about 20 per cent by 1990–1991. In contrast, the interest component increased from around 8 per cent to about 15 per cent across the same period (Figure 1.5).

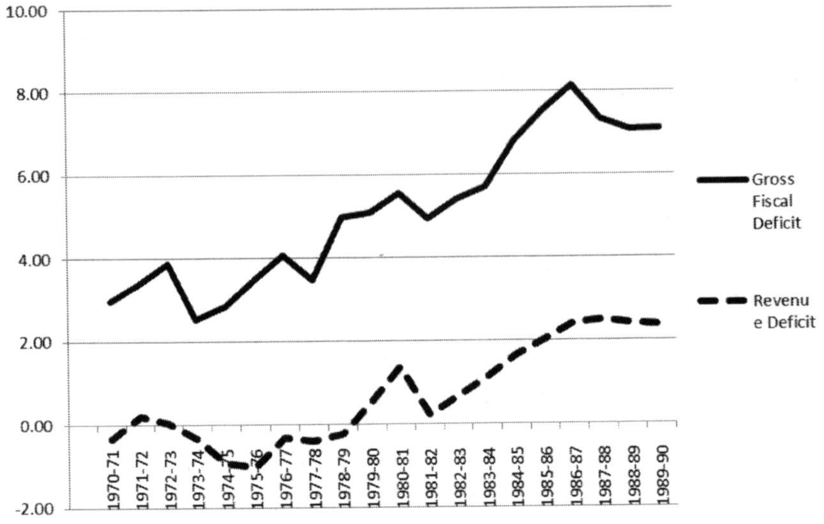


**FIGURE 1.3 Deficits of the central government as percentage of GDP (1970–1971 to 1989–1990).**

*Source*: Database on the Indian Economy, http://dbie.rbi.org.in (Reserve Bank of India, 2016).

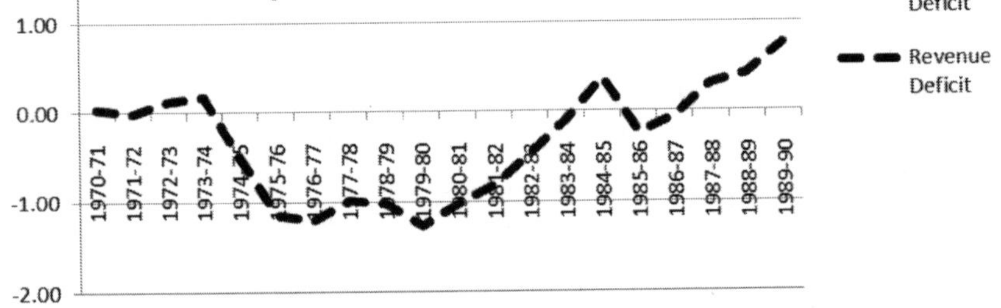


**FIGURE 1.4 Deficits of the state governments as percentage of GDP (1970–1971 to 1989–1990).**

*Source*: Database on the Indian Economy, http://dbie.rbi.org.in (Reserve Bank of India, 2016).

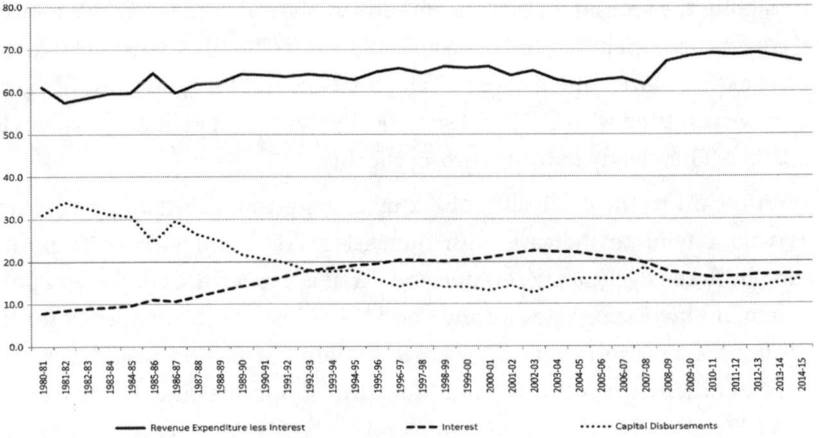


**FIGURE 1.5 Composition of aggregate disbursements of central and state governments (as percentage of aggregate disbursements).**

*Source*: Database on the Indian Economy, http://dbie.rbi.org.in (Reserve Bank of India, 2016).

Within revenue expenditures, in 1970–1971, defence expenditures had the highest share of 34 per cent, interest component was 19 per cent while subsidies were only 3 per cent (Figure 1.2). However, by 1990–1991, the largest component was the interest share of 29 per cent with subsidies constituting 17 per cent and defence only 15 per cent (Figure 1.2). Therefore, besides the burden of servicing the public debt, the subsidy burden was also quite great. The steady build-up of debt resulted in a large interest burden. The large-scale attempts to shield citizens from price increases of items such as food, petroleum products and fertilizers mediated through a complex and inefficient production system dominated by public enterprises resulted in a large subsidy burden.

While India's external debt and expenditure patterns were heading for unsustainable levels, the proximate causes of the BoPs crisis came from certain unforeseen external and domestic political events. The First Gulf War caused a spike in oil prices leading to a sharp increase in the government's fuel subsidy burden. Furthermore, the assassination of former Prime Minister Rajiv Gandhi increased political uncertainties leading to the withdrawal of some foreign funds. The subsequent economic reforms changed the Indian economy forever.

While in the long-run, pre-1991 fiscal policy was clearly unsustainable, its short-run cyclical behaviour is also questionable (Table 1.2). In view of the discussion in the section 'Basic concepts and analytical framework', we focus on total government spending and its various indicators. For the 1973–1990 period, revenue expenditure, capital expenditure, total expenditure and subsidies are all positively correlated with GDP in a statistically significant manner (*p*-values less than 0.05). This clearly indicates pro-cyclicality.

With regard to the cyclicality of tax revenue, given a certain tax rate, since taxes would tend to increase with increasing GDP and vice versa positive relation between cyclical tax revenue and GDP is expected. Stabilization policy may demand increasing rates during good times leading to a tendency for this. But if tax policy is pro-cyclical, negative or zero correlation would arise. The analysis of different types of taxes in India provides interesting insights. For the period 1973–1990, overall tax revenues and central excise revenue are positively correlated with GDP (Table 1.3). But both corporate income tax and personal

**TABLE 1.2 Correlation between cyclical components of government expenditure and primary balance indicators with cyclical GDP (1973–1990)**

| Revenue Expenditure | Capital Expenditure | Total Expenditure | Subsidies | Gross Primary Balance | Gross Primary Balance/ GDP |
|---|---|---|---|---|---|
| **0.5002** | **0.7455** | **0.6646** | **0.4828** | −0.3345 | −0.1497 |
| *0.0345* | *0.0004* | *0.0026* | *0.0424* | *0.1749* | *0.5533* |

*Notes*: Cyclical components of series extracted using the HP filter with smoothing parameter 6.25. Correlation *p*-values in italics. Statistically significant values are in bold.
*Source*: Database on the Indian Economy, http://dbie.rbi.org.in (Reserve Bank of India, 2016).

**TABLE 1.3 Correlation between cyclical components of revenue indicators with cyclical GDP (1973–1990)**

| Tax Revenue | Personal Income Tax | Personal Income Tax/GDP | Corporate Income Tax | Corporate Income Tax/GDP | Central Excise | Central Excise/ GDP |
|---|---|---|---|---|---|---|
| **0.7487** | 0.209 | 0.0234 | 0.2653 | 0.1156 | **0.7432** | **0.5524** |
| *0.0004* | *0.4053* | *0.9265* | *0.2873* | *0.6478* | *0.0004* | *0.0174* |

*Notes*: Cyclical components of series extracted using the HP filter with smoothing parameter 6.25. Correlation *p*-values in italics. Statistically significant values are in bold.
*Source*: Database on the Indian Economy, http://dbie.rbi.org.in (Reserve Bank of India, 2016).

income tax are not correlated with GDP in a statistically significant manner for 1973–1990. Probably due to the high tax rates targeting a narrow base, the two direct taxes were adjusted upwards to garner revenues during downturns. This indicates that direct tax policy was pro-cyclical prior to the reforms of 1991.

## Liberalization, growth, inclusion and fiscal consolidation (1991–2008)

Following the BoPs crisis of 1991, the government commenced on a path of economic liberalization whereby the economy was opened up to foreign investment and trade, the private sector was encouraged and the system of quotas and licences was dismantled. Fiscal policy was re-oriented to cohere with these changes.

The Tax Reforms Committee provided a blue print for reforming both direct and indirect taxes. Its main strategy was to reduce the proportion of trade taxes in total tax revenue, to increase the share of domestic consumption taxes by converting the excise into a VAT and to enhance the contribution of direct taxes to total revenue. It recommended reducing the rates of all major taxes, minimizing exemptions and deductions, simplifying laws and procedures, improving tax administration, and increasing computerization and information system modernization (Rao and Rao, 2006).

As a part of the subsequent direct tax reforms, the personal income tax brackets were reduced to three with rates of 20, 30 and 40 per cent in 1992–1993. Financial assets were removed from the imposition of wealth tax and the maximum rate of wealth tax was reduced to 1 per cent. Personal income tax rates were reduced again to 10, 20 and 30 per cent in 1997–1998. The rates have largely remained the same since with the exemption limit being increased and slab structure changed from time to time. A subsequent 2 per cent surcharge to fund education was later made applicable to all taxes. The basic corporate tax rate was reduced to 50 per cent and the rates for different closely held companies made uniform at 55 per cent. In 1993–1994, the distinction between the closely held and the widely held companies was removed and the uniform tax rate was brought down to 40 per cent. The rate was further reduced to 35 per cent with a 10 per cent tax on distributed dividends in 1997–1998 (Rao and Rao, 2006).

Despite these reforms, the tax system continued to have preferential exemptions and deductions as tax incentives for various socio-economic goals including location of industries in backward areas, export promotion and technology development. This led to the phenomenon of 'zero-tax companies' whereby imaginative arrangements were used to leverage all these tax incentives with an intent to minimize tax liabilities. To counter this trend, the Minimum Aalternative Ttax (MAT) was introduced in 1996–1997. It required a company to pay a minimum of 30 per cent of book profits as tax. Further attempts to expand the tax base and increase revenues were the introduction of the securities transaction tax (STT) in 2004 and the fringe benefit tax (FBT) in the budget of 2005–2006 (Rao and Rao, 2006).

In indirect taxes, the MODVAT credit system for excise was expanded to cover most commodities and provide a comprehensive credit system by 1996–1997. The eleven rates were merged into three with a few luxury items subject to additional non-rebatable tax in 1999–2000. In 2000–2001, the three rates were merged into a single rate and renamed as central VAT (CENVAT). There remained three additional excises of 8, 16 and 24 per cent. In case of custom duties, in 1991–1992 all duties on non-agriculture goods that were above 150 per cent were brought down to this rate. The 'peak rate' was brought down to 40 per cent in 1997–1998, 30 per cent in 2002–2003, 25 per cent in 2003–2004 and 15 per cent in 2005–2006. The number of major duty rates was also brought down from 22 in 1990–1991 to 4 in 2003–2004. These four rates covered almost 90 per cent of customs collected from items. This period also saw the introduction of the service tax in 1994–1995, which was subsequently expanded to cover more and more services. Given that the Indian economy was having an increasingly large service component, this increasingly became a major source of revenue. Eventually, provisions were made for allowing input tax credits for both goods and services at the central indirect tax level (Rao and Rao, 2006).

Despite the reforms in central taxes, even after the economic reforms of 1991, state government tax reforms were inadequate and sporadic. A major move in this direction was the coordinated simplification of the state sales tax system in 1999. This eventually led to the introduction of a VAT in 21 states in 2005. The value-added tax gives credit to taxes paid on inputs and provides relief from cascading. Implemented at the retail level, this replaced the cascading sales tax providing great relief to consumers and traders alike while enhancing the revenues of the state government. The administrative design of the VAT ensures reporting of inputs and outputs resulting in substantial reduction in tax evasion. The basic features of the tax include two rates of 4 per cent for common consumption commodities and inputs and 12.5 per cent for the others. Some essential items are exempted and precious metals are taxed at 1 per cent. The credit system covers inputs and purchases as also capital goods for manufacturers as well as dealers. Credit for capital goods taxes can be availed over three years of sales. The tax credit operates fully only for intra-state sales (Rao and Rao, 2006). This is a major hindrance to the formation of a smooth nationwide market and is to be addressed by the proposed GST.

In consonance with the tax reform plans, the sources of central government revenue shifted from indirect taxes towards direct taxes. In 1995–1996, about 54 per cent of revenues came from indirect taxes while around 20 per cent were from direct taxes (Figure 1.1). In 2000–2001, the share of indirect taxes had gone down dramatically to around 45 per cent while the contribution from direct taxes had increased to about 26 per cent (Figure 1.1). By 2005–2006, indirect taxes accounted for approximately 43 per cent while the direct taxes share was about 35 per cent (Figure 1.1).

The post-1991 expenditure strategy focussed on reducing subsidies and cutting down on non-capital expenditures. However, the large debt burden meant that the interest component would take a long time to ebb. In 1995–1996, of the central government's revenue expenditures, 9 per cent went to subsidies, 13 per cent to defence and 36 per cent to interest (Figure 1.2).

Five years later in 2000–2001, defence and interest remained at 13 and 36 per cent, respectively, while subsidies increased slightly to 10 per cent (Figure 1.2). This reveals that the composition of government expenditure generally does not change very fast. By 2005–2006, the interest component had come down to 30 per cent and defence and subsidies each took up 11 per cent (Figure 1.2). As a component of aggregate disbursements of the central and state governments, the interest component continued to rise till around 2002–2003 and then started to decline. Capital disbursements showed just the opposite trend falling till around 2002–2003 and then rising till 2007–2008 (Figure 1.5).

The rising revenues from tax administration reforms and expenditure control resulted in the deficits being brought under control.[12] The central government's revenue deficit went down to 2.37 per cent of GDP in 1996–1997 while the GFD was 4.84 per cent (Figure 1.6). The government was also more prudent about its external debt. The debt to GDP ratio went down to 4.3 per cent of GDP in 1995–1996 and reached a further low point of 2.99 per cent in 1999–2000. However, government debt and fiscal discipline again seemed to give way in the

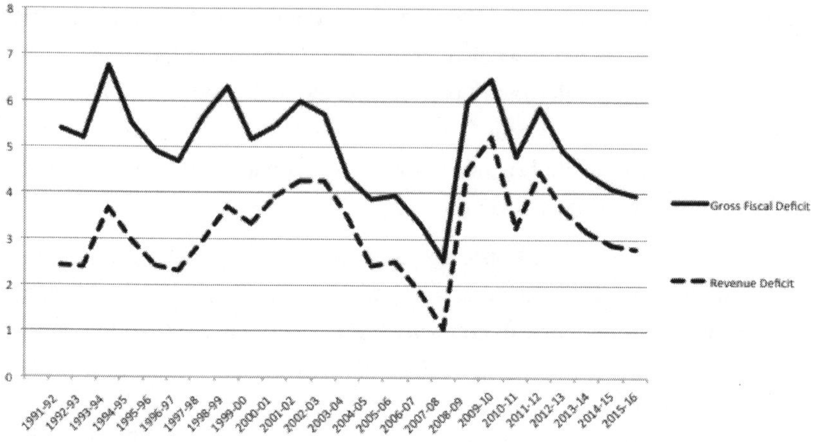


**FIGURE 1.6 Deficits of the central government as percentage of GDP (1990–1991 to 2015–2016).**

*Source*: Database on the Indian Economy, http://dbie.rbi.org.in (Reserve Bank of India, 2016).

early 2000s. The central government's revenue deficit climbed up to 4.4 per cent of GDP in 2002–2003 while the GFD was at 5.91 per cent of GDP. By 2003–2004, the combined liabilities of the centre and the states were up at 81.09 per cent of GDP from 70.59 per cent in 2000–2001. The external liabilities were, however, kept under control at only 1.67 per cent of GDP in 2003–2004.

It was obvious that a new fiscal discipline framework was urgently required. After around three years of discussions, the FRBMA was adopted in 2003. This Act gave a medium-term target for balancing current revenues and expenditures and set overall limits to the fiscal deficit at 3 per cent of GDP to be achieved according to a phased deficit reduction roadmap. The FRBMA enhanced budgetary transparency by requiring the government to place before the Parliament on an annual basis reports related to its economic assessments, taxation and expenditure strategy, and three-year rolling targets for the revenue and fiscal balance. It also required quarterly progress reviews to be placed in Parliament. A large number of state governments also brought out their own fiscal discipline legislations (Herd and Leibfritz, 2008).

These fiscal discipline legislations seemed to have had good impact at both the central and state levels. The year before the GFC in 2007–2008, the central government's revenue deficit came down to 1.06 per cent of GDP while the GFD was 3.33 per cent (Figure 1.6). The state governments achieved a

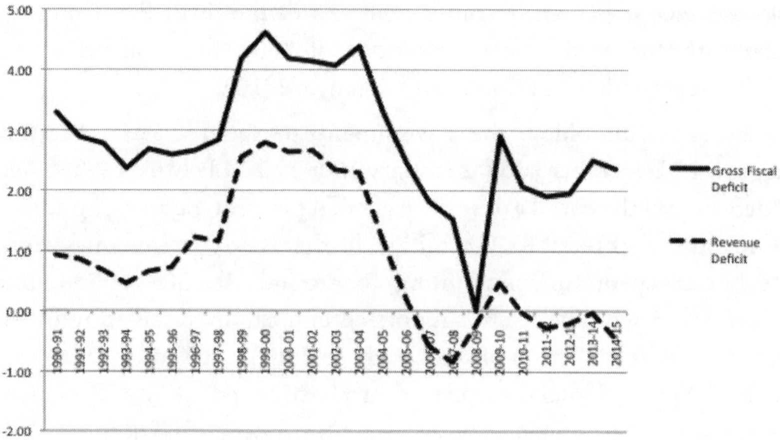


**FIGURE 1.7 Deficits of the state governments as percentage of GDP (1990–1991 to 2014–2015).**

revenue surplus of 0.58 per cent of GDP and a GFD of 1.81 per cent of GDP by 2006–2007. Even in the year of the crisis, in 2008–2009 they had a small revenue surplus of 0.19 per cent of GDP and a GFD of 3.2 per cent of GDP (Figure 1.7). This fiscal discipline fed into other economic variables in a positive manner. The aggregate disbursements of the central and state governments showed an increase in capital outlays from 11.87 per cent in 2002–2003 to 18.59 per cent 2007–2008. Inflation was moderate and growth was buoyant at 9.6 per cent in 2006–2007. This benign macroeconomic environment was disturbed by the GFC.

## Crisis and return to fiscal consolidation: The maturing of Indian fiscal policy

The GFC that erupted around September 2008 saw Indian fiscal policy being tested to its limits. The policymakers had to grapple with the impact of the crisis that was affecting the Indian economy through three channels; contagion risks to the financial sector; the negative impact on exports; and the effect on exchange rates (Kumar and Soumya, 2010). Somewhat serendipitously, the government already had an expansionary fiscal stance in view of a rural farm loan waiver scheme, the expansion of social security schemes under the Mahatma Gandhi National Rural Employment Guarantee Act (MNREGA) and the implementation of revised salaries and compensations for the central public servants as per the recommendations of the Sixth Pay Commission. Furthermore, the parliamentary elections of 2008 also resulted in further government expenditures (Kumar and Soumya, 2010).

As the crisis unfolded, the government activated a series of stimulus packages on 7 December 2008, 2 January 2009 and 24 February 2009. Actions included an overall central excise duty cut of 4 per cent, ramping up additional plan expenditure of about Rs. 200 billion, further state government borrowings for planned expenditure amounting to around Rs. 300 billion, interest subsidies for export finance to support certain export-oriented industries, a further 2 per cent reduction of central excise duties and service tax for export industries (that is, a total 6 per cent central excise reduction). The impact of these measures is estimated to be around 1.8 per cent of GDP in 2008–2009. If the increase in public expenditure across the budgets of 2007–2008 and 2008–2009 is taken together it amounted to about 3 per cent of GDP (Kumar and Soumya, 2010).

Given its inherent strengths, which include: a strong and prudently regulated financial sector, a well-managed capital account policy, large foreign exchange reserves, strong domestic consumption and effective fiscal policy interventions, the Indian economy weathered the financial crisis rather well. GDP growth declined to 5.8 per cent (year-on-year) in the second half of 2008–2009 compared to 7.8 per cent in the first half. By 2009–2010, India's GDP was growing at 8 per cent (quick estimates [QE]). This increased to 8.5 per cent in 2010–2011 (revised estimates [RE]).

At this stage, we pause to analyse the cyclical stance of post-1991 fiscal policy. During 1991–2010, only subsidies have a statistically significant negative correlation with GDP (Table 1.4). This indicates counter-cyclicality and a certain maturing of fiscal policy whereby at least subsidies were used to moderate the business cycle.

The corporate income tax is positively correlated with GDP in a statistically significant manner for 1990–2010 (Table 1.5). However, the personal income tax does not have a statistically significant correlation with GDP indicating continuing pro-cyclicality of this tax.

Following the growth spurt after the GFC, it was important to reinstate the process of fiscal consolidation. This was a delicate process where the fiscal tightening had to be achieved without prematurely choking off the growth process. The 13th FC in its report was keenly conscious of the need to return

**TABLE 1.4 Correlation between cyclical components of government expenditure and primary balance indicators with cyclical GDP (1991–2010)**

| Revenue Expenditure | Capital Expenditure | Total Expenditure | Subsidies | Gross Primary Balance | Gross Primary Balance/ GDP |
|---|---|---|---|---|---|
| −0.3357 | 0.0933 | −0.2114 | **−0.6752** | **0.7313** | **0.6276** |
| *0.1479* | *0.6956* | *0.3709* | *0.0011* | *0.0002* | *0.0031* |

*Notes*: Cyclical components of series extracted using the HP filter with smoothing parameter 6.25. Correlation *p*-values in italics. Statistically significant values are in bold.
*Source*: Database on the Indian Economy, http://dbie.rbi.org.in (Reserve Bank of India, 2016).

**TABLE 1.5 Correlation between cyclical components of revenue indicators with cyclical GDP (1991–2010)**

| Tax Revenue | Personal Income Tax | Personal Income Tax/GDP | Corporate Income Tax | Corporate Income Tax/GDP | Central Excise | Central Excise/ GDP |
|---|---|---|---|---|---|---|
| **0.6762** | 0.224 | 0.1085 | **0.5218** | 0.284 | **0.5147** | 0.1874 |
| *0.0011* | *0.3424* | *0.6489* | *0.0183* | *0.225* | *0.0202* | *0.4289* |

*Notes*: Cyclical components of series extracted using the HP filter with smoothing parameter 6.25. Correlation *p*-values in italics. Statistically significant values are in bold.
*Source*: Database on the Indian Economy, http://dbie.rbi.org.in (Reserve Bank of India, 2016).

to the path of fiscal prudence and provided a roadmap charting a set of desired fiscal deficit targets. The budget of 2010–2011 adopted a calibrated exit policy targeting a fiscal deficit of 5.5 per cent of GDP in 2010–2011 from a level of 6.5 per cent (inclusive of bonds in lieu of securities) in 2009–2010 (Ministry of Finance, 2011).

In course of 2010–2011, the non-tax revenues from auction of telecom spectrum (3G and broadband) resulted in higher than anticipated receipts. A conscious decision was taken to increase allocation to priority sectors while adhering to the fiscal deficit target. Ultimately, the fiscal deficit for 2010–2011 declined to a better than targeted 4.8 per cent of GDP. This was also an improvement over the 13th FC roadmap target of 5.7 per cent. The government's medium-term fiscal policy statement as mandated by the FRBMA for the annual budget 2011–2012 projected continuing on a path of gradual adjustment at a pace faster than that prescribed by the 13th FC. The 2011–2012 fiscal deficit target was set at 4.6 per cent of GDP as against the 13th FC target of 4.8 per cent. The rationale for this was that reducing the debt to GDP ratio at an accelerated pace would unlock more resources for use in developmental programmes instead of debt servicing (Ministry of Finance, 2011). The subsequent budget enacted through Finance Act 2012 saw the introduction of a negative list concept of service tax to widen the tax base. This essentially meant that all services not included in the negative list were liable to service tax.

By 2009–2010, direct taxes were contributing around 48 per cent of revenues while the indirect taxes share was about 32 per cent (Figure 1.1). In 2011–2012, the share of direct taxes was about 45 per cent of the central government's projected revenue while the indirect taxes contribution was around 39 per cent (Figure 1.1). The move to increase the share of direct taxes as envisaged in 1991 had therefore been achieved.

In terms of tax policy, after the conscious slackening of the tax to GDP ratio in the wake of the crisis, a tightening was seen to be desirable. The budget of 2011–2012 aimed at dovetailing both direct and indirect tax policy with medium-term objectives of fiscal consolidation and the proposed adoption of major new tax legislations; the Direct Tax Code (DTC) for direct taxes and the GST in case of indirect taxes. In indirect taxes, among major proposals, the central excise merit rate was increased from 4 to 5 per cent, branded readymade garments were subjected to excise duty of 10 per cent and few additional services were brought in under the service tax net. In the case of direct taxes, the personal income tax exemption limit was increased and the surcharge on corporate income tax for domestic companies was reduced from 7.5 to 5 per cent resulting in the overall rate coming down from 33.2 to 32.4 per cent. Certain changes were also made to the minimum alternate tax (MAT) provisions to maintain revenue neutrality and preserve horizontal equity as far as possible (Ministry of Finance, 2011).

The government's expenditure management initiatives also seemed to have gathered momentum with a focus on outcomes rather than allocations. For this selected departments are mandated to develop their 'Result Framework Document' with an emphasis on tracking measurable outcomes. In 2009–2010, defence expenditures made up around 10 per cent, subsidies 16 per cent and interest 23 per cent of revenue expenditures (Figure 1.2). The situation remained more or less the same in the budget of 2011–2012, revealing once again the largely slow changing nature of the composition of government expenditures. Of the government's revenue expenditures for 2011–2012, defence constitutes 9 per cent, subsidies 18 per cent and interest 24 per cent (Figure 1.2). A burgeoning subsidy bill linked to imported petroleum-related subsidies remained the Achilles' heel of India's fiscal policy.

Financial year 2011–2012 saw a major global slowdown necessitating mid-year fiscal correction. Early in the fiscal year it became apparent that due to a slowing down of the economy linked largely to external factors, revenue collections would be subdued.

The budget of 2012–2013 envisaged a fiscal deficit of 5.1 per cent and a revenue deficit of 3.5 per cent. As the fiscal year advanced, it became increasing apparent that the fiscal situation was deteriorating. The central government set up the Kelkar Committee to examine the issue and suggest corrective action. The Committee opined that if decisive action were not taken the fiscal deficit could come close to 6.1 per cent of GDP. The government's borrowing requirement would feed into the external sector through the 'twin deficit' effect. The fiscal stress would impact the CAD, which was already high at 4.2 per cent of GDP in the previous year. Things could worsen given the vulnerability of the rupee and falling foreign exchange reserves. The other effect was the 'crowding-out' of private sector financing for investment, because the gross borrowing requirement, already high, was likely to exceed the previous year's level by a large margin (5.8 per cent of GDP versus 5.4 per cent of GDP in the previous year). The fuel subsidy was also increasing the debt burdens of public sector oil marketing companies (OMCs). This forced a major revision in the diesel subsidy and allocation of subsidized domestic liquefied petroleum gas (LPG). In September 2012, it was decided to increase the price of diesel by Rs. 5 a litre and put a cap on subsidized domestic LPG to six cylinders per annum (later revised to nine in January 2013). While the politically difficult step of controlling fuel subsidies was taken, this was partly possible since these subsidies were largely being absorbed by the comparatively well to do sections of the populace. Given that India continues to have a large number of poor people, certain subsidies meant for the poor and basic welfare measures were not compromised upon. The government announced additional allocation of food grains in 2012–2013. The Kelkar Committee estimated that this would result in additional expenditures of Rs. 10,000 crore. However, it was obvious that expenditures for social causes could not be compressed beyond a certain extent. For instance, the Kelkar

Committee suggested that benefits to malnourished children and lactating and pregnant mothers, as well as expenditures related to employment generation to protect vulnerable segments could not be compromised. This, in essence, is the most vexing dilemma of India's recent fiscal policy.

The interim budget of 2014–2015 was the last of the second UPA regime. It witnessed two rather divergent policy directions: a desire to keep the fiscal deficit under control and a continuing commitment to social expenditures. It came at a time of growth deceleration and falling revenues. In view of the manufacturing slowdown, excise duty was reduced for the automobile industry (small vehicles from 12 to 8 per cent, SUVs from 30 to 24 per cent and larger cars from 27/24 to 24/20 per cent). Domestic production of mobile handsets was encouraged through restructuring excise duties to 6 per cent with CENVAT credit or 1 per cent without. The 2014–2015 fiscal deficit was estimated at 4.1 per cent.

The new NDA regime presented an interim budget after its formation. This recorded a fiscal deficit of 4.5 per cent in 2013–2014 indicating that the fiscal tightening of the earlier regime had been successful. However, it noted that this was by way of expenditure reduction rather than higher revenue realization. It continued with the earlier target of 4.1 per cent fiscal deficit for 2014–2015. The task was acknowledged to be difficult in view of a growth slowdown, sluggish industrial growth, subsidy burden and reduced tax buoyancy. Its fiscal consolidation roadmap envisaged a fiscal deficit of 3.6 per cent for 2015–2016 and 3 per cent for 2016–2017. The personal income tax exemption limit was raised by Rs. 50,000. In personal income tax, there were also changes in the deductions for savings invested in specified schemes (section 80C of Income Tax Act) with an increase in the limit from Rs. 100,000 to Rs. 150,000. Deduction on interest paid on loan for self-occupied house property was increased from Rs. 150,000 to Rs. 200,000. In view of the manufacturing slowdown, the investment allowance of 15 per cent to manufacturing companies investing over Rs. 25 crore (Rs. 250 million) in new plant and machinery was extended for three years. The ten-year tax holiday on power generation, distribution and transmission undertakings was also extended.

In indirect taxes, the issue of inverted duties was addressed by reducing basic customs duties on certain items. The service tax base was expanded to include sale of space or time for media advertisements (other than print media), services by air-conditioned contract carriages and drug testing on human participants. On the other hand, services provided by Indian tour operators to foreign tourists outside India were taken out of the service tax net. CENVAT credit was available for rent-a-cab and tour operators to encourage tourism. Micro-insurance schemes were also exempted.

The budget of 2015–2016 was the first full budget of the new NDA regime. In terms of strategic shift, it gave importance to domestic manufacturing (Make in India), improved governance, infrastructure, financial inclusion, steps against black money and greater focus on the aspirations of the middle class. It was presented in a backdrop of improving GDP growth and more benign inflation. The aim of reaching a fiscal deficit target of 3 per cent was to be achieved in three years instead of two years as planned earlier. The fiscal deficit targets are 3.9, 3.5 and 3 per cent for FY 2015–2016, 2016–2017 and 2017–2018, respectively. There was an increase in outlays for roads and railways together with increased capital expenditure by public sector units. A separate Public Debt Management Agency was to be set up to manage both external and domestic borrowings.

There were no changes in personal income tax rates. But a reduction in corporate tax rates from the next financial year moving from 30 to 25 per cent over four years was envisaged. A new law on black money with rigorous imprisonment of up to ten years and penalty of 300 per cent was to be introduced. Several steps were directed at domestic manufacturing and investment promotion. Additional investment allowance (15 per cent) and additional depreciation (35 per cent) were to be given to new manufacturing units in notified backward areas of the newly separated states of Andhra Pradesh and Telangana. To improve inflow of technology, rate of income tax on royalty and fees for technical services was reduced from 25 to 10 per cent. Basic custom duty on certain inputs and intermediates in 22 items was reduced. The wealth tax was replaced by an additional surcharge of 2 per cent for persons with annual taxable income over Rs. 1 crore. The domestic transfer pricing threshold limit was increased from Rs. 5 crore to Rs. 20 crore. For middle-class taxpayers, health insurance premium deduction was increased from Rs. 15,000 to Rs. 25,000 (Rs. 30,000 for senior citizens). Furthermore, for persons above eighty years, not covered by health insurance, a deduction of Rs. 30,000 for medical expenditures was instituted. Deductions for contributions to pension schemes were also increased. Since most provisions of the proposed Direct Taxes Code were already included in the tax legislations, plans to have a separate new DTC were shelved.

It now appears that Indian fiscal policy is caught in a dilemma. On the one hand, there appears to be a preference for fiscal prudence and growth enhancement. On the other hand, certain social expenditures and the tendency to revert back to selective tax incentives to boost growth during difficult times remains a recurring theme. The desire to limit the public debt through better revenue and expenditure outcomes has been fairly institutionalized in the Indian policy matrix. This is probably partly attributable to the anchoring role played by the FRBMA and the deficit reduction roadmaps put forward by the 13th FC. Despite the temporary deviation from stringent fiscal consolidation targets necessitated by the GFC, Indian fiscal policy is being steered rapidly back to the path of prudence. The determination displayed by policymakers to set for themselves strict deficit reduction targets, often exceeding those mandated by the 13th FC appear to demonstrate that fiscal discipline is here to stay. Recent developments, such as the politically difficult step to address diesel subsidies indicate that policymakers have come to accept strict budgetary constraints. Nevertheless, subsidies and tax incentives may act as built-in pro-cyclical destabilizers. While instituted in troubled economic times, they are rarely withdrawn during cyclical up-turns. This would continue to erode the effectiveness of the Indian fiscal policy unless addressed proactively.

With regard to tax policy, changes can be expected in terms of legislation as well as administrative reforms to improve efficiency. The main legislative proposal is the GST. The GST aims at bringing a fairly unified system of input tax credits across the value chain and at an inter-state level. Currently, the central excise and service taxes have limited credit facilities up to the manufacturing stage. The state VAT is not geared to provide inter-state input tax credits. It is proposed to institute a dual GST structure with separate central and state GSTs. This required a constitutional amendment to allow both the central and state governments to have concurrent jurisdiction over the entire value chain. Inter-state GST credit and full credit for the central GST is envisaged. This would also require an advanced information technology (IT) infrastructure (Empowered Committee of State Finance Ministers, 2009). IT is also likely to be further leveraged for improving the direct tax administration. Moves in this direction include increasing the number of centralized processing centres (CPCs) that carry out bulk processing functions from one to four. The number of taxpayer help centres and web-based taxpayer interface facilities are also to be increased substantially (Ministry of Finance, 2011). It also appears that there are moves to improve social expenditure outcomes and target subsidies in a better manner. Much of this would hinge on the adoption of new techniques and technologies including IT-based identification systems as proposed by the Aadhar Unique Identification system.

## Conclusion

This chapter traced major developments in India's fiscal policy from the early stages of planned development in the 1950s, through the country's BoPs crisis of 1991, the subsequent economic liberalization and rapid growth phase, the response to the GFC of 2008 and the recent post-crisis moves to return to a path of fiscal consolidation. India's fiscal policy in the phase of planned development commencing from the 1950s to economic liberalization in 1991 was largely characterized by a strategy of using the tax system to transfer private resources to massive investments in the public sector industries and also achieve greater income equality. The result was high maximum marginal income tax rates and the consequent tendency of tax evasion. The public sector investments and social expenditures were also not efficient. Given these apparent inadequacies, there were limited attempts to reform the system in the 1980s. However, the path of debt-induced growth that was pursued partly contributed to the BoPs crisis of 1991.

Following the crisis of 1991, the government charted out a path of economic liberalization. Tax reforms focussed on lowering of rates and broadening of the tax base. There were attempts to curb subsidies and disinvest government holdings in public sector industries. While initially the fiscal deficit and public debt were brought under control, the situation again started to deteriorate in the early 2000s. This induced the adoption of fiscal responsibility legislations at the central and state levels. There were also reforms in the state-level tax system with the introduction of VAT. Consequently, there were major improvements in the public finances. This probably contributed to the benign macro-fiscal environment of high growth, low deficits and moderate inflation that prevailed around 2008. The GFC brought an end to this phase as the government was forced to undertake sharp counter-cyclical measures to prop up growth in view of the global downturn. Measures included, excise duty cuts, fiscal support to selected export industries and ramping up public expenditure.

The Indian economy weathered the global crisis rather well with growth going down to only 5.8 per cent in the second half of 2008–2009 and then bouncing back to 8.5 per cent in 2009–2010. In view of the recovery, a slow exit from the fiscal stimulus was attempted in a manner whereby fiscal consolidation was achieved without hurting the recovery process. Recent policy developments such as the attempt to address diesel subsidies indicate that the fiscal consolidation mindset is fairly well institutionalized in the country's policy establishment. This is partly reinforced by institutional structures like fiscal responsibility legislations and the regular FCs that mandate the federal fiscal transfer regime. The National Democratic Alliance regime is focussing on manufacturing industries, rebalancing centre–state relations, focussing on economic needs of the middle class, improving financial inclusion and governance. In the future, it appears that the government would focus on tax reforms and better targeting of social expenditures to achieve fiscal consolidation while maintaining the process of growth.

## Notes

1 The government's exclusive right and privilege to print money is known as 'seigniorage'.

2 In the Indian fiscal statements, the terms gross and net fiscal deficit are used. 'The *gross fiscal deficit* (GFD) of government is the excess of its total expenditure, current and capital, including loans net of recovery, over revenue receipts (including external grants) and non-debt capital receipts'. The net fiscal deficit is the gross fiscal deficit reduced by net lending by government (Dasgupta and De, 2011). The gross primary deficit is the GFD less interest payments while the primary revenue deficit is the revenue deficit less interest payments.

3 Some governments with recurring surpluses, such as Singapore, have 'sovereign wealth funds' that deploy these surpluses in international markets.

4 For details, see Chuhan (2005).

5 Some textbooks denote government consumption separately as G.

6 Most economic time series, including GDP, exhibit a core slow changing component, the trend, and a more rapidly changing component that fluctuates around the trend, namely the cyclical component. (See "Introduction to Time Series Using Stata", by Sean Becketti, Stata Press, College Station, Texas.) Each time series, $y_t$, can be decomposed into the trend, $\tau_t$, and cyclical, $c_t$, components, i.e. $y_t = \tau_t + c_t$. The cyclical component can be extracted from a time series using different methodologies: Hodrick–Prescott (HP) detrending, Baxter–King (BK) filter or polynomial trend removal.

7 Economic theory indicates that the incidence of a tax depends on various factors. In the case of commodity taxes, these include the respective elasticities of supply and demand.

8 A capital gain (or loss) arises when a person sells off a capital asset. The gain (or loss) is the difference between the price at which the asset was purchased and the price at which it is sold and represents an appreciation (or fall) in value. Often an adjustment to the basic value of the asset is made to include factors like cost inflation or economic depreciation due to wear and tear.

9 Some other forms of direct taxation that existed in India from time to time but were removed as part of various reforms include the estate duty, gift tax, expenditure tax and fringe benefits tax. The estate duty was levied on the estate of a deceased person. The fringe benefits tax was charged on employers on the value of in-kind non-cash benefits or perquisites received by employees from their employers. Such perquisites are now largely taxed directly in the hands of employees and added to their personal income tax. Some states charge a tax on professions. Most local governments also charge property owners a tax on land and buildings.

10 The Indian fiscal year commences on the 1st April of a calendar year and ends on the 31st March of the next calendar year.

11 Specific duties are levied in terms of a certain amount for every unit, for instance a tax amount per litre of alcohol or per hundred cigarettes. Ad valorem taxes are based on the value of the article or service to be taxed at a certain rate. For instance, a 10 per cent ad valorem sales or consumption tax rate would mean that if a good worth Rs. 100 were purchased, a tax of Rs. 10 would be paid.

12 Tax administration reforms included the introduction of computerization, significant expansion of the scope of tax deduction at source (TDS) (whereby payers of amounts liable to tax were mandated to deduct tax and pay the same to government), simplified procedures for smaller taxpayers and an active program to expand the tax net and identify new taxpayers.

## References

Burnside, Craig. 2005. 'Theoretical Prerequisites for Fiscal Sustainability Analysis.' In *Fiscal Sustainability in Theory and Practice: A Handbook*, edited by Craig Burnside. Washington, DC: World Bank.

Chuhan, Punam. 2005. 'Debt and Debt Indicators in the Measurement of Vulnerability.' In *Fiscal Sustainability in Theory and Practice: A Handbook*, edited by Craig Burnside. Washington, DC: World Bank.

Dasgupta, Dipak and Supriyo De. 2011. 'Fiscal Deficit.' In *New Oxford Companion to Economics in India*, edited by Kaushik Basu and Annemie Maertens. New Delhi: Oxford University Press.

Empowered Committee of State Finance Ministers. 2009. 'First Discussion Paper on Goods and Services Tax in India.'

Fischer, Stanley and William Easterly. 1990. 'The Economics of the Government Budget Constraint.' *The World Bank Research Observer* 5 (2): 127–42.

Herd, Richard and Willi Leibfritz. 2008. 'Fiscal Policy in India: Past Reforms and Future Challenges.' *Organisation for Economic Co-operation and Development, Economics Department Working Paper No. 595.*

Kaminsky, Graciela L., Carmen M. Reinhart and Carlos A. Vegh. 2005. 'When Its Rains, It Pours: Procyclical Capital Flows and Macroeconomic Policies.' *NBER Macroeconomics Annual 2004* 19.

Kumar, Rajiv and Alamuru Soumya. 2010. 'Fiscal Policy Issues for India after the Global Financial Crisis (2008–2010).' *Asian Development Bank Institute, Working Paper No. 249.*

Ministry of Finance. 2011. 'Fiscal Policy Strategy Statement (Budget 2011–2012).'

——— 2013. 'Economic Survey 2012–2013.'

Planning Commission. 2011. 'Approach to the Twelfth Five Year Plan. '

Rao, N. Govinda and R. Kavita Rao. 2006. 'Trends and Issues in Tax Policy and Reform in India.' *India Policy Forum, NCAER*. http://www.ncaer.org/downloads/Journals/ipf0506-paper2.pdf.

Reserve Bank of India. 2016. 'Database on the Indian Economy.' Accessed October 19, 2011. http://dbie.rbi.org.in.

Singh, Nirvikar and T. N. Srinivasan. 2004. 'Fiscal Policy in India: Lessons and Priorities. ' Paper for the NIPFP-IMF Conference on Fiscal Policy in India, New Delhi.

Subbarao, D. 2016. 'India - Overhaul of the Budget Process.' ISAS Brief No. 448. Institute of South Asian Studies, Singapore.

2

# Decentralization, Indirect Tax Reform and Fiscal Federalism in India

Raghbendra Jha*

*India can develop only if its states develop.*

—Prime Minister Narendra Modi (2 June 2014)

## Introduction

It is a time honoured cliché that India is a country of immense diversity. In operational terms, a well-established and functioning federalism is a dire necessity for effective governance of the country. A fundamental requirement for this is the establishment of a relationship of trust between all principal stakeholders in India's federal set-up: the central government, states, regions and even villages and panchayats. This involves *inter alia* that all stakeholders be clear about their responsibilities and rights and that financial flows between these stakeholders are predictable and easily understood. This, of course, does not imply a financial straitjacket but the clear enunciation of rules and circumstances under which departures from the established norms would be undertaken. Such arrangements would require constant review, updating and recalibration of the entire gamut (and not piecemeal) of federal relations – tax, expenditure and transfers. This is particularly important at this time since there is widespread agreement that states have become the new engines of economic growth in India whence inter-state and centre–state financial relations should remain positioned on an even keel to ensure high economic growth and the consequent poverty reduction.[1]

* I am grateful to the editor, two anonymous referees and participants in a seminar at the Arndt-Corden Department of Economics at the Australian National University for helpful comments on an earlier draft. The usual disclaimer applies.

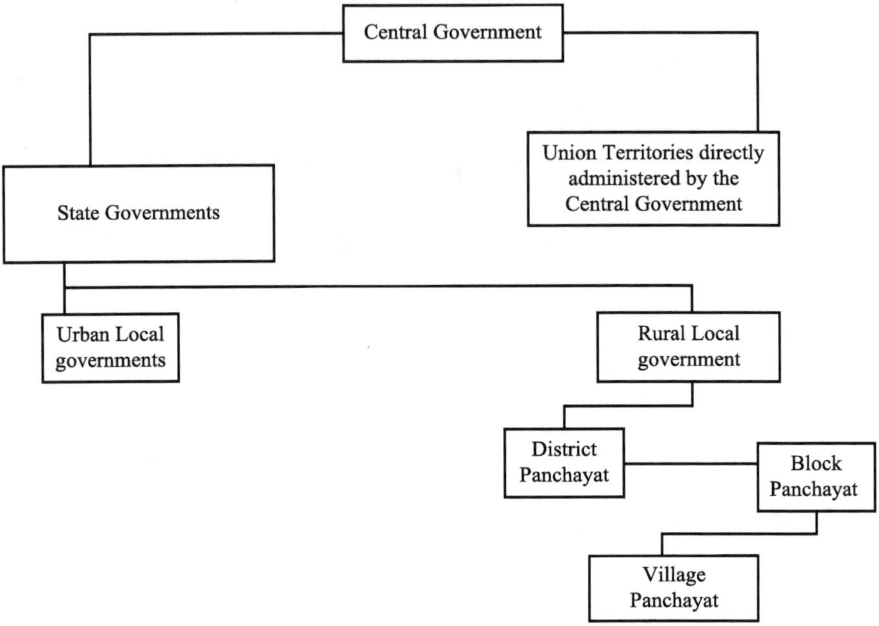


**FIGURE 2.1 Structure of fiscal federalism in India.**

Figure 2.1 lays out the structure of fiscal federalism in India. As indicated in this figure, the Government of India (GOI) delegates some responsibilities to union territories directly controlled and administered by it and to state governments which, in turn, delegate some responsibilities, in the case of urban areas, to urban local bodies. In the case of rural areas, some responsibilities are delegated to rural local government following from which there is subsequent delegation to district panchayat and block panchayat. Following the *Panchayati Raj* amendments to the Constitution of India, there is a further delegation of responsibilities to village panchayats. Both administrative and financial powers are so delegated. The Constitution of India clearly earmarks the areas which fall exclusively within the purview of: (1) the central government (the union list); (2) state governments (the state list) and (3) central and state governments (the concurrent list).

This complex delegation of responsibilities has been altered several times since the promulgation of the Constitution. In any event, the Constitution permits the GOI to bypass state and local governments in crisis situations and in the implementation of programmes such as centrally sponsored schemes (CSS).

Against the background of fundamental indirect tax reform (the proposed implementation of the Goods and Services Tax [GST]), this chapter attempts a broad overview of the current status of Indian federal fiscal relations, particularly with respect to GOI and state governmental relations and is organized as follows. The section 'Economic Disparities across Indian states' gives a broad overview of economic disparity across various states of India and discusses the rationale for and modalities of transfers from the central to state governments. The section 'The GST and the role of the FC' overviews the recommendations of recent Finance Commissions (FCs) and emphasizes the issues of the integration of the indirect tax structure through the introduction of a GST. The section 'Structure of transfers from the central government to state governments' overviews the structure of central transfers to state governments through FC, Planning Commission (PC) and CSS and issues arising therefrom. The section 'Transfers to PRIs and urban bodies' discusses transfers to Panchayati Raj Institutions (PRIs) and local bodies. Finally, conclusions are presented in the last section.

## Economic disparity across Indian states

Although there are considerable linguistic, political and cultural variations across states, our focus in this chapter is on economic disparities. Table 2.1 provides summary statistics (mean, standard deviation [SD] and coefficient of variation [CV]) of real per capita net state domestic product (PCNSDP) for Indian states. Different base years are used for various blocks of years implying that only the CV is comparable for the entire period 1980–1981 to 2010–2011, but the mean and SD are comparable within every block of years. All three series as plotted in Figure 2.2 show a distinct upward trend. Particularly, significant is the distinct upward trend of the CV.

**TABLE 2.1 Characteristics of real PCNSDP at factor cost**

| Year | SD (Rupees) | Mean (Rupees) | CV |
|---|---|---|---|
| 1980–1981 | 716.20 | 1,819 | 0.39 |
| 1981–1982 | 707.10 | 1,862 | 0.37 |
| 1982–1983 | 774.75 | 1,897 | 0.40 |
| 1983–1984 | 728.53 | 1,944 | 0.37 |

*(continued)*

**TABLE 2.1 Characteristics of real PCNSDP at factor cost (*continued*)**

| Year | SD (Rupees) | Mean (Rupees) | CV |
|---|---|---|---|
| 1984–1985 | 740.36 | 1,953 | 0.38 |
| 1985–1986 | 808.78 | 2,024 | 0.40 |
| 1986–1987 | 830.58 | 2,057 | 0.40 |
| 1987–1988 | 877.18 | 2,104 | 0.42 |
| 1988–1989 | 944.68 | 2,305 | 0.41 |
| 1989–1990 | 997.06 | 2,372 | 0.42 |
| 1990–1991 | 1,046.40 | 2,458 | 0.43 |
| 1991–1992 | 1,110.83 | 2,473 | 0.45 |
| 1992–1993 | 1,188.93 | 2,527 | 0.47 |
| 1993–1994 | 3,942.47 | 8,801 | 0.45 |
| 1994–1995 | 4,225.89 | 9,152 | 0.46 |
| 1995–1996 | 4,359.81 | 9,394 | 0.46 |
| 1996–1997 | 4,953.493 | 10,026 | 0.49 |
| 1997–1998 | 5,243.51 | 10,493 | 0.50 |
| 1998–1999 | 5,716.75 | 10,933 | 0.52 |
| 1999–1900 | 9,182.45 | 18,611 | 0.49 |
| 2000–2001 | 9,512.57 | 18,832 | 0.51 |
| 2001–2002 | 9,703.60 | 19,484 | 0.50 |
| 2002–2003 | 10,690.63 | 20,187 | 0.53 |
| 2003–2004 | 11,082.8 | 21,364 | 0.52 |
| 2004–2005 | 16,090.18 | 30,054 | 0.53 |
| 2005–2006 | 17,642.1 | 32,199 | 0.55 |
| 2006–2007 | 19,155.54 | 34,720 | 0.55 |
| 2007–2008 | 19,836.88 | 36,942 | 0.54 |
| 2008–2009 | 20,869.97 | 39,115 | 0.53 |
| 2009–2010 | 22,363.32 | 41,904 | 0.53 |
| 2010–2011 | 24,093.67 | 44,777 | 0.54 |
| 2011–2012 | 25,852.19 | 46,007 | 0.56 |

*Source*: Computed from Reserve Bank of India Handbook of Statistics on the Indian Economy. Data for 1980–1981 to 1993–1994 use 1980–1981 as base, data from 1993–1994 to 1999–1900 use 1993–1994 as base, data from 1999–1900 to 2003–2004 use 1999–1900 as base and data from 2004–2005 to 2011–2012 use 2004–2005 as base.

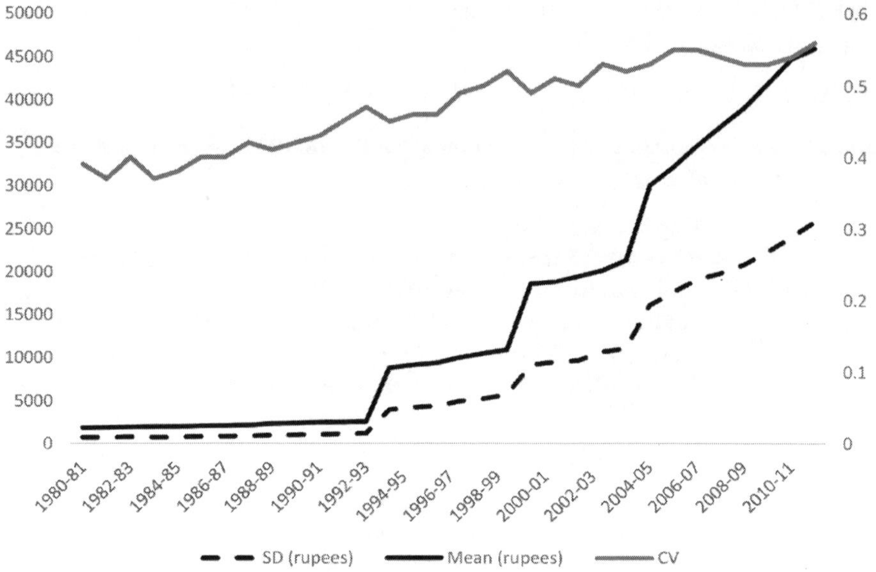


**FIGURE 2.2 Mean real PCNSDP, its SD and COV.**

Details of the three series are not included here, in order to save space but, suffice it to say that there is considerable persistence in the ranking of states according to real PCNSDP. Hence, Bihar has the lowest real PCNSDP for every year. Uttar Pradesh (UP), Rajasthan and Odisha are also nearly always close to the bottom of this ranking along with some North-eastern states such as Assam and Tripura. Delhi, Goa, Chandigarh, Punjab and Haryana are almost always at the top of the rankings. Hence, economic disparity across Indian states seems well entrenched.

Table 2.2 and Figure 2.3 show the extent of the gap in respect of real PCNSDP across states. Three measures of such gaps are reported: (1) the gap between real PCNSDP of richest and poorest state as percentage of mean real PCNSDP across all states (G1); (2) the gap between real PCNSDP of richest and poorest state as percentage of real PCNSDP of poorest state (G2) and (3) the gap between real PCNSDP of richest and poorest state as percentage of real PCNSDP of richest state (G3). These magnitudes are quite large with G2 rising to more than 900 per cent in 2005–2006 before tapering off. As expected, G3 is uniformly lower with G1 in between G2 and G3. It is also worth noting that G2 has accelerated after the onset of the reforms in the early 1990s. Thus, not only are the gaps between states' real PCNSDP entrenched, these gaps, if anything, have grown over time, with only a mild downturn in very recent times.

**TABLE 2.2 Percentage gap between mean real PCNSDP between richest and poorest states – alternative measures**

| Year | Gap between Real PCNSDP of Richest and Poorest State as Percentage of Mean Real PCNSDP across All States (G1) | Gap between Real PCNSDP of Richest and Poorest State as Percentage of Real PCNSDP of Poorest State (G2) | Gap between Real PCNSDP of Richest and Poorest State as Percentage of Real PCNSDP of Richest State (G3) |
|---|---|---|---|
| 1980–1981 | 171.10 | 339.48 | 77.24 |
| 1981–1982 | 172.72 | 339.60 | 77.26 |
| 1982–1983 | 187.69 | 380.75 | 79.20 |
| 1983–1984 | 164.74 | 319.34 | 76.15 |
| 1984–1985 | 160.07 | 291.15 | 74.43 |
| 1985–1986 | 177.39 | 334.35 | 76.98 |
| 1986–1987 | 176.49 | 319.82 | 76.18 |
| 1987–1988 | 186.55 | 373.81 | 78.89 |
| 1988–1989 | 174.72 | 347.75 | 77.67 |
| 1989–1990 | 182.20 | 387.27 | 79.48 |
| 1990–1991 | 172.92 | 355.05 | 78.02 |
| 1991–1992 | 199.82 | 447.15 | 81.72 |
| 1992–1993 | 198.88 | 494.10 | 83.17 |
| 1993–1994 | 189.25 | 550.67 | 84.63 |
| 1994–1995 | 192.83 | 535.84 | 84.27 |
| 1995–1996 | 210.06 | 725.66 | 87.89 |
| 1996–1997 | 213.91 | 644.61 | 86.57 |
| 1997–1998 | 212.37 | 721.61 | 87.83 |
| 1998–1999 | 214.21 | 732.33 | 87.98 |
| 1999–1900 | 208.02 | 669.13 | 86.99 |
| 2000–2001 | 221.63 | 636.83 | 86.43 |
| 2001–2002 | 228.29 | 742.11 | 88.12 |
| 2002–2003 | 244.37 | 740.96 | 88.11 |

| Year | Gap between Real PCNSDP of Richest and Poorest State as Percentage of Mean Real PCNSDP across All States (G1) | Gap between Real PCNSDP of Richest and Poorest State as Percentage of Real PCNSDP of Poorest State (G2) | Gap between Real PCNSDP of Richest and Poorest State as Percentage of Real PCNSDP of Richest State (G3) |
|---|---|---|---|
| 2003–2004 | 249.43 | 871.16 | 89.70 |
| 2004–2005 | 229.76 | 872.55 | 89.72 |
| 2005–2006 | 226.81 | 934.73 | 90.33 |
| 2006–2007 | 222.08 | 842.70 | 89.39 |
| 2007–2008 | 209.52 | 799.17 | 88.87 |
| 2008–2009 | 206.70 | 735.41 | 88.03 |
| 2009–2010 | 210.09 | 732.92 | 87.99 |
| 2010–2011 | 212.71 | 698.68 | 87.48 |

*Source*: Computed from data from Handbook of Statistics on the Indian Economy, Reserve Bank of India.

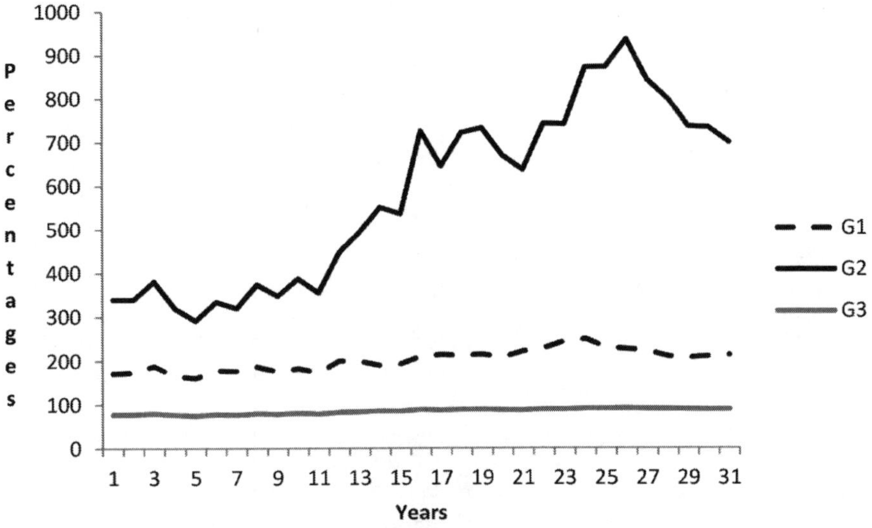


**FIGURE 2.3 Percentage gap between mean per capita real PCNSDP between richest and poorest states – alternative measures.**

Table 2.3 shows that inequality and its persistence across states extends to more comprehensive indicators of human development (such as HDI) than income.[2]

**TABLE 2.3 Ranking of states according to HDI value**

| State | HDI 1999–2000 | HDI 2007–2008 | Rank 1999–2000 | Rank 2007–2008 |
|---|---|---|---|---|
| Kerala | 0.677 | 0.790 | 2 | 1 |
| Delhi | 0.783 | 0.750 | 1 | 2 |
| Goa | 0.581 | 0.652 | 4 | 3 |
| Punjab | 0.595 | 0.617 | 3 | 4 |
| NE (excluding Assam) | 0.543 | 0.605 | 5 | 5 |
| Maharashtra | 0.501 | 0.572 | 6 | 7 |
| Tamil Nadu | 0.480 | 0.570 | 8 | 8 |
| Haryana | 0.501 | 0.552 | 7 | 9 |
| Jammu and Kashmir | 0.465 | 0.529 | 11 | 10 |
| Gujarat | 0.466 | 0.527 | 10 | 11 |
| Karnataka | 0.432 | 0.519 | 12 | 12 |
| West Bengal | 0.422 | 0.492 | 13 | 13 |
| Uttarakhand | 0.339 | 0.490 | 16 | 14 |
| Andhra Pradesh | 0.368 | 0.473 | 15 | 15 |
| Assam | 0.336 | 0.444 | 17 | 16 |
| Rajasthan | 0.387 | 0.434 | 14 | 17 |
| Uttar Pradesh | 0.316 | 0.380 | 18 | 18 |
| Jharkhand | 0.268 | 0.376 | 23 | 19 |
| Madhya Pradesh | 0.285 | 0.375 | 20 | 20 |
| Bihar | 0.292 | 0.367 | 19 | 21 |
| Orissa | 0.275 | 0.362 | 22 | 22 |
| Chattisgarh | 0.278 | 0.358 | 21 | 23 |
| All India | 0.387 | 0.467 | – | – |

*Source*: Institute of Applied Manpower Research and Planning Commission, Government of India (2011).

Sharp differences in the performance of Indian states with respect to private investment and foreign direct investment (FDI) inflows are both cause and effect of the persistence of economic inequality across Indian states. Using Annual Survey of Industries data, Table 2.4 provides details of private investment in manufacturing in 20 major Indian states for two time periods 1993–1999 and 2000–2007. States with high economic performance (such as Maharashtra and Gujarat) do well whereas states such as Bihar and Assam are lagging. Mallick (2012) indicates that economic conditions in the states have had a significant effect on private investment.

**TABLE 2.4 Share of private investment in manufacturing (in per cent) in 20 major states**

| State | 1993–1999 | 2000–2007 | Change in Rank | 1993–2007 |
|---|---|---|---|---|
| Maharashtra | 22.55(1) | 16.95(1) | 0 | 18.87(1) |
| Gujarat | 17.81(2) | 16.88(2) | 0 | 17.20(2) |
| Tamil Nadu | 9.26(4) | 12.27(3) | −1 | 11.24 |
| Uttar Pradesh | 9.33(3) | 7.26(4) | +1 | 7.97(4) |
| Karnataka | 8.86(5) | 7.11(5) | 0 | 7.71(5) |
| Andhra Pradesh | 5.40(6) | 5.94(6) | 0 | 5.75(6) |
| Haryana | 3.32(9) | 4.07(7) | −2 | 3.81(7) |
| Madhya Pradesh | 5.11(7) | 2.46(13) | +6 | 3.37(8) |
| Rajasthan | 4.01(8) | 2.80(11) | +3 | 3.21(9) |
| Punjab | 2.07(10) | 2.66(12) | +2 | 2.46(10) |
| West Bengal | 1.74(12) | 2.83(10) | −2 | 2.45(11) |
| Odisha | 1.07(14) | 3.14(8) | −6 | 2.43(12) |
| Chattisgarh | 0.070(17) | 2.94(9) | −8 | 2.17(13) |
| Jharkhand | 2.03(11) | 2.05(14) | +3 | 2.04(14) |
| Uttarakhand | 0.17(19) | 1.68(15) | −4 | 1.16(15) |
| Himachal Pradesh | 1.21(13) | 0.90(16) | +3 | 1.01(16) |
| Kerala | 1.04(15) | 0.84(17) | +2 | 0.90(17) |
| Delhi | 0.91(16) | 0.56(18) | +2 | 0.68(18) |
| Assam | 0.33(18) | 0.35(19) | +1 | 0.34(19) |

*(continued)*

**TABLE 2.4 Share of private investment in manufacturing (in per cent) in 20 major states (*continued*)**

| State | 1993–1999 | 2000–2007 | Change in Rank | 1993–2007 |
|---|---|---|---|---|
| Bihar | 0.13(20) | 0.12(20) | 0 | 0.12(20) |
| 20 major states | 97.04 | 93.80 | | 94.91 |

*Notes*: Figures in parentheses indicate ranks according to share of states in total private investment.
*Source*: Mallick (2012).

Further, as Table 2.5 indicates and, as would be expected, FDI flows into Indian states are also highly correlated with economic performance.

Hence, there are structural reasons for entrenched and even growing spatial inequality in India.

The 2009 World Development Report (WDR; World Bank, 2009) entitled 'Spatial Disparities and Development Policy' demonstrates that economic activity and growth are spatially concentrated in many developing countries due to agglomeration benefits deriving from networks, technological change and human capital externalities. India does not appear to be an exception to this rule. The WDR argues that countries should embrace this development rather than insist on geographically balanced growth. However, the report further argues that policymakers should explore opportunities to ensure that the benefits from such spatially concentrated growth are distributed broadly across the population. A well-designed fiscal transfer mechanism that is also spatially redistributive in nature would go a considerable distance in achieving this. Public expenditure programmes that are sensitive to spatial inequality could also complement this effort. However, this is easier said than done.

Against this background it is pertinent to inquire into the capacity of Indian states, particularly the less developed ones, to sustain high rates of economic growth. In particular, given their relatively lacklustre performance in attracting private investment (both domestic and FDI) the fiscal capacity of these states to support high rates of economic growth is critical; hence their fiscal position becomes pertinent. Table 2.6 shows the deficit/liabilities positions of various state governments and the GOI. Relatively less well-off states such as Bihar, UP, Rajasthan and West Bengal consistently have debt/GDP ratios in excess of 40 per cent. Whereas debt levels of all states hover around 20–25 per cent and that of the GOI plus states is in excess of 70 per cent.[3] Fiscal deficits of GOI

**TABLE 2.5 FDI equity (equity capital and component) inflows to Indian states**

| | 2008–2009 | 2009–2010 | 2010–2011 | 2011–2012 | 2008–2009 | 2009–2010 | 2010–2011 | 2011–2012 |
|---|---|---|---|---|---|---|---|---|
| | U(US$ Million) | | | | (Per Cent of Total) | | | |
| Maharashtra | 12,431 | 8,249 | 6,097 | 9,553 | 45.5 | 31.9 | 31.4 | 26.2 |
| Delhi | 1,868 | 9,695 | 2,677 | 7,983 | 6.8 | 37.5 | 13.8 | 21.9 |
| Karnataka | 2,026 | 1,029 | 1,332 | 1,533 | 7.4 | 4.0 | 6.9 | 4.2 |
| Gujarat | 2,826 | 807 | 724 | 1,001 | 10.3 | 3.1 | 3.7 | 2.7 |
| Tamil Nadu | 1,724 | 774 | 1,352 | 1,422 | 6.3 | 3.0 | 7.0 | – |
| Andhra Pradesh | 1,238 | 1,203 | 1,262 | 848 | 4.5 | 4.7 | 6.5 | 2.3 |
| West Bengal | 489 | 115 | 95 | 394 | 1.8 | 0.4 | 0.5 | 1.1 |
| Chandigarh | 0 | 224 | 416 | 130 | 0.0 | 0.9 | 2.1 | 0.4 |
| Goa | 29 | 169 | 302 | 38 | 0.1 | 0.7 | 1.6 | 0.1 |
| Madhya Pradesh | 44 | 54 | 451 | 123 | 0.2 | 0.2 | 2.3 | 0.3 |
| Kerala | 82 | 128 | 37 | 471 | 1.3 | 0.5 | 0.2 | 1.3 |
| Rajasthan | 343 | 31 | 51 | 33 | 0.3 | 0.1 | 0.3 | 0.1 |
| Uttar Pradesh | 0 | 48 | 112 | 140 | 0.0 | 0.2 | 0.6 | 0.4 |
| Odisha | 9 | 149 | 15 | 28 | 0.0 | 0.6 | 0.1 | 0.1 |
| Assam | 42 | 11 | 8 | 1 | 0.2 | 0.0 | 0.0 | 0.0 |

(*continued*)

**TABLE 2.5 FDI equity (equity capital and component) inflows to Indian states (*continued*)**

| | 2008–2009 | 2009–2010 | 2010–2011 | 2011–2012 | 2008–2009 | 2009–2010 | 2010–2011 | 2011–2012 |
|---|---|---|---|---|---|---|---|---|
| | U(US$ Million) | | | | (Per Cent of Total) | | | |
| Bihar | 0 | 0 | 5 | 24 | 0.0 | 0.0 | 0.0 | 0.1 |
| Region not indicated | 4,181 | 3,148 | 4,491 | 12,782 | 15.3 | 12.2 | 23.1 | 35.0 |
| Total | 27,332 | 25,834 | 19,427 | 36,504 | 100.0 | 100.0 | 100.0 | 100.0 |
| Top six states | 22,113 | 21,757 | 13,444 | 22,340 | 80.9 | 84.2 | 69.2 | 61.2 |
| Top two states | 14,299 | 17,944 | 8,774 | 17,536 | 52.3 | 69.5 | 45.2 | 48.0 |

*Notes*: (1) Maharashtra includes Dadra and Nagar Haveli and Daman and Diu; (2) Delhi includes New Delhi and parts of UP and Haryana; (3) Tamil Nadu includes Puducherry; (4) West Bengal includes Sikkim and Andaman and Nicobar Islands; (5) Chandigarh includes Punjab, Haryana and Himachal Pradesh; (6) Madhya Pradesh includes Chattisgarh; (7) Kerala includes Lakshwadeep; (8) UP includes Uttarakhand and (9) Assam includes Arunachal Pradesh, Manipur, Meghalaya, Mizoram, Nagaland and Tripura.
*Source*: Mukherjee (2011).

and states alone are in excess of 7 per cent and, in each of the post-crisis years 2008–2009 to 2013–2014, both the central and the state governments were running primary deficits with the combined primary deficit in 2011–2012 being in the vicinity of 3 per cent of GDP. Table 2.7 indicates the fiscal deficit and revenue deficit of individual states. Both remain quite significant for most states, particularly states with low PCNSDP.

Together Tables 2.6 and 2.7 reveal that debt/deficit positions of GOI and state governments are concerning. See also Asher (2012). In particular, it is important to note that these deficits are entrenched and, at the state level, structural in nature with poorer states having persistently high debt ratios. Hence, any tax reform that involves both the state and the central governments, such as the proposed extension of the value-added tax (VAT) to a harmonized GST, should recognize the fact that the ensuing changes in state revenue positions may persist for a considerable time.

## The GST and the role of the FC

In a deservedly celebrated report, Bagchi (2002) had described India's indirect tax structure prior to 2005 as 'archaic, irrational, and complex – according to knowledgeable experts, the most complex in the world'. In essence the commodity tax structure involved states imposing sales taxes (at different rates) at the first point of sale within their jurisdiction.

Indirect tax reform has always been constrained by provisions of India's Constitution which do not allow either the central government or state governments the authority to levy taxes on a comprehensive base of all goods and services and at all stages of production and supply. The GOI is not permitted to tax goods beyond the point of manufacturing whereas the states are not permitted to tax services. All indirect tax reform in India must operate within these constitutional constraints.

### *Some recent reforms in indirect taxation and their beneficial effects*

Notwithstanding these constraints and in perhaps the most significant indirect tax reform in independent India, in 2005 a state-level VAT on goods was instituted and replaced the state sales tax and some other state-level indirect taxes. Unlike sales tax, VAT is an intra-state multi-point tax system and is levied

**TABLE 2.6 Debt positions of centre and state governments**

**Panel A: Debt Position of States Actual and Forecasts**

| | 2009–2010 | 2010–2011 | 2011–2012 | 2012–2013 | 2013–2014 | 2014–2015 |
|---|---|---|---|---|---|---|
| AP | 30.9 | 30.3 | 29.6 | 28.9 | 28.2 | 27.6 |
| AR | 64.0 | 61.3 | 58.2 | 55.2 | 52.5 | 50.1 |
| AS | 28.1 | 28.2 | 28.3 | 28.4 | 28.4 | 28.5 |
| BI | 49.4 | 48.2 | 46.4 | 44.6 | 43.0 | 41.6 |
| Chh | 21.3 | 22.0 | 22.5 | 23.0 | 23.5 | 23.9 |
| Go | 33.7 | 33.0 | 31.9 | 30.8 | 29.9 | 29.1 |
| Gu | 30.1 | 29.4 | 28.8 | 28.1 | 27.6 | 27.1 |
| Ha | 22.0 | 22.4 | 22.6 | 22.7 | 22.8 | 22.9 |
| HP | 52.1 | 49.7 | 47.0 | 44.4 | 42.1 | 40.1 |
| JK | 56.4 | 56.1 | 55.1 | 53.6 | 51.6 | 49.3 |

**Panel B: Liabilities Position of the Centre and States (Per cent of GDP) at the End of March**

| | 2004–2005 | 2005–2006 | 2006–2007 | 2007–2008 | 2008–2009 | 2009–2010 | 2010–2011 | 2011–2012 (RE) | 2012–2013 (BE) |
|---|---|---|---|---|---|---|---|---|---|
| Centre (total) | 61.5 | 61.2 | 59.1 | 56.9 | 56.1 | 54.5 | 50.5 | 49.8 | 49.5 |
| Internal | 39.4 | 37.6 | 36.0 | 36.1 | 35.9 | 35.9 | 34.2 | 35.7 | 36.8 |
| External | | | | | | | | | |
| States | 26.3 | 26.8 | 25.5 | 23.7 | 23.6 | 23.3 | 21.6 | 20.6 | 20.3 |
| Centre + states | 87.9 | 88.0 | 84.6 | 80.6 | 79.7 | 77.7 | 72.1 | 70.4 | 69.8 |

**Panel C: Fiscal Deficit of Centre and States (Per cent of GDP)**

| | 2004–2005 | 2005–2006 | 2006–2007 | 2007–2008 | 2008–2009 | 2009–2010 | 2010–2011 (RE) | 2011–2012 | 2012–2013 | 2013–2014 (RE) |
|---|---|---|---|---|---|---|---|---|---|---|
| Centre | 3.88 | 3.96 | 3.32 | 2.54 | 5.99 | 6.48 | 5.23 | 4.60 | 4.8 | 4.6 |
| States | 3.11 | 2.33 | 1.82 | 1.49 | 2.26 | 2.94 | 2.62 | 2.16 | | |
| Combined (centre + states) | 7.05 | 6.38 | 5.10 | 3.97 | 8.17 | 9.38 | 7.81 | 6.75 | | |

| | | | | | | |
|---|---|---|---|---|---|---|
| Jh | 29.0 | 29.0 | 28.5 | 27.8 | 27.3 | 26.9 |
| Ka | 25.9 | 26.2 | 26.0 | 25.7 | 25.4 | 25.2 |
| Ke | 33.2 | 32.8 | 32.3 | 31.7 | 30.7 | 29.8 |
| MP | 38.8 | 38.4 | 37.6 | 36.8 | 36.0 | 35.3 |
| MH | 26.4 | 26.3 | 26.1 | 25.8 | 25.5 | 25.3 |
| MA | 68.9 | 65.8 | 62.9 | 60.1 | 57.0 | 54.3 |
| ME | 33.5 | 33.1 | 32.7 | 32.3 | 32.0 | 31.7 |
| MI | 87.5 | 87.3 | 85.7 | 82.9 | 79.2 | 74.8 |
| NA | 57.7 | 56.8 | 55.8 | 54.9 | 53.5 | 52.3 |
| OD | 31.5 | 31.0 | 30.6 | 30.2 | 29.8 | 29.5 |
| PU | 43.0 | 42.5 | 41.8 | 41.0 | 39.8 | 38.7 |
| RA | 41.5 | 40.4 | 39.3 | 38.3 | 37.3 | 36.5 |
| SI | 71.8 | 68.4 | 65.2 | 62.1 | 58.8 | 55.9 |
| TN | 23.6 | 24.1 | 24.5 | 24.8 | 25.0 | 25.2 |
| TR | 44.9 | 45.2 | 44.9 | 44.6 | 44.2 | 43.8 |
| UP | 49.9 | 48.7 | 46.9 | 45.1 | 43.4 | 41.9 |
| UT | 43.3 | 42.2 | 41.1 | 40.0 | 38.5 | 37.2 |
| WB | 42.0 | 40.6 | 39.1 | 37.7 | 35.9 | 34.3 |

| | **Panel D: Primary Surplus (+)/Deficit (−) of Centre and States** | | | | | | | | | |
|---|---|---|---|---|---|---|---|---|---|---|
| | **2004–2005** | **2005–2006** | **2006–2007** | **2007–2008** | **2008–2009** | **2009–2010** | **2010–2011 (RE)** | **2011–2012 (BE)** | **2012–2013** | **2013–2014 (RE)** |
| Centre | 0.04 | −0.37 | 0.18 | 0.88 | −2.57 | −3.18 | −2.09 | −1.61 | −1.8 | −1.3 |
| States | −0.38 | 0.01 | 0.40 | 0.41 | −0.53 | −1.15 | −0.93 | −0.56 | | |
| Combined (centre + states) | −1.12 | −0.79 | 0.33 | 1.02 | −3.24 | −4.46 | −3.12 | −2.28 | | |

*(continued)*

**TABLE 2.6 Debt positions of centre and state governments (*continued*)**

| Panel A: Debt Position of States Actual and Forecasts | | | | | | |
|---|---|---|---|---|---|---|
| TGC | 33.1 | 32.6 | 31.9 | 31.2 | 30.5 | 29.8 |
| TSC | 43.5 | 42.7 | 41.7 | 40.7 | 39.5 | 38.3 |
| GT | 33.7 | 33.2 | 32.5 | 31.7 | 31.0 | 30.3 |

*Notes*: AP = Andhra Pradesh, AR = Arunachal Pradesh, AS = Assam, BI = Bihar, Chh = Chhatisgarh, GO = Goa, GU = Gujarat, HA = Haryana, HP = Himachal Pradesh, JK = Jammu and Kashmir, Jh = Jharkhand, Ka = Karnataka, Ke = Kerala, MP = Madhya Pradesh, MH = Maharashtra, MA = Manipur, ME = Meghalaya, MI = Mozoram, NA = Nagaland, OD = Odisha, PU = Punjab, RA = Rajasthan, SI = Sikkim, TN = Tamil Nadu, TR = Tripura, UP = Uttar Pradesh, UT = Uttarakhand, WB = West Bengal, TGC = total general category states, TSC = total special category states, GT = grand total across all states, * = until December 2013. BE = budget estimates, RE = revised estimates, 2013–2014 figures are from the Budget of the GOI, 2014–2015.

*Source*: Panel A Ministry of Finance: Report of the Thirteenth Finance Commission, Panels B, C and D: Ministry of Finance *Indian Public Finance Statistics*.

**TABLE 2.7 Fiscal position of Indian states and projections (per cent of GSDP)**

| | 2005–2006 | | 2006–2007 | | 2007–2008 | | 2011–2012 | | 2012–2013 | | 2013–2014 | | 2014–2015 | |
|---|---|---|---|---|---|---|---|---|---|---|---|---|---|---|
| | FD | *RD* | *FD* | *RD* | *FD* | *RD* | *FD* | *RD* | *FD* | *RD* | *FD* | *RD* | *FD* | *RD* |
| AP | 3.4 | 0.0 | 2.0 | −1.0 | 2.7 | 0.0 | 3.0 | 0.0 | 3.0 | 0.0 | 3.0 | 0.0 | 3.0 | 0.0 |
| AR | 8.6 | −6.1 | −3.0 | −19.4 | 0.2 | −18.5 | 3.0 | 0.0 | 3.0 | 0.0 | 3.0 | 0.0 | 3.0 | 0.0 |
| AS | −0.6 | −2.5 | −1.1 | −3.4 | −1.0 | −3.4 | 3.0 | 0.0 | 3.0 | 0.0 | 3.0 | 0.0 | 3.0 | 0.0 |
| BI | 4.4 | −0.1 | 3.4 | −2.8 | 1.7 | −4.7 | 3.0 | 0.0 | 3.0 | 0.0 | 3.0 | 0.0 | 3.0 | 0.0 |
| Chh | 0.8 | −2.5 | −0.1 | −4.4 | 0.2 | −4.3 | 3.0 | 0.0 | 3.0 | 0.0 | 3.0 | 0.0 | 3.0 | 0.0 |
| Go | 4.5 | 0.2 | 3.2 | −0.9 | 3.0 | −0.9 | 3.0 | 0.0 | 3.0 | 0.0 | 3.0 | 0.0 | 3.0 | 0.0 |
| Gu | 2.9 | 0.2 | 2.2 | −0.7 | 1.6 | −0.7 | 3.0 | 0.0 | 3.0 | 0.0 | 3.0 | 0.0 | 3.0 | 0.0 |
| Ha | 0.3 | −1.2 | −1.0 | −1.3 | 0.9 | −1.6 | 3.0 | 0.0 | 3.0 | 0.0 | 3.0 | 0.0 | 3.0 | 0.0 |
| HP | 2.6 | −0.3 | 3.0 | −0.6 | 1.6 | −2.4 | 3.0 | 0.0 | 3.0 | 0.0 | 3.0 | 0.0 | 3.0 | 0.0 |
| JK | 9.5 | −1.4 | 6.3 | −1.9 | 7.6 | −3.1 | 4.7 | 0.0 | 4.2 | 0.0 | 3.6 | 0.0 | 3.0 | 0.0 |
| Jh | 8.3 | 0.0 | 1.4 | −1.4 | 2.5 | −1.5 | 3.0 | 0.0 | 3.0 | 0.0 | 3.0 | 0.0 | 3.6 | 0.0 |
| Ka | 2.0 | −1.2 | 2.2 | −1.9 | 2.2 | −1.5 | 3.0 | 0.0 | 3.0 | 0.0 | 3.0 | 0.0 | 3.0 | 0.0 |
| Ke | 3.3 | 2.5 | 2.6 | 1.8 | 3.6 | 2.3 | 3.5 | 1.4 | 3.5 | 0.0 | 3.0 | 0.0 | 3.0 | 0.0 |
| MP | 3.8 | 0.0 | 2.1 | −2.5 | 1.9 | −3.4 | 3.0 | 0.0 | 3.0 | 0.0 | 3.0 | 0.0 | 3.0 | 0.0 |
| MH | 3.9 | 0.9 | 2.2 | −0.2 | −0.5 | −2.5 | 3.0 | 0.0 | 3.0 | 0.0 | 3.0 | 0.0 | 3.0 | 0.0 |
| MA | 5.4 | −8.1 | 8.7 | −8.2 | −1.7 | −19.9 | 3.5 | 0.0 | 3.5 | 0.0 | 3.0 | 0.0 | 3.0 | 0.0 |
| ME | 2.8 | −1.1 | 1.0 | −3.1 | 2.4 | −2.1 | 3.0 | 0.0 | 3.0 | 0.0 | 3.0 | 0.0 | 3.0 | 0.0 |
| MI | 13.8 | −2.3 | 6.0 | −8.0 | 11.2 | −3.7 | 6.4 | 0.0 | 5.2 | 0.0 | 4.1 | 0.0 | 3.0 | 0.0 |

*(continued)*

**TABLE 2.7 Fiscal position of Indian states and projections (per cent of GSDP) (*continued*)**

| | 2005–2006 | | 2006–2007 | | 2007–2008 | | 2011–2012 | | 2012–2013 | | 2013–2014 | | 2014–2015 | |
|---|---|---|---|---|---|---|---|---|---|---|---|---|---|---|
| | FD | *RD* | *FD* | *RD* | *FD* | *RD* | *FD* | *RD* | *FD* | *RD* | *FD* | *RD* | *FD* | *RD* |
| NA | 5.6 | −3.8 | 2.7 | −9.4 | 6.2 | −6.6 | 3.5 | 0.0 | 3.5 | 0.0 | 3.0 | 0.0 | 3.0 | 0.0 |
| OD | 0.3 | −0.6 | −0.9 | −2.4 | −1.2 | −3.8 | 3.0 | 0.0 | 3.0 | 0.0 | 3.0 | 0.0 | 3.0 | 0.0 |
| PU | 2.4 | 1.1 | 0.5 | −1.7 | 3.5 | 2.9 | 3.5 | 1.8 | 3.5 | 1.2 | 3.0 | 0.6 | 3.0 | 0.0 |
| RA | 3.8 | 0.5 | 2.5 | −0.4 | 1.9 | −0.9 | 3.0 | 0.0 | 3.0 | 0.0 | 3.0 | 0.0 | 3.0 | 0.0 |
| SI | 7.9 | −10.4 | 4.8 | −11.3 | 2.8 | −15.3 | 3.5 | 0.0 | 3.5 | 0.0 | 3.0 | 0.0 | 3.0 | 0.0 |
| TN | 1.0 | −0.8 | 1.4 | −1.0 | 1.2 | −1.4 | 3.0 | 0.0 | 3.0 | 0.0 | 3.0 | 0.0 | 3.0 | 0.0 |
| TR | 1.2 | −6.6 | −1.3 | −8.3 | 0.1 | −8.2 | 3.0 | 0.0 | 3.0 | 0.0 | 3.0 | 0.0 | 3.0 | 0.0 |
| UP | 3.5 | 0.4 | 3.0 | −1.5 | 3.9 | −1.0 | 3.0 | 0.0 | 3.0 | 0.0 | 3.0 | 0.0 | 3.0 | 0.0 |
| UT | 7.5 | 0.3 | 3.0 | −3.0 | 5.1 | −1.9 | 3.5 | 0.0 | 3.5 | 0.0 | 3.0 | 0.0 | 3.0 | 0.0 |
| WB | 4.1 | 3.1 | 4.3 | 3.1 | 3.7 | 2.7 | 3.5 | 1.6 | 3.5 | 1.1 | 3.0 | 0.5 | 3.0 | 0.0 |
| TGC | 3.1 | 0.4 | 2.1 | −0.7 | 1.8 | −1.0 | 3.1 | 0.3 | 3.1 | 0.2 | 3.0 | 0.1 | 3.0 | 0.0 |
| TSC | 3.8 | −2.1 | 1.9 | −3.7 | 2.3 | −4.1 | 3.4 | 0.0 | 3.3 | 0.0 | 3.1 | 0.0 | 3.0 | 0.0 |
| GT | 3.1 | 0.2 | 2.1 | −0.9 | 1.9 | −1.2 | 3.1 | 0.2 | 3.1 | 0.2 | 3.0 | 0.1 | 3.0 | 0.0 |

*Notes*: FD = fiscal deficit, RD = revenue deficit, AP = Andhra Pradesh, AR = Arunachal Pradesh, AS = Assam, BI = Bihar, Chh = Chhatisgarh, GO = Goa, GU = Gujarat, HA = Haryana, HP = Himachal Pradesh, JK = Jammu and Kashmir, Jh = Jharkhand, Ka = Karnataka, Ke = Kerala, MP = Madhya Pradesh, MH = Maharashtra, MA = Manipur, ME = Meghalaya, MI = Mozoram, NA = Nagaland, OD = Odisha, PU = Punjab, RA = Rajasthan, SI = Sikkim, TN = Tamil Nadu, TR = Tripura, UP = Uttar Pradesh, UT = Uttarakhand, WB = West Bengal, TGC = total general category states, TSC = total special category states, GT = grand total across all states.

Indicates a surplus.

*Source*: Ministry of Finance: Report of the Thirteenth Finance Commission.

on the value added at each stage. Under the VAT regime, the VAT paid by registered persons on goods (including capital goods) purchased from within the state is available for input tax credit. The input tax credit can be used to offset periodic liability either under VAT or the central sales tax (CST). This ensures that the cascading effect of taxes is avoided and that only the value addition is taxed. Currently, there is no VAT on imports into India and exports are zero-rated. This means that while exports are not charged with VAT, VAT charged on inputs purchased and used in the manufacture of export goods or goods purchased for export, is available to the purchaser as a refund. State VAT is charged at varying rates, for example 0 per cent on natural produce and essentials, 1 per cent on bullion, 4/5 per cent on industrial inputs, and 20 per cent on alcohol. Goods other than those covered under the above rates are charged at a general rate ranging from 12.5 per cent to 15 per cent.

In addition, there is a service tax on specified taxable service. This classifies about 114 services as taxable. The current rate is 12 per cent. Further, there is an education cess of 3 per cent which makes the effective rate of tax 12.36 per cent. Service providers can claim credit for certain specified taxes, for example service tax, excise tax, a portion of the customs duty paid on capital goods. The structure of this tax is undergoing radical overhauls with the implementation of the negative list of services. All services except those specified in the negative list will be liable to service taxation.

The CST is an origin-based tax that makes it inconsistent with the VAT which is a destination-based tax. As such it is proposed to merge the CST with the VAT in the proposed harmonized GST. In recent times, the CST was reduced from 4 to 3 per cent and has been 2 per cent since June 2008. The entire revenue accruing under levy of CST is collected and kept by the state in which the sale originates. The CST Act excludes taxation of imports and exports.

The GOI introduced and took responsibility for a service tax with the stipulation that the base for this tax would be expanded considerably. An additional element of the tax reform involved rationalization of the central value-added tax (CENVAT) with a reduction of the number of rates and replacing several specific taxes with *ad valorem* taxes and a new system of CENVAT credits.

CENVAT is an (excise) tax levied at an *ad valorem* rate (expressed as a percentage of the transaction value or the maximum retail price of the good) on the manufacture or production of movable and marketable goods in India. Manufacturers are permitted to claim input tax credit of specified taxes, that is service tax, excise duty, a portion of the customs duty, and so on, paid on capital goods, inputs and services procured and used in the manufacture of dutiable goods.

The rationalization of the VAT rate structure across states meant that harmful tax competition among them has been reduced. Further, this move eased the cascading of taxes. Application of CENVAT has resulted in a reduction in the number of disputes about classification and in tax cascading as well as making the tax more neutral.

## Some remaining issues with the indirect tax structure

In operational terms, however, not all the benefits associated with these reforms could be realized. The most important reason for this is that although the base of the service tax has been expanded services have themselves been classified into a large number of categories with consequent disagreement about the scope of each such category. This disagreement has been compounded by a large expansion in the number and scope of services in recent years and, in contrast to manufactured goods, the absence of a nomenclature for services. As indicated above, states are precluded from taxing services.

In the case of the CENVAT Poddar and Ahmad (2009) argue, manufacturing has a narrow base in India and there are issues with respect to what constitutes manufacturing and their valuation. Further, the burden of the tax depends on where in the supply chain it is levied relative to value added after that point.[4]

A major new drawback from the fact that state governments are barred from taxing services is that the traditional distinction between goods and services and the separation of the powers of states and the centre to tax these has now been rendered archaic. Telecommunication services, for example, involve mobile phones which could be considered goods. A number of similar examples exist and underscore the importance of integrating manufacturing and services into an integrated GST. Thus, an artificial distinction between goods and services appears seriously outdated.

Further, the fact that states cannot tax services (and services remain the most rapidly growing sector of the economy) means that their tax revenues are less buoyant even when economic growth accelerates. This would be a matter of concern in light of the debt and deficit burdens of states that I have commented on earlier. Indeed, under current constitutional demarcation of taxation authority state-level fiscal deficits would appear to be structural, implying that the fear of states about lost revenue in the aftermath of tax reform, particularly commodity tax reform, is a matter of genuine concern.

A further drawback of the current tax structure is that the partial coverage of both state and central taxes leads to cascading of both central and state taxes. Thus, several sectors, such as oil and gas production, mining, agriculture, wholesale and retail trade, and several services are not subject to CENVAT or the central service tax (CST). However, although these sectors still pay both CENVAT and CST on their inputs, they are not permitted to claim any credit for these tax payments. This naturally creates a cost disadvantage for these sectors not just locally but also in international transactions.

A similar logic is extended to state VAT where sectors exempt from state taxes are not allowed any deductions for taxes paid on inputs. Such sectors include the entire service sector, real estate, agriculture, oil, gas production and mining.

Another major distortion results from the fact that no deductions are allowed for CST on inter-state sales by any level of government.[5] The multiplicity of rates and the irrational structure of exemptions and levies in the case of both CENVAT and CST contribute to cascading and exacerbation of cost disadvantage for Indian producers (Thirteenth Finance Commission, 2009).

Problems with the existing structure of VAT include the classification of goods and assignment of goods to different tax schedules. Partly as a consequence of this, both central and state tax administrations are severely inadequate which increases the cost of compliance and reduces revenue collection with serious impacts of the fiscal deficits at both central and state levels.

Although the tax structure under the proposed GST is slated to be comprehensive, there are a few caveats. Some essential consumption goods are kept out of the tax regime. Others such as natural gas and crude petroleum, petrol, diesel, aviation turbine fuel and alcohol are subject to tax but are kept out of the tax credit mechanism. Hence, there is no input tax credit for taxes paid on inputs used in the production of these goods. Moreover, activities which use these goods as inputs will not be able to net out taxes paid on these goods. Since petroleum products in particular are an essential input into many production processes major avenues for cascading remain in the proposed GST structure.[6] Mukherjee and Rao (2014) discuss various options for including these goods within the proposed GST. Any consequent revision to the rate of the GST to facilitate such inclusion and yet remain revenue neutral would still be within acceptable levels.

## *Agenda for indirect tax reform*

Any proposed reform of the indirect tax structure should address these issues. Apart from being efficient and simple to administer, indirect taxes should be neutral in their application, progressive in distribution and prevent leakages from the system. The tax structure should raise enough revenue for both central and state governments, and there should be clear, predictable rules for both central and state taxation as well as vertical transfer of funds from the central to the state governments. Sustained practice of tax reform and fiscal federalism along these lines would engender trust between different levels of government and make India's economy and society more resilient to shocks and better able to capitalize on incipient opportunities.

The need for large and buoyant indirect tax revenues would indicate that the base of this tax should be large and should comprise all or almost all items in the consumer basket including goods, services, real estate and so on. Some particular considerations arise from the fact that this tax base is to be shared between the central and state governments. First, goods and services that are close substitutes should not be taxed at very different rates in any part of the country. Second, efficiency and neutrality would require that irrespective of the supply chain management and distribution the tax on a good/service should be a uniform percentage of the final retail price. Cascading of taxes should be avoided by ensuring that all taxes paid on inputs are creditable. Further, all the tax revenue should accrue to the jurisdiction where final consumption occurs, that is taxation should follow the destination principle.

These principles necessitate the implementation of a destination-based GST. Clearly, multiple tax rates (particularly if these vary across jurisdictions) will go against the canons of simplicity and neutrality of the tax structure.

If the representative consumer's utility function is weakly separable between leisure and consumption goods then a flat tax on consumption goods approximates a lump-sum tax and is, therefore, efficient (for an elaboration see Jha, 2009). However, such taxes will be regressive. Many countries such as Australia, New Zealand, Singapore and Japan have chosen to apply the GST at a low flat rate and address the accompanying redistributive issues through direct taxes and transfers.

In any reform of the indirect tax structure, simplification of tax administration and ease of compliance are critical. The first critical factor for attaining these is the design of the tax itself. A GST levied at a single rate on a very broad base with very few exceptions would minimize record keeping, permit easy enforcement and encourage voluntary compliance.

The extant literature has discussed three approaches to the design of such a tax, namely, (1) concurrent dual GST; (2) national GST and (3) state-level GST (Rangarajan and Srivastava, 2008). All these three models would require amendments to the Constitution. The national GST would closely approximate the Australian case. In this model, the entire GST would be collected by the GOI with the result that India would become a unified common market. That would be its major advantage. Its major disadvantage would be that the current constitutional authority of states to impose sales taxes would disappear and states would become overly dependent upon the central government for revenues (disbursements from the GST collected by the central government), that is a large vertical imbalance would be created.

The model for concurrent central and state GST has two variants. In the first version, both the central and state governments would levy a GST on goods but the central government alone would impose a GST on services. The central GST would therefore apply to all goods and services, whereas the state GST would largely be confined to goods. A more recent version of this variant of GST (Kelkar Committee Report, 2012) would have both state and central governments impose GST on goods and services. Taxation would follow the destination principle but since the destination of many inter-state services is hard to determine the state GST on services would be collected by the central government and then distributed among the states in some manner. State and central governments would cooperate in the levying and administration of the GST. This is the version being favoured by policymakers.

A third version is the state-level VAT, which is the other extreme from the national GST. The GST is levied exclusively by the state governments (whence vertical imbalances will be sharply reduced) but the central government's power to make equalizing transfers will be reduced (whence horizontal imbalances will be exaggerated) unless it can fall back upon a separate excise tax. The United States is the prime example of a country following this rule where the general sales tax is relegated to the states within the United States. Cascading is eliminated within this arrangement as the states would agree to provide input credit for taxes levied by the centre, and the central government would provide input credits for taxes collected by the states. In this case, the central government could face revenue shortfalls some of which could be neutralized through reduction in central transfers to states. Although this arrangement would lower vertical imbalances it could widen horizontal imbalances since the better off states would be able to collect more revenue (per capita or per unit of GDP) and hence be better off. Furthermore, the central government would be needed for coordinating state taxes, a role it could play better if it is actively involved in the taxation process (Jha et al., 1999).

Clearly, one of the principal reasons for the difference between the two variants is uncertainty about how to define the destination of inter-state services. It is presumed that state taxes on inter-state services will be collected by the centre and apportioned among states in some manner.

Yet another proposal would have the states collecting all the state GSTs and even the central GST (under the CENVAT) and returning the latter to the central government. Tax returns would be filled out in duplicate with one copy given to the state government concerned and the second to the central government. Thus, a consistent cross-check would be applied. This model has some distinct advantages. By enabling both levels of governments to tax a comprehensive base of goods and service it strikes a balance between the fiscal autonomy of the central and state governments. It allows a ready base for incorporation of other GSTs into the GST and eliminates cascading and empowers both levels of governments to tax a comprehensive base of goods and services.

A single national VAT would be ideal for the establishment of a common market in India and would eliminate cascading but may not be acceptable to states as they would become too dependent on the central government for their revenue and lose flexibility over their tax sources. States may also have the apprehension that the formula for disbursements of central revenues to states may become prone to political influences and wheeling-dealing. Indian federalism could lose its vitality.

The logic of the GST requires that for it to be an efficient tax it should be imposed on a comprehensive tax base of all goods and services and at a single rate. However, governments often violate these principles. In Australia, for example, food is exempt from GST. While such exemptions are often granted on the basis of redistributive arguments they create complications for tax administration and can have spillover effects benefiting the rich – although the poor spend a larger proportion of their incomes on food, the rich spend larger amounts and would, hence, benefit more in absolute terms. Redistributive concerns are better addressed through direct taxation and public spending programmes. In this context, there is considerable scope for improving and revitalizing the targeted public distribution system (see Jha et al., 2013).

However, the current debate in India has argued for a dual GST – one for the centre and the second for the states. Under this arrangement, tax harmonization between the states and the central government and across state governments becomes important. Whereas the first issue has been much discussed; there is need to take cognizance of and address the second issue as well.

Nevertheless, there are several caveats to be considered. First, all these arrangements (including the provision of inter-state services) pertain to the formal sector of the economy whereas the Indian economy has a large, even dominant, informal sector.[7] In many cases of inter-state supply, for example group health insurance or business to business transactions, destination points are hard to identify. It is also unclear how land and property sales and services would be treated.

Harmonization, itself, is an amalgam of three factors: tax rate, tax base, and the tax administration and compliance system. The first two elements would clearly be of considerable interest to the states and have been discussed earlier. In both the central and the state governments, administration and compliance are the most important element of tax harmonization. This involves registration of taxpayers, automation of services, ensuring that the size of the informal economy is minimized and adequate IR systems (especially cross-border IT systems).

India's CST provides a good example of tax harmonization. It is a state-level tax on inter-states sales of goods based on the origin principle. Although it is a central tax its proceeds are collected and kept by the states.

The institution of a GST in India in any form requires a paradigm change and, hence, a substantial re-alignment of the taxation powers of the states and the centre (Rao, 2008). Indeed such paradigm change is long overdue even in cases such as the personal income tax. Separation of tax powers between centre and state governments based on whether the income is non-agricultural or agricultural has been a major source of tax evasion in India, especially because agricultural income is not covered under the income tax and the agricultural sector itself is being rapidly transformed into business.

The 13th FC (with validity between 2010 and 2015) argued the case for a 'grand bargain' among the central and state governments in the implementation of the GST. This model GST would be entirely consumption based and not distinguish between goods and services. It would be applied at a positive rate on all goods and services with exports being zero rated. The central GST would subsume all of the following: (1) central excise duty and additional excise duty; (2) service tax; (3) additional customs duty and (4) all surcharges and cesses. The state GST would include the VAT, CST, entry tax (octroi), luxury tax, taxes on lotteries and gambling, entertainment tax, purchase tax, state excise duties, stamp duty, taxes on vehicles, tax on goods and passengers, taxes on duties and electricity, all state-level cesses and surcharges (Thirteenth Finance Commission, 2009). The Commission also argued against all exemptions and the zero rating of all inter-state transactions (no tax on inter-state transactions). The tax would be collected by the consuming state, consistent with the destination principle.

Using the report of the 13th Finance Commission as a point of departure an empowered Committee (EC) of the Union Ministry of Finance and State Finance Ministers has considered various proposals for the GST. However, implementation of the GST has been put off several times although there is common agreement between the central government and all state governments that it will ultimately be the law. Two principal issues seem to be deterring the enthusiasm of the state governments for this tax. First principle is the states' apprehension that they will lose control and flexibility over their tax and, therefore, revenue structures. Second, and more importantly, in an economy such as India's with a large unorganized sector the implementation of a tax such as the GST may lead to considerable amounts of potential activity going underground.[8] This may lead to a sharp drop in states' revenue. The EC has recommended compensating states for any revenue losses for a limited time period after the implementation of the GST. However, as we have seen, the fiscal deficits of many (particularly less well-off states) are structural. Hence, shortfalls in revenue may persist. If that is the case then state governments may have to increase their public expenditure to attract votes, thus increasing their fiscal deficits. This will, in turn, place additional demands on transfers from the central to the state government and exacerbate pressures on the GOI's fiscal deficit.

On 3rd August 2016 the Upper House of the Indian Parliament passed the Constitutional amendment to facilitate the imposition of a GST in the country. The final version adopted will merge large number of state and central taxes into the GST and exclude only a small number of commodities, e.g., potable alcohol. Even petroleum products are to be brought into the ambit of the tax in due course of time. This amendment does not envisage a constitutional limit on the rate of the GST.

An important point to underscore here is that a large part of states' revenues come from own sources (Table 2.8). Thus, during 2004–2008 states' aggregate

**TABLE 2.8 Aggregate receipts of state governments (amount in Rs. Billion)**

| Item | 2004–2008 | 2008–2010 | 2010–2011 | 2011–2012 | 2012–2013 (RE) | 2013–2014 (BE) |
|---|---|---|---|---|---|---|
| | Average | | | | | |
| Aggregate receipts (1 + 2) | | | | | | |
| 1. Revenue receipts (a + b) | 5,814.6<br>(14.3) | 8,951.3<br>(14.8) | 11,026.9<br>(14.1) | 12,943.4<br>(14.4) | 15,652.8<br>(15.6) | 17,779.5<br>(15.6) |
| a. States' own revenue (i + ii) | 4,872.1<br>(12.0) | 7,314.0<br>(12.1) | 9,353.5<br>(12.0) | 10,985.3<br>(12.2) | 13,421.4<br>(13.4) | 15,260.1<br>(13.4) |
| i. States' own tax | 2,333.6<br>(5.8) | 3,425.0<br>(5.7) | 4,607.1<br>(5.9) | 5,574.0<br>(6.2) | 6,613.9<br>(6.6) | 7,638.5<br>(6.7) |
| ii. State's own non-tax | 587.5<br>(1.4) | 854.2<br>(1.4) | 916.5<br>(1.2) | 991.3<br>(1.1) | 1,196.8<br>(1.2) | 1,280.9<br>(1.1) |
| b. Current transfers (i + ii) | 1,951.0<br>(4.8) | 3,034.8<br>(5.0) | 3,829.9<br>(4.9) | 4,420.1<br>(4.9) | 5,610.7<br>(5.6) | 6,340.7<br>(3.0) |
| i. Shareable taxes | 1,110.7<br>(2.7) | 1,630.3<br>(2.7) | 2,194.9<br>(2.8) | 2,555.9<br>(2.8) | 2,962.3<br>(3.0) | 3,440.7<br>(3.0) |
| ii. Grants-in-aid | 840.4<br>(2.1) | 1,404.5<br>(2.3) | 1,635.0<br>(2.1) | 1,864.2<br>(2.1) | 2,648.4<br>(2.6) | 2,900.1<br>(2.6) |

*(continued)*

**TABLE 2.8 Aggregate receipts of state governments (amount in Rs. Billion) (*continued*)**

| Item | 2004–2008 | 2008–2010 | 2010–2011 | 2011–2012 | 2012–2013 (RE) | 2013–2014 (BE) |
|---|---|---|---|---|---|---|
| | Average | | | | | |
| 2. Capital receipts (a + b) | 942.5<br>(2.3) | 1,637.3<br>(2.7) | 1,673.4<br>(2.1) | 1,958.1<br>(2.2) | 2,231.4<br>(2.2) | 2,519.4<br>(2.2) |
| a. Non-debt capital receipts (i + ii) | 102.9<br>(0.3) | 101.2<br>(0.2) | 62.4<br>(0.1) | 178.2<br>(0.2) | 116.7<br>(0.1) | 69.3<br>(0.1) |
| i. Recovery of loans and advances | 81<br>(0.2) | 96<br>(0.2) | 49.9<br>(0.1) | 171.6<br>(0.2) | 115.3<br>(0.1) | 66.9<br>(0.1) |
| ii. Miscellaneous capital receipts | 22<br>(0.1) | 5<br>(0.0) | 12.4<br>(0.0) | 6.7<br>(0.0) | 1.4<br>(0.0) | 2.4<br>(0.0) |
| b. Debt receipts (i + ii) | 839.6<br>(2.1) | 1,536.1<br>(2.5) | 1,611.1<br>(2.1) | 1,779.8<br>(2.0) | 2,114.7<br>(2.1) | 2,450.1<br>(2.2) |
| i. Market borrowings | 292<br>(0.7) | 1,083<br>(1.8) | 887.8<br>(1.1) | 1,354.0<br>(1.5) | 1,683.9<br>(1.7) | 2,161.8<br>(1.9) |
| ii. Other debt receipts | 547<br>(1.4) | 453<br>(0.7) | 723.3<br>(0.9) | 425.9<br>(0.5) | 430.8<br>(0.4) | 288.3<br>(0.3) |

*Notes*: RE = revised estimates, BE = budget estimates. (1) The period averages provided reflect the different fiscal phases of the states; (2) Figures in parentheses are percentages to GDP and (3) Debt receipts are on net basis.
*Source*: Reserve Bank of India, State Finances: A Study of Budgets of 2013–2014.

receipts amounted to 14.3 per cent of GDP of which more than half was states' own revenue. This trend has been maintained to date. Thus, states' apprehension about losing revenue is a genuine concern.

As per the statues of the Constitutional amendment bill passed on 3rd August 2016 states will be compensated for any revenue loss for five years. This should help smoothen the impact of the states. This amendment now needs to be endorsed by majority vote in at least 50 % of state legislatures in the country. It is possible that this tax may become law by 1 April 2017.

Hence, whereas the efficiency case for switching over to a GST regime is strong there are several operational caveats to be considered. The fiscal federalism structure of the country needs to be sensitive to such concerns and, in particular, needs to look beyond and modify the formulae determining transfers from the central to state governments.

## Structure of transfers from the central government to state governments

Central assistance to state governments occurs through three major channels: (1) FC transfers; (2) PC transfers and (3) CSS.[9] The FC is a Constitutional Body, set up every five years to advise the GOI on the sharing of central taxes and is the principal means of federal transfers. The FC is answerable to the Parliament.

PC transfers were meant to augment productive capacity and work towards reducing inter-state disparities in economic outcome. The PC was accountable to the prime minister, but not the Parliament. The PC was set up through an executive order in March 1950 and its discretionary mandate was expanded in 1970s. This involved some dilution of the FC's constitutional mandate. Among the then 28 states of India, PC transfers distinguished between special and general category states. The special category states are (1) Arunachal Pradesh; (2) Assam; (3) Himachal Pradesh; (4) Jammu and Kashmir; (5) Manipur; (6) Meghalaya; (7) Mizoram; (8) Nagaland; (9) Sikkim; (10) Tripura and (11) Uttarakhand. These states have the common characteristics that they are remote (typically these are border states) and would have low-potential GDP growth without the help of the GOI. Finally, there are a number of CSS which are carried out under the auspices of the GOI.

## *FC transfers*

One of the principal reasons for FC transfers in a federal country is that in the absence of such transfers horizontal equity across states will be compromised. The basic argument in favour of this was put forward by Buchanan (1950) and Boadway and Flatters (1982). Thus, income taxes levied by the central government cannot ensure horizontal equity across states since they ignore the redistributive effects of states' fiscal operations. Further, in a country with regional inequality federal transfers will be necessary to ensure broad equality of access to public goods in various parts of the country. Thus, there is a clear rationale for FC transfers.

With respect to the FC transfers, the first issue to be considered is the share of central government tax collections and grants in state governments' revenue. Table 2.9 shows that between 1984–1989 and 2009–2010 this share first rose (peaking during the period of the 10th FC, i.e. 1995–2000) and then tapered off to a value, in 2009–2010, just above that during 1984–1989 but lower than the mean value for the entire period. However, this share has remained broadly unchanged with a CV between 1984–1989 and 2009–2010 of just 0.05. The share of grants in states' total revenue from the centre more than doubled between 1984–1989 and 2005–2006 (the first year of the 12th FC) before tapering off. However, this value in 2009–2010 was substantially higher than during 1984–1989 and the mean value for the entire period. As a result, the CV of grants over this time period is much higher compared to that of states' revenue from taxes shared (0.26 compared to 0.05). The share of total FC transfers in total central transfers to states hovers around the 2/3 mark. This share rose from 1984–1989 (value 60.13) per cent to 2005–2006 (value 71.94 per cent) and then fell. Its value in 2009–2010 was higher than that in 1984–1989 but below the mean value for the entire period. The CV over this period was low at 0.06.

The 13thFC has noted that states have been asking for augmentation of their share in central taxes.[10] Table 2.10 reveals that over the period 1984–1989 to 2009–2010 the share of states in central taxes rose to a peak in 2008–2009 and then fell, although the latter figure was marginally higher than its value during 1984–1989 but lower than the mean for the period 1984–1989 to 2009–2010. The CV over the period was only 0.03. Hence, there is considerable stability in the share of central taxes going to states.[11] Outright grants peaked in 2005–2006, its value in 2009–2010 was higher than that in 1984–1989 and the average for the period and the CV over the period 1984–1989 to 2009–2010

**TABLE 2.9 Percentage composition of revenue transfers from the centre to states**

| Years | FC Transfers | | | Other Transfers | | | Total Transfers | Total Transfers as Percentage of GDP |
|---|---|---|---|---|---|---|---|---|
| | *Share in Central Taxes* | *Grants* | *Total FC Transfers (2 + 3)* | *Plan Grants* | *Non-Plan Grants* | *Total Other Transfers (5 + 6)* | (4 + 7) | |
| *1* | 2 | 3 | 4 | 5 | 6 | 7 | 8 | 9 |
| FC-VIII (1984–1989) | 53.48 | 6.65 | 60.13 | 35.80 | 4.07 | 39.87 | 100.00 | 4.83 |
| FC-IX (1989–1995) | 52.98 | 8.48 | 61.46 | 35.91 | 2.63 | 38.54 | 100.00 | 4.89 |
| FC-X (1995–2000) | 62.06 | 6.55 | 68.61 | 29.52 | 1.87 | 31.39 | 100.00 | 4.09 |
| FC-XI (2000–2005) | 58.38 | 11.0 | 69.38 | 28.65 | 1.97 | 30.62 | 100.00 | 4.16 |
| FC-XII (2005–2010) | 56.48 | 11.55 | 68.03 | 28.55 | 3.43 | 31.97 | 100.00 | 5.21 |
| 2005–2006 | 57.00 | 14.95 | 71.94 | 25.36 | 2.70 | 28.06 | 100.00 | 4.69 |
| 2006–2007 | 57.93 | 13.47 | 71.40 | 25.54 | 3.05 | 28.60 | 100.00 | 5.11 |
| 2007–2008 | 58.82 | 10.21 | 69.02 | 27.69 | 3.29 | 30.98 | 100.00 | 5.46 |
| 2008–2009 (RE) | 56.04 | 9.69 | 65.74 | 30.92 | 3.34 | 34.26 | 100.00 | 5.37 |
| 2009–2010 (BE) | 53.62 | 11.22 | 64.84 | 30.88 | 4.28 | 35.16 | 100.00 | 5.23 |

*(continued)*

**TABLE 2.9 Percentage composition of revenue transfers from the centre to states (*continued*)**

| | FC Transfers | | | Other Transfers | | | Total Transfers | Total Transfers as Percentage of GDP |
|---|---|---|---|---|---|---|---|---|
| Mean | 56.68 | 10.38 | 67.06 | 29.88 | 3.06 | 32.95 | – | 4.90 |
| SD | 2.82 | 2.70 | 3.96 | 3.67 | 0.80 | 3.96 | – | 0.48 |
| CV | 0.05 | 0.26 | 0.06 | 0.12 | 0.26 | 0.12 | – | 0.10 |

*Notes*: Source Report of the Thirteenth Finance Commission, Last three rows author's calculations. FC = Finance Commission, Prior to FC-XII Plan assistance also carried a loan component, which varied as a share of total assistance from 70 per cent for general category states to 10 per cent for special category states. Prior to 1999–2000, there was also on-lending by the centre to states of net collections in small savings schemes.

**TABLE 2.10 Revenue transfers from centre to states as percentage of gross revenue receipts of the centre**

| | FC Transfers | | | Other Transfers | | | Total Transfers |
|---|---|---|---|---|---|---|---|
| Years | *Share in Central Taxes* | *Grants* | *Total FC Transfers (2 + 3)* | *Plan Grants* | *Non-Plan Grants* | *Total Other Transfers (5 + 6)* | *(4 + 7)* |
| *1* | *2* | *3* | *4* | *5* | *6* | *7* | *8* |
| FC-VIII (1984–1989) | 20.25 | 2.52 | 22.77 | 13.56 | 1.54 | 15.10 | 37.86 |
| FC-IX (1989–1995) | 21.37 | 3.42 | 24.79 | 14.49 | 1.06 | 15.55 | 40.33 |
| FC-X (1995–2000) | 22.22 | 2.34 | 24.56 | 10.57 | 0.67 | 11.24 | 35.79 |
| FC-XI (2000–2005) | 20.59 | 3.88 | 24.47 | 10.10 | 0.70 | 10.80 | 35.27 |
| FC-XII (2005–2010) | 21.75 | 4.45 | 26.20 | 10.99 | 1.32 | 12.31 | 38.51 |
| 2005–2006 | 21.71 | 5.69 | 27.41 | 9.66 | 1.03 | 10.69 | 38.09 |
| 2006–2007 | 21.97 | 5.11 | 27.08 | 9.69 | 1.16 | 10.85 | 37.93 |
| 2007–2008 | 21.88 | 3.80 | 25.68 | 10.30 | 1.22 | 11.53 | 37.21 |
| 2008–2009 (RE) | 22.17 | 3.83 | 26.01 | 12.23 | 1.32 | 13.56 | 39.57 |
| 2009–2010 (BE) | 21.10 | 4.42 | 25.52 | 12.15 | 1.69 | 13.84 | 39.35 |
| Mean | 21.50 | 3.95 | 25.45 | 11.37 | 1.17 | 12.55 | 37.99 |
| SD | 0.67 | 1.04 | 1.37 | 1.67 | 0.33 | 1.84 | 1.60 |
| CV | 0.03 | 0.26 | 0.05 | 0.15 | 0.28 | 0.15 | 0.04 |

*Notes*: Source Report of the 13th FC, last three rows author's calculations.

was much higher than that of states' share in central taxes (0.26 compared to 0.05). Total FC transfers represent about a one-fourth of central government revenue with a low CV (0.05) over the entire period. The share peaked in 2005–2006 and then fell to a value, in 2009–2010, higher than that in 1984–1989 and the mean for the entire period.

Tables 2.9 and 2.10 lead to some interesting conclusions. The share of central taxes going to states as well states' share in central taxes has remained relatively stable over a twenty-five-year period. Grants, although marginal in comparison to share in central taxes, are playing a larger role in fiscal transfers. Indeed various FC reports have advocated the need for stability in central government transfers to states.

This stability, particularly in FC transfers, is all the more surprising since the criteria for FC transfers to states have changed considerably over time. Table 2.11 depicts the criteria for federal transfers in the last three FCs.

The first argument in the transfer function, the population of the state in the 1971 census of India, clearly needs to be updated in view of major changes in state population growth since 1971. The weight of population has ranged from 10 per cent in the 11th FC to 25 per cent in the 12th and 13th FCs.

The second argument in the transfer function is income distance as a proxy for the fiscal capacity of individual states. The 12th FC measured this by applying a single average tax/gross state domestic product (GSDP) ratio to individual

**TABLE 2.11 Criteria and weights for tax devolution by recent FCs**

| | Weight (Per cent) | | |
|---|---|---|---|
| **Criteria** | **11th FC (2000–2005)** | **12th FC (2005–2010)** | **13th FC (2010–2015)** |
| Population | 10 | 25 | 25 |
| Income distance | 62.5 | 50 | – |
| Fiscal capacity distance | – | – | 47.5 |
| Area | 7.5 | 10 | 10 |
| Tax effort | 5.0 | 7.5 | – |
| Infrastructure index | 7.5 | – | – |
| Fiscal discipline | 7.5 | 7.5 | 17.5 |
| Total | 100 | 100 | 100 |

*Source*: 11th, 12th and 13th FC Reports.

state per capita GSDPs to measure the fiscal capacity distance between states. This argument was substituted for in the 13th FC by a fiscal capacity distance computed as follows. First, three-year average per capita GSDPs were worked out for individual states for the years 2004–2005 to 2006–2007. Second, average tax to comparable GSDP ratio was computed as a weighted mean separately for general category and special category states. These averages are then applied to all states in each of the two categories. This enables one to calculate the potential per capita tax revenue in each state available at the average tax to GSDP ratio. Fiscal distance is obtained for each state as the difference between the potential per capita tax revenue of that state and that of Haryana, the state with the highest per capita tax revenue after Goa.

Another argument in the transfer function (index of fiscal discipline) is arrived at by relating improvement in ratio of a state's own revenue receipts relative to its total revenue expenditure compared to average ratio across all states. The 'area' criterion got a weight of 10 per cent. Small states with less than 2 per cent share in total area of the country were deemed to have an area of 2 per cent.

Infrastructure index, tax effort and income distance were not used as elements of the fiscal transfer function in the 13th FC. It can be argued that the omission of the income distance measure is not a major omission since a proxy is incorporated in the Gadgil-Mukherjee formula for disbursements by the PC. The omission of the infrastructure index and tax effort is an issue of concern since these factors certainly affect the tax collected by states.[12]

## PC transfers

India's planning heritage goes back to the First Five-Year Plan (1951–1956) and for a long while, at least until the economic reforms of 1991, planned economic development was a key element of India's economic strategy. The 'socialistic' pattern of economic development was ingrained in the Second Five-Year Plan. The 11th Five-Year Plan completed its term in March 2012 and currently the country is going through the 12th Five-Year Plan (2012–2017).

Table 2.12 gives the evolution of the formula (known as the Gadgil-Mukherjee formula) for disbursements of PC assistance to states. These transfers are heavily geared towards redistribution to less well-off states. Figure 2.4 gives details of variation of real PCNSDP and its mean value for the 11 special category states

**TABLE 2.12 Gadgil-Mukherjee formula: Alternative versions (Weightage: percentage)**

| Criteria | | Modified Gadgil Formula (1980) | NDC Revised Formula 1990 | NDC Revised Formula 1991 |
|---|---|---|---|---|
| A. | Special Category States (10) | 30% share of 10 States excluding North Eastern Council | 30% share of 10 States including North Eastern Council | 30% share of 10 States excluding North Eastern Council |
| B. | General Category States (15) | | | |
| (i) | Population (1971) | 60.0 | 55.0 | 60.0 |
| (ii) | Per Capita income Of which | 20.0 | 25.0 | 25.0 |
| a. | According to the 'deviation' method covering only the states with per capita income below the national average | 20.0 | 20.0 | 20.0 |
| b. | According to the 'distance' method covering all the fifteen states | – | 5.0 | 5.0 |
| (iii) | Performance Of which | 10.0 | 5.0 | 7.5 |
| a. | Tax Effort | 10.0 | – | 2.5 |
| b. | Fiscal Management | – | 5.0 | 2.5 |
| c. | National Objectives | – | – | 2.5 |
| d. | Special Problems | 10.0 | 15.0 | 7.5 |
| Total | | 100.0 | 100.0 | 100.0 |

*Notes*: (1) Fiscal management is assessed as the difference between states' own total plan resources estimated at the time of finalizing Annual Plans and their actual performance, considering latest five years.

(2) Under the criterion of the performance in respect of certain programmes of national priorities the approved formula covers four objectives, namely: (i) population control; (ii) elimination of illiteracy; (iii) on-time completion of externally aided projects and (iv) success in land reforms.

*Source*: Planning Commission, GOI.

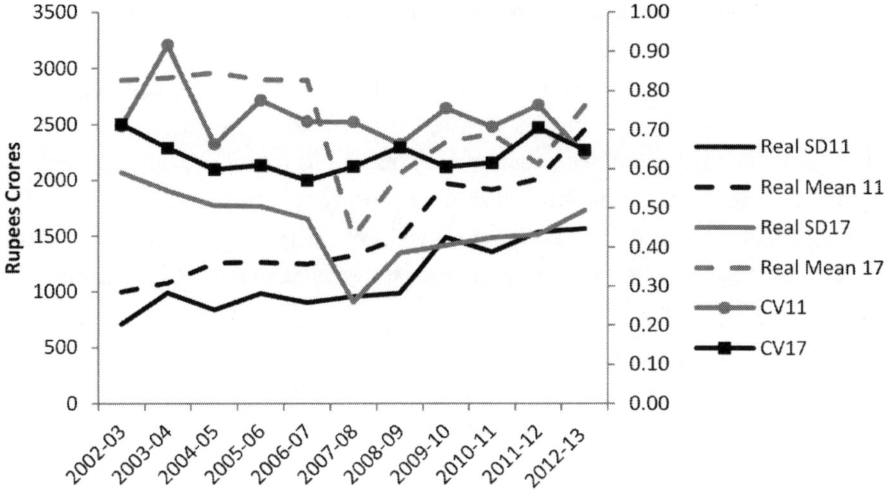


**FIGURE 2.4 Real mean, real SD of central assistance loans and grants for special and other programmes.**

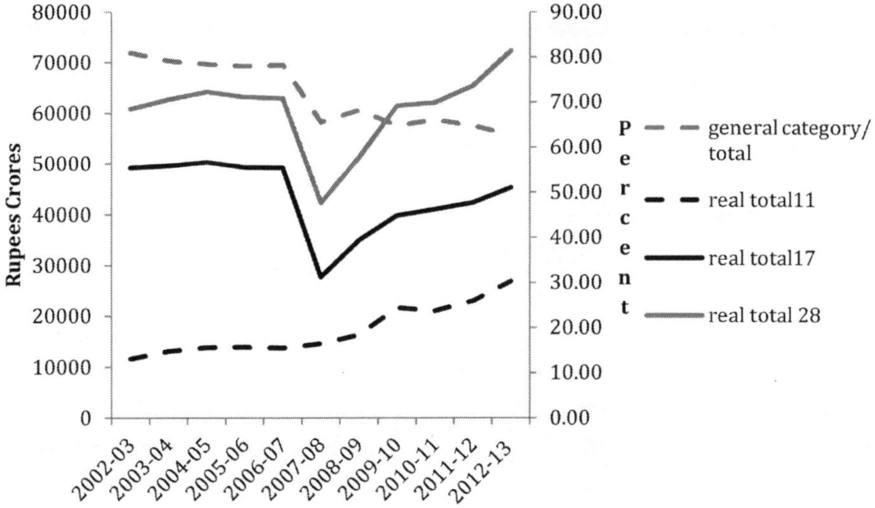


**FIGURE 2.5 Total real transfers.**

and 17 general category states whereas Figure 2.5 gives corresponding values of real transfers for these states.

The special category states are supposed to receive a pre-determined share (30 per cent). The dominant factor in the division of the rest of the funds among the states is population. Per capita income is the next most significant argument with a quarter of this weightage arising from the 'distance' argument already discussed. The performance of states with respect to national priorities such as population control, elimination of illiteracy, on-time completion of externally aided projects and tax effort each get a weight of 2.5 per cent in the last version of the formula whereas special problems of states get a weight of 7.5 per cent.

Tables 2.10 and 2.11 provide information on transfers through plan and non-plan grants in comparison to those from the FC for the period 1984–1989 to 2009–2010. Plan grants constitute typically more than 50 per cent of transfers through FC grants. Non-plan grants are slightly above 10 per cent of plan grants.

Table 2.13 indicates some basic characteristics of PC grants (in nominal and real terms) to state governments. It distinguished between the 11 special category states and the 17 general category states. RSD11 (the SD of real transfers to special category states) has more than doubled during the period 2002–2003 to 2012–2013 and Rtotal11 (the total of real transfers to 11 special category states) has gone up by about 2.5 times over the same period. RSD17 (the SD of real transfers to general category states) has, however, shown no real trend. It fell between 2002–2003 and 2007–2008 and rose thereafter. What is worth noting is that Rtotal17 (the total of real transfers to 17 general category states) has actually fallen over this period. There is a rise in Rtotal28 (the total of real transfers to all 28 states) but this is accounted for by the increase to special category states. The share of general category states in total transfers has fallen steadily from 80.90 per cent in 2002–2003 to 62.71 per cent in 2012–2013.[13]

The Gadgil-Mukherjee formula had been widely criticized for the following reasons. (1) The designation of 30 per cent of the funds to the special category states has no explicit rationale. This division was initially meant to cover revenue expenditure on plans and has long since become irrelevant. (2) Further, shares of transfers based on tax effort were unscaled for size of state. Thus, if a large state and a small state had the same tax effort they would receive the same absolute transfer so that the per capita transfer to the small state would be very large in comparison to that for the large state. (3) There was considerable arbitrariness in the allocation of funds to individual special category states from the 30 per cent share allocated to them. (4) The formula

**TABLE 2.13 Characteristics of PC transfers to states**

| Year | SD11 | CV11 | Total11 | SD17 | CV17 | Total17 | Total28 | RSD11 | Rtotal11 | RSD17 | Rtotal17 | Rtotal28 | Share (%) |
|---|---|---|---|---|---|---|---|---|---|---|---|---|---|
| 2002–2003 | 630.99 | 0.71 | 10,349.82 | 1,841.61 | 0.71 | 43,829.92 | 54,179.74 | 708.54 | 11,621.83 | 2,067.95 | 49,216.69 | 60,838.52 | 80.90 |
| 2003–2004 | 929.19 | 0.92 | 12,294.28 | 1,790.28 | 0.65 | 46,568.41 | 58,862.69 | 989.41 | 13,091.06 | 1,906.31 | 49,586.49 | 62,677.55 | 79.11 |
| 2004–2005 | 837.33 | 0.66 | 13,880.23 | 1,773.41 | 0.60 | 50,343.89 | 64,224.13 | 837.33 | 13,880.23 | 1,773.41 | 50,343.89 | 64,224.13 | 78.39 |
| 2005–2006 | 1,027.03 | 0.78 | 14,559.73 | 1,845.89 | 0.61 | 51,499.59 | 66,059.32 | 982.80 | 13,932.75 | 1,766.40 | 49,281.90 | 63,214.66 | 77.96 |
| 2006–2007 | 1,004.68 | 0.72 | 15,310.34 | 1,841.09 | 0.57 | 54,820.41 | 70,130.75 | 901.86 | 13,743.57 | 1,652.68 | 49,210.42 | 62,953.99 | 78.17 |
| 2007–2008 | 1,113.95 | 0.72 | 17,016.96 | 1,055.28 | 0.61 | 32,375.23 | 49,392.19 | 955.36 | 14,594.30 | 905.05 | 27,766.06 | 42,360.37 | 65.55 |
| 2008–2009 | 1,240.04 | 0.66 | 20,551.40 | 1,698.78 | 0.66 | 44,081.30 | 64,632.70 | 984.15 | 16,310.63 | 1,348.23 | 34,985.16 | 51,295.79 | 68.20 |
| 2009–2010 | 1,945.60 | 0.76 | 28,336.72 | 1,852.24 | 0.60 | 52,086.29 | 80,423.01 | 1,487.46 | 21,664.15 | 1,416.08 | 39,821.32 | 61,485.48 | 64.77 |
| 2010–2011 | 1,942.89 | 0.71 | 30,176.59 | 2,128.37 | 0.62 | 58,826.90 | 89,003.49 | 1,355.81 | 21,058.33 | 1,485.25 | 41,051.57 | 62,109.90 | 66.10 |
| 2011–2012 | 2,394.95 | 0.76 | 35,971.98 | 2,359.10 | 0.71 | 66,078.75 | 102,050.73 | 1,534.56 | 23,049.11 | 1,511.60 | 42,340.08 | 65,389.19 | 64.75 |
| 2012–2013 | 2,685.13 | 0.64 | 46,255.36 | 2,966.32 | 0.65 | 77,787.13 | 124,042.49 | 1,564.76 | 26,955.33 | 1,728.62 | 45,330.50 | 72,285.83 | 62.71 |

*Notes*: (1) Source: Calculations based on Planning Commission data; (2) SD11 = standard deviation across 11 special category states, CV = coefficient of variation across 11 special category states, Total11 = total grants to 11 special category states, SD17 = standard deviation across 17 regular states, CV17 = coefficient of variation across 17 regular states, Total17 = total across 17 regular states, Total28 = total across all states, RSD11 = standard deviation of real transfers across 11 special category states, RTotal11 = total real grants to 11 special category states, RSD17 = standard deviation of real transfers across 17 regular states, Rtotal17 = total real transfers across 17 regular states, Rtotal28 = total real transfers to all 28 states, share = share of general category states in total transfers.

Deflator used WPI (all commodities), 2004–2005 = 100. Rupee magnitudes in crores of rupees.

Special category states are: (1) Arunachal Pradesh; (2) Assam; (3) Himachal Pradesh; (4) Jammu and Kashmir; (5) Manipur; (6) Meghalaya; (7) Mizoram; (8) Nagaland; (9) Sikkim; (10) Tripura and (11) Uttaranchal.

did not monitor costs and benefits of programmes already executed in states so that performance in plan expenditure had no impact on the transfer formula used by the PC (Rajaraman, 2007).

Further, there were several issues related to the interaction of transfers through FC and PC. Transfers through FC and PC followed different rules and were uncoordinated. Whereas FC is answerable to the Parliament, PC was not. There was inefficiency in the system of transfers. Not only was the coordination of current transfers through FC and PC important but there were intertemporal issues to be considered as well since any plan transfer generates three major liabilities for periods beyond the plan: interest payments on funds borrowed for financing the plan, maintenance of assets created during the plan and salaries of people employed in plan schemes who remain in government employment after the plan has ended. To service these liabilities after the plan is over states often looked to the FC. This then generated dependence over time between PC and FC which the current structure of transfers does not recognize. The FC is interested only in the non-plan revenue expenditures whereas the PC only looked at new schemes. The current financial implications of previous plan expenditures were ignored by both agencies. This lack of coordination, therefore, set up a system of perverse incentives for both FC and PC.

Another complication with PC transfers was that they mixed grants and loans. In principle, these disbursements should be guided by different procedures. When resources are deficient but the social benefits from a project are large, for example primary health, education, and so on, resources should ideally be transferred through grants. With a loan the ability of the state to service the repayments of the loan should also be a key concern. But, the structure of PC grants had not laid down explicit criteria for making such distinctions.

The artificial dichotomy between plan and non-plan expenditures also induces a number of inefficiencies. There is an undue emphasis on taking up new schemes, while uncompleted projects of the past plans and maintenance of assets acquired in the past get little attention. In effect, plan schemes, as originally envisaged cannot be taken up fully, because the contemplated 'balance from current revenues' (BCRs) are often not realized. Plan finances are diverted to non-plan items, and time overruns increase costs. As a result, many schemes remain half done. The maintenance and efficient operation of existing projects are given inadequate attention.

The formation of the FC was extensively discussed during the deliberations of the Constituent Assembly. The FC is a constitutional body, constituted every five years and is designed with the enunciation of explicit formulae for federal fiscal transfers. These formulae were often at variance with those used by the PC, which meant that there needed to be more coordination between the two organizations.

Any coordination of the FC and PC transfer criteria should have recognized that FC and PC transfers were performing entirely different tasks. FC's primary traditional role is to provide equalization transfers to states so that states with relatively similar tax capacity and tax effort get similar public goods outcomes. PC transfers, on the other hand, attempted to equalize over time some indicator of development, for example per capita GSDP, across states. Hence, the equalization criterion used for PC transfers should have been different from that used in FC transfers. In this context, Singh and Srinivasan (2013) advocated the formation of a Fiscal Review Council analogous to the Trade Policy Review Mechanism of the World Trade Organization (WTO).[14] Indeed they go one step ahead and advocated the concentration of federal transfers with the FC with PC transfers being used for facilitating private investment in states. With the dissolution of PC and formation of NITI Aayog, a large part of these discrepancies have been addressed. Indeed a review of the PC by an Independent Evaluation Office (IEO, 2014) set up by the PC itself has recommended unequivocally that the PC be scrapped. The PC was seen as often diluting, if not working against, the provisions of the FC and was, therefore, inimical to the federal structure of the country. The IEO should be replaced with a Reform and Solutions Commission with broad representation from technical experts, academics, bureaucrats and civil society organizations. This commission should function as a think tank of the government and provide broad guidelines for twenty- or even fifty-year horizons. More reforms could be useful. The distinction between revenue and capital expenditure should be done away with (Planning Commission, 2011a), the FC should be made a permanent body and be solely responsible for federal transfers and a newly created department of planning in the Ministry of Finance should be asked to apportion funds amongst the various ministries of the central government to meet their capital expenses. If and when implemented these proposals would provide substantial efficiency dividends in fiscal transfers.

## *Centrally sponsored schemes*

CSS represent yet another form in which central assistance is given to states. Starting with the Second Five-Year Plan funds were provided under CSS to states. These CSS were then implemented by states as part of their plan. But, the pattern of financing of these CSS has varied considerably over time. Thus, in the Fourth Five-Year Plan there were 90 CSS of which 59 were eligible for 100 per cent funding, 12 for 75 per cent funding 3 for 60 per cent funding and 15 for 50 per cent funding. As Planning Commission (2011b) reveals this variation of sources of funding for CSS has persisted over time. As Table 2.14 indicates the proportions of CSS to other central assistance is high and has grown over time.

Two models have been used to transfer funds through CSS (Planning Commission, 2011a). In the Treasury Model, the central government transfers funds to the state government which, in turn, transfers funds to CSS. In the Society Mode, the central government bypasses the state governments to transfer funds directly to CSS. Since the mid-1990s, the Society Mode of transfer has been followed. This has the implication that it is captured in the accounts of state governments only in respect of expenditures actually incurred by them. There are very few exceptions to this rule, for example funds transferred under the Mahatma Gandhi National Rural Employment Guarantee Scheme, the Sarva Shiksha Abhiyan and the National Rural Health Mission. Thus, actual expensed on CSS are difficult to track.[15]

Clearly, the CSS route of the centre influencing state expenditures appeals for its rationale to the 'Concurrent' list of the Constitution of India and ambiguities therein. Table 2.15 indicates the overwhelming importance of CSS in successive five year plans of India whereas Table 2.16 indicates that, despite the number of CSS coming down, expenditure on CSS has grown very significantly both in nominal and in real terms.[16]

State governments naturally view CSS as an infringement on their rights and argue for their curtailment. The 2011 Report of the Committee on Restructuring of CSS argued that smaller CSS should be handed over to the states and recommended the re-classification of other CSS into three broad categories: (1) Flagship schemes.[17] (2) Sub-sector scheme where the core element would be supported by the centre and segments for operation by states could be identified. The report was of the opinion that such sub-sectoral schemes could be particularly in areas such as Education, Animal Husbandry and Health. (3) Umbrella schemes which are basically small-scale schemes.

**TABLE 2.14 CSS: Proportion to allocation (gross budgetary support) (percentages)**

| Sl. No. | Description | 2007–2008 | 2008–2009 | 2009–2010 | 2010–2011 | 2011–2012 | Grand Total (2007–2012) |
|---|---|---|---|---|---|---|---|
| A | Total Central Sector Schemes | 34.54 | 32.10 | 31.59 | 33.11 | 35.13 | 33.39 |
| B | Total CSS and Total Central Assistance | 65.46 | 67.90 | 68.41 | 66.89 | 64.87 | 66.61 |
| (i) | Normal Central Assistance | 8.22 | 8.04 | 6.45 | 6.41 | 5.84 | 6.74 |
| (ii) | CSS | 41.01 | 41.84 | 42.18 | 42.09 | 40.85 | 41.59 |
| (iii) | Total Central Assistance | 24.46 | 26.06 | 26.24 | 24.79 | 24.01 | 25.02 |
| (iv) | CSS Flagship | 31.40 | 31.59 | 34.15 | 32.56 | 31.76 | 32.36 |
| (v) | ACA/CS Flagship | 8.06 | 10.44 | 12.60 | 12.32 | 10.96 | 11.16 |
| (vi) | Total CSS (including CSS and ACA/CS Flagship) | 49.07 | 52.27 | 54.78 | 54.41 | 51.82 | 52.75 |
| (vii) | Total CSS and Central Assistance other than Normal Central Assistance | 57.25 | 59.85 | 61.96 | 60.48 | 59.03 | 59.87 |
| (viii) | Central Assistance to states other than Normal Central Assistance | 16.24 | 18.02 | 19.79 | 18.38 | 18.17 | 18.28 |

*Notes*: ACA = additional central assistance to states, CS = central scheme.

*Source*: Planning Commission (2011b).

**TABLE 2.15 Number of central assistance to CSS**

| Plan | Number of CSS | Percentage of CSS to GBS | Percent of Central Assistance to GBS |
|---|---|---|---|
| Ninth Plan (1997–2002) | 360 | 31.30 | 43.75 |
| Tenth Plan (2002–2007) | 155 | 38.64 | 34.15 |
| Eleventh Plan (2007–2012) | 147 | 41.59 | 25.02 |

*Source*: Planning Commission (2011b).

**TABLE 2.16 Centrally sponsored schemes**

| Year | Number of CSS | Budgeted Expenditure (Nominal) Rs. Crore | Budgeted Expenditure (Real) Rs. Crore | Central Assistance to State Plans (Nominal) Rs. Crore | Central Assistance to State Plans (Real) Rs. Crore |
|---|---|---|---|---|---|
| 2002–2003 | 188 | 31,389 | 35,248.74 | 44,344 | 49,796.74 |
| 2003–2004 | 213 | 32,141 | 34,445.40 | 49,814 | 53,385.49 |
| 2004–2005 | 207 | 38,312 | 38,312.00 | 51,766 | 51,766.00 |
| 2005–2006 | 204 | 55,924 | 53,515.79 | 34,901 | 33,398.09 |
| 2006–2007 | 155 | 71,996 | 64,628.37 | 45,518 | 40,859.96 |
| 2007–2008 | 99 | 81,620 | 70,000.00 | 61,614 | 52,842.20 |
| 2008–2009 | 133 | 101,824 | 80,812.70 | 77,075 | 61,170.63 |
| 2009–2010 | 138 | 137,137 | 104,844.80 | 84,490 | 64,594.80 |
| 2010–2011 | 139 | 157,051 | 109,595.95 | 96,412 | 67,279.83 |
| 2011–2012 | 147 | 180,389 | 115,584.58 | 106,026 | 67,936.35 |

*Source*: Planning Commission (2011b) and author's calculations.

It was recommended that the Central Ministries would provide guidelines for the operation of the umbrella schemes (in order to provide uniformity of standards across the country) with the actual operation being conducted by state governments. The report is, however, silent on how the CSS would fit in with FC transfers and other plan transfers. It also does not deal with spillover effects of CSS. The take away message from this analysis is that not only the structure of indirect taxation but also that of intergovernmental transfers needs overall coordination. At the present point in time lack of clarity on this point leads to the possibility of arbitrariness (particularly political expediency) creeping into the transfer criteria. The budget of the GOI for 2014–2015 (Ministry of Finance, 2014) has hinted at some rationalization of CSS.

## Transfers to PRIs and urban bodies

PRIs form the third tier of India's federal structure and are seen as key to delivering local public goods to Indian villages. In its submission to the 13th FC, the Ministry of Panchayati Raj highlighted the importance of PRI in implementing many CSS as well as programmes of individual state governments. While the PRI have considerable funds to implement CSS they lack funds for conducting their own administration. In this connection the Ministry asked for 4 per cent of the divisible funds allocated to local bodies be given to PRI for the construction of village infrastructure. Another 1 per cent was to be given as a specific purpose grant-in-aid to panchayats for preparation of databases and incentivizing state governments to empower panchayats. Table 2.17 provides details of disbursements to PRI in 2010–2011 and 2011–2012.

For 2010–2011 and 2011–2012, Table 2.17 depicts basic grants to states under two headings: general areas and special areas. General purpose grants are of much larger magnitude than special purpose grants but overall transfers to PRI are relatively modest in comparison to FC and PC grants to states. However, there has been a substantial increase in (real and nominal transfers) over the period 2010–2011 to 2011–2012. As expected large states get larger shares, that of UP is dominant.

Grants to municipalities are in a 'highly unsatisfactory state' (Mathur, 2013, p. 23). The 11thFC earmarked Rs. 2,000 crores for municipalities, the 12th FC allocated Rs. 5,000 crores and the 13th Commission Rs. 8,000 crores. The 11th and 12th FCs allocated a fixed amount whereas the 13th FC advocated that a fixed percentage of the divisible pool be given to all states as a grant. Municipal expenditure as a percentage of GSDP was only 1.08 in 2002–2003, rising to a meagre 1.24 in 2007–2008.

However, there have been very few objective evaluations of the impact of two-tier, let alone three-tier decentralization on balanced regional growth.

**TABLE 2.17 Grants to panchayats under 13th FC (Rs. Crore)**

| | | Allocation Based on the Divisible Pool 2010–2011 | | | Allocation Based on the Divisible Pool 2011–2012 (Nominal) | | | Allocation Based on the Divisible Pool 2011–2012 (Real, Comparable with 2010–2011) | | |
|---|---|---|---|---|---|---|---|---|---|---|
| | | Basic Grant | | | Basic Grant | | | Basic Grant | | |
| S. No. | State | General Areas | Special Areas | Total | General Areas | Special Areas | Total | General Areas | Special Areas | Total |
| 1 | Andhra Pradesh | 480.74 | 5.9 | 486.64 | 609.39 | 5.9 | 615.29 | 559.42 | 5.42 | 564.84 |
| 2 | Arunachal Pradesh | 25.2 | 0 | 25.2 | 31.95 | 0 | 31.95 | 29.33 | 0.00 | 29.33 |
| 3 | Assam | 145.11 | 7.3 | 152.41 | 183.94 | 7.3 | 191.24 | 168.86 | 6.70 | 175.56 |
| 4 | Bihar | 455.7 | 0 | 455.7 | 577.65 | 0 | 577.65 | 530.28 | 0.00 | 530.28 |
| 5 | Chattisgarh | 153.67 | 21.1 | 174.77 | 194.79 | 21.1 | 215.89 | 178.82 | 19.37 | 198.19 |
| 6 | Goa | 8.32 | 0 | 8.32 | 10.55 | 0 | 10.55 | 9.68 | 0.00 | 9.68 |
| 7 | Gujarat | 214.61 | 14.4 | 229.01 | 272.05 | 14.4 | 286.45 | 249.74 | 13.22 | 262.96 |
| 8 | Haryana | 99.94 | 0 | 99.94 | 126.68 | 0 | 126.68 | 116.29 | 0.00 | 116.29 |
| 9 | Himachal Pradesh | 51.2 | 0.3 | 51.5 | 64.9 | 0.3 | 65.2 | 59.58 | 0.28 | 59.85 |
| 10 | Jammu and Kashmir | 84.48 | 0 | 84.48 | 107.09 | 0 | 107.09 | 98.31 | 0.00 | 98.31 |
| 11 | Jharkhand | 139.48 | 35 | 174.48 | 176.81 | 35 | 211.81 | 162.31 | 32.13 | 194.44 |
| 12 | Karnataka | 414.33 | 0 | 414.33 | 525.21 | 0 | 525.21 | 482.14 | 0.00 | 482.14 |
| 13 | Kerala | 179.35 | 0 | 179.35 | 227.34 | 0 | 227.34 | 208.70 | 0.00 | 208.70 |
| 14 | Madhya Pradesh | 378.43 | 26.5 | 404.93 | 479.7 | 26.5 | 506.2 | 440.37 | 24.33 | 464.69 |

| | | | | | | | | | | |
|---|---|---|---|---|---|---|---|---|---|---|
| 15 | Maharashtra | 505.78 | 7.9 | 513.68 | 641.14 | 7.9 | 649.04 | 588.57 | 7.25 | 595.82 |
| 16 | Manipur | 20.13 | 1.8 | 21.93 | 25.52 | 1.8 | 27.32 | 23.43 | 1.65 | 25.08 |
| 17 | Meghalaya | 28.77 | 4.6 | 33.37 | 36.47 | 4.6 | 41.07 | 33.48 | 4.22 | 37.70 |
| 18 | Mizoram | 18.54 | 1.8 | 20.34 | 23.51 | 1.8 | 25.31 | 21.58 | 1.65 | 23.23 |
| 19 | Nagaland | 28.05 | 4 | 32.05 | 35.56 | 4 | 39.56 | 32.64 | 3.67 | 36.32 |
| 20 | Odisha | 238.31 | 21.6 | 259.91 | 302.08 | 21.6 | 323.68 | 277.31 | 19.83 | 297.14 |
| 21 | Punjab | 103.5 | 0 | 103.5 | 131.2 | 0 | 131.2 | 120.44 | 0.00 | 120.44 |
| 22 | Rajasthan | 362.26 | 3.6 | 365.86 | 459.2 | 3.6 | 462.8 | 421.55 | 3.30 | 424.85 |
| 23 | Sikkim | 16.96 | 0 | 16.96 | 21.5 | 0 | 21.5 | 19.74 | 0.00 | 19.74 |
| 24 | Tamil Nadu | 283.64 | 0 | 283.64 | 359.55 | 0 | 359.55 | 330.07 | 0.00 | 330.07 |
| 25 | Tripura | 26.95 | 2.4 | 29.35 | 34.16 | 2.4 | 36.56 | 31.36 | 2.20 | 33.56 |
| 26 | Uttar Pradesh | 900.3 | 0 | 900.3 | 1,141.23 | 0 | 1,141.23 | 1,047.65 | 0.00 | 1,047.65 |
| 27 | Uttarakhand | 54.37 | 0 | 54.37 | 68.92 | 0 | 68.92 | 63.27 | 0.00 | 63.27 |
| 28 | West Bengal | 381.2 | 1.6 | 382.8 | 483.21 | 1.6 | 484.81 | 443.59 | 1.47 | 445.06 |
| | Total | 5,799.3 | 159.8 | 5,959.1 | 7,351.3 | 159.8 | 7,511.1 | 6,748.50 | 146.70 | 6,895.20 |

*Source*: Ministry of Panchayati Raj, Government of India (2012) Annual report 2011–2012 and author's calculations. Deflator used WPI.

Kalirajan and Otsuka (2012) show that two-tier decentralization (between centre and states) has been helpful in fostering growth through health and education expenditures. However, the performance of PRI and other local bodies has been dismal.

## Conclusions

The urgency for indirect reform in India has never been greater and is only growing. Furthermore, such indirect tax reform must take place against the background high fiscal deficits for the central government and structurally high deficits for several state governments. This, then, makes transparency and consistency of all financial relations between states and between state and central governments an integral part of such reform.

This chapter has provided a broad overview of fiscal issues facing various levels of government in India. In a society as complex and varied as India's fiscal federalism is an essential element of the economic landscape. Already it is becoming clear that states are the new engines of India's economic growth. Thus, the *Economist Intelligence Unit* in a report dated 25th June 2013 argued that during 2011–2012 over 80 per cent of states had GSDP growth rates of above 6 per cent when the national growth rate was 6.2 per cent and that this trend is likely to continue. Some traditionally laggard states have been growing well above the national average indicating that nurturing state-level economic growth can have considerable payoffs for national economic growth and, hence, poverty reduction.

These factors underscore the benefits of putting centre–state fiscal relations on an even keel to encourage buoyant economic growth. Concurrently, the risks of having adverse incentives in fiscal relations can risk economic crises as the example of Argentina suggests.

Reform of fiscal federalism in India is an ongoing process and is currently facing the twin additional challenges of moving to a harmonized central and state GST and addressing a persistent fiscal deficit level problem at both central and state levels (Rao and Sen, 2011). Indeed there is apprehension, at least on the part of states, that moving to a GST will exacerbate their fiscal deficits and compromise their revenue flexibility.

A difficulty with the enactment and promulgation of the GST is that states perceive that much of the power rests with the GOI. A way out would be to constitute a body for arbitration and dispute resolution along the lines of the EC which has a strong record in reforming the tax system. Like the EC the GST Council should have members who are proficient and have high credibility among the GOI and all state governments. It would be preferable to make the GST Council a regulatory constitutional body with punitive powers, unlike the EC which was a 'society' registered under the Societies Registration Act. By implementing these measures, the new government will find it possible to bring all states on board to introduce GST in the near future by ensuring the removal of all the bumps and road blocks in the path of its introduction.

Furthermore, if the role of the PC is removed with the new NITI Aayog, then any perceived conflict between transfers completely through the FC and PC would be seen to diminish with transfers being made according to a unified federal transfer structure. This in itself will reduce the states' skepticism about the GST.

Against this background this chapter has underscored the substantial spatial disparities across India. It has evaluated the case for putting together (various versions) of the GST and also indicated the risks involved in the process. This chapter argues that, on balance, there is a case for an appropriately constituted GST but that the federal transfer formula must be sensitive to any fallout from such a move.

The chapter also argues that there is an urgent need to review the totality of transfers from the central to state governments and local bodies. This review would include transfers through FC and CSS. There is a compelling necessity to review and recalibrate the entire gamut (and not piecemeal) of federal relations – tax, expenditure and transfers. This is critical to ensure the stability and predictability needed to ensure that India's state driven growth blossoms and attains full fruition.

## Notes

1 The Economist Intelligence Unit in a report dated 25th June 2013 has underscored the recent centrality of state-level growth to national growth in India with many traditionally backward states posting strong growth performances.

2 In a similar vein, Jha and Sharma (2014) have reported rising inequality using household data for the period 1993–1994 to 2009–2010.

3 Until very recent times much of this debt has been in the nature of internal debt with long-term maturity. Nevertheless, there are good reasons to be concerned about India's debt situation (Asher, 2012).

4 Countries such as Australia which are not encumbered by such constitutional restrictions have replaced a tax on manufacturing level by a GST and extended this to the retail level. However, constitutional provisions preclude this policy in India.

5 Estimates of the extent of cascading in the case of India do not exist. However, estimates for Canada's retail sales tax (similar to India's state VAT) indicate that cascading could be as high as 35–40 per cent of tax revenue. This is partly due to the fact that most of such taxes are applied to business-to-business transactions.

6 I am grateful to an anonymous referee for indicating this literature to me.

7 For the effects of a large informal sector on VAT see Emran and Stiglitz (2005).

8 See Emran and Stiglitz (2005) for a lucid discussion of this point.

9 The PC has now been disbanded with the NITI Aayog taking up some of its policy functions.

10 Although proceeds from most central taxes are included in the pool that is distributed to states revenue from central government cesses (such as the education cess) is not included. The 13th FC Report, for instance, provides detailed justification for this omission. This practice goes back to the days before the 10th FC when revenue from some taxes was not shared with central governments.

11 Indeed reports of various FCs have emphasized the importance of stability in FC transfers.

12 There is the further issue of whether the infrastructure index and tax effort, as computed and used by earlier FCs, are meaningful indicators of tax effort (Jha et al., 1999) and the availability of infrastructure.

13 It is hardly surprising, therefore, that there is a clamor among some relatively less well-off states, such as Bihar, to have the criteria for special category state tweaked in order to gain entry.

14 Indeed Singh and Srinivasan (2013) emphasize that such coordination and setting the parameters of centre state transfers on an even keel is essential for macroeconomic stability. In the past Argentina paid a high cost for ignoring this.

15 I am grateful to an anonymous referee for suggesting this line of argument.

16 Much of the recent growth in CSS expenditure has been on account of relatively new programs such as the National Rural Employment Guarantee Schemes, Pradhan Mantri Gram Sadak Yojana, Sarva Shiksha Abhiyan and so on.

17 The criteria for identifying a 'flagship scheme' are unclear. In 2011, the PC recognized fifteen flagship schemes.t

## References

Asher, M. 2012. 'Public Debt Sustainability and Fiscal Management in India.' In *Public Debt Sustainability in Developing Asia*, edited by B. Ferrarini, R. Jha and A. Ramayandi, 139–69. London and New York: Routledge.

Bagchi, A. 2002. *Fifty Years of Fiscal Federalism in India: An Appraisal*. Working Paper No. 3, 2002, Kale Memorial Lecture, Gokhale Institute of Politics and Economics.

Boadway, R. and F. Flatters. 1982. *Equalization in a Federal State: An Economic Analysis*. Economic Council of Canada, Ottawa: Canadian Government Publishing Center.

Buchanan, J. 1950. 'Federalism and Fiscal Equity.' *American Economic Review* 40 (4): 421–32.

Emran, S. and J. Stiglitz. 2005. 'On Selective Indirect Tax Reform in Developing Countries.' *Journal of Public Economics* 89 (3): 599–623.

Independent Evaluation Office. 2014. 'Reforming the Planning Commission.' Mimeo The Planning Commission.

Institute of Applied Manpower Research and Planning Commission, Government of India. 2011. *India Human Development Report: Towards Social Inclusion*. New Delhi: Oxford University Press.

Jha, R. 2009. *Modern Public Economics*. 2nd ed. London and New York: Routledge.

Jha, R. and A. Sharma. 2014. 'Poverty and Inequality: Redesigning Intervention.' In *The Oxford Handbook of the Indian Economy in the 21st Century*, edited by A. Goyal, 249–73. New Delhi: Oxford University Press.

Jha, R., R. Gaiha, N. Kaicker and M. Pandey. 2013. 'Food Subsidy, Income Transfers and the Poor: A Comparative Analysis of the Public Distribution System in India's States.' *Journal of Policy Modelling* 35: 887–908.

Jha, R., M. Mohanty, S. Chatterjee and P. Chitkara. 1999. 'Fiscal Efficiency in Selected Indian States.' *Empirical Economics* 24 (3): 641–54.

Kalirajan, K. and K. Otsuka. 2012. 'Fiscal Decentralization and Development Outcomes in India: An Exploratory Analysis.' *World Development* 40 (8): 1511–521.

Kelkar Committee Report. 2012. *Report of the Committee on Roadmap for Fiscal Consolidation*. Ministry of Finance, Government of India.

Mallick, J. 2012. 'Estimation of Private Investment in Manufacturing Sector and Determinants in Indian States.' New Delhi: Institute for Studies in Industrial Development Working Paper 2012/06.

Mathur, O. 2013. 'Finances of Municipalities: Issues before the 14th Finance Commission.' *Economic and Political Weekly* 48 (22): 23–27.

Ministry of Finance. 2014. 'Budget of the Union of India for 2014–2015.' Accessed July 21. http://www.finmin.nic.in/.

Ministry of Panchayati Raj, Government of India. 2012. Annual Report 2011–2012.

Mukherjee, A. 2011. 'Regional Inequality in Foreign Investment Flows to India: The Problem and the Prospects.' *Reserve Bank of India Occasional Papers* 32 (2): 99–127.

Mukherjee, S. and K. Rao. 2014. *Exploring Policy Options to Include, Petroleum, Natural Gas and Electricity Under the Goods and Services Tax Regime in India*. Working Paper No. 2014–136, National Institute of Public Finance and Policy, New Delhi.

Planning Commission. 2011a. *Report of the High Level Expert Committee on Efficient Management of Public Expenditure*. New Delhi: Government of India.

Planning Commission. 2011b. *Report of the Committee on Restructuring of Centrally Sponsored Schemes*. New Delhi: Government of India.

Poddar, S. and E. Ahmad. 2009. *GST Reforms and Intergovernmental Consideration in India*. Working Paper No.1/2009-DEA, Ministry of Finance, Government of India.

Rajaraman, I. 2007. 'The Political Economy of the Indian Federation.' *India Policy Forum* 4: 1–52.

Rangarajan, C. and D. K. Srivastava. 2008. 'Reforming India's Fiscal Transfer System: Resolving Vertical and Horizontal Imbalances.' *Economic and Political Weekly* 43 (23): 47–60.

Rao, M. G. 2008. 'Unfinished Reform Agendum: Fiscal Consolidation and Reforms – A Comment.' In *Sustaining India's Growth Miracle*, edited by Jagdish Bhagwati and Charles W. Colomiris, 104–14. New York, NY: Columbia Business School.

Rao, M. and T. Sen. 2011. *Federalism and Fiscal Reforms in India*. Working Paper 2011-84, National Institute of Public Finance and Policy, New Delhi.

Singh, N. and T. N. Srinivasan. 2013. 'Federalism and Economic Development in India: An Assessment.' In *Economic Reform in India: Challenges, Prospects and Lessons*, edited by N. Hope, A. Kochar, R. Noll and T. N. Srinivasan. Cambridge, UK and New Delhi: Cambridge University Press.

Thirteenth Finance Commission. 2009. *Report of the Thirteenth Finance Commission*. New Delhi: Government of India.

World Bank. 2009. World Development Report entitled *Spatial Disparities and Development Policy*. Washington, DC: The World Bank.

3

# Fiscal Implications of Energy Subsidies

S. Narayan

## Introduction

Fiscal deficits have been a worry for the Indian economy for over two decades. The initial budget making years focussed on a planned model of economic growth, and capital expenditures out of the government budget were used largely for plan expenditure. The focus was much more on revenue deficit figures, that is, the difference between revenue receipts and revenue expenditure. The austerity models of the early political leaders and a socialist model of growth led to a focus on high levels of personal taxation, barriers to imports, an import substitution model of growth, and reliance on the public sector for economic growth. In this model, public finances were a tool for capital formation, aided by funds from the banking sector that had been substantially nationalized by the early seventies.

Towards the second half of the seventies, and subsequently thereafter, expenditure on social sectors started to grow both at the state and central levels. Government increasingly found it necessary to borrow to maintain the infrastructure for schools, hospitals and water supply that it had funded. Government borrowing was used not just for capital funding, but also for revenue expenditure gaps. At about this time, the role of subsidies in expenditure started increasing. The food grains procurement and distribution programmes devolved substantial expenditure on to the central government budget starting from wheat, and then rice, procurement operations. Fertilizer subsidies increased after the Green Revolution initiatives focussed on fertilizer application as an important production input. Finally, the change in fuel pricing policies after the 1973–1974 oil price shock added a big burden to the budgets in the form of fuel and energy subsidies. Figures 3.1 and 3.2 trace the growth in fiscal deficits from 1992 at the centre and state level (Ministry of Finance).

The year 2008–2009 represents an inflection point in the fiscal deficit strategy of the central government. In that year, fiscal expansion increased the fiscal

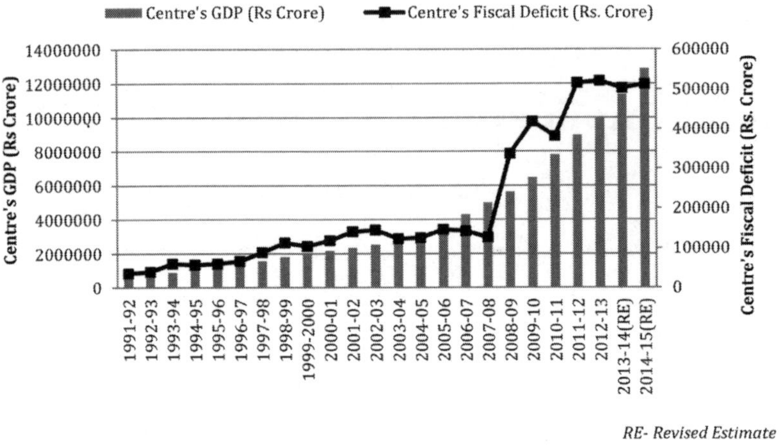


**FIGURE 3.1 Centre's fiscal deficit.**

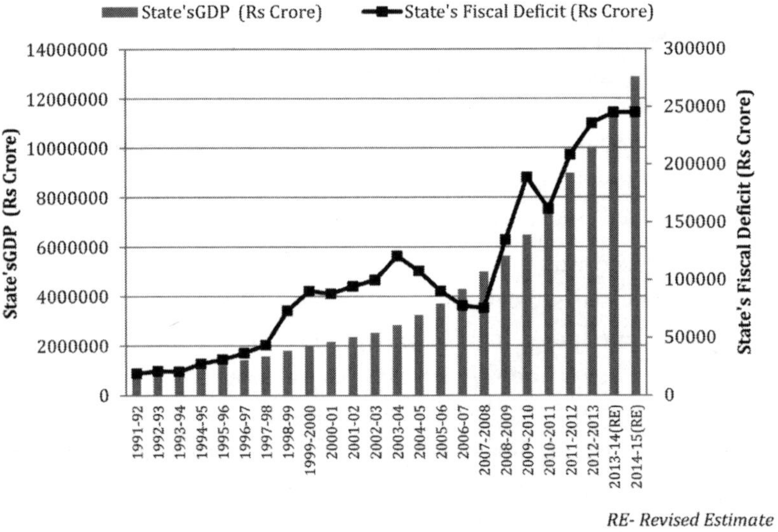


**FIGURE 3.2 State's fiscal deficit.**

deficit from Rs. 126,912 crores to Rs. 336,992 crores, from 2.54 per cent of gross domestic product (GDP) to 5.99 per cent. It was argued by government that, this fiscal expansion was required to cushion the economy from the impact of the global financial crisis of 2008. Critics have argued that such an expansion in fact, led to inflationary pressures arising from supply side constraints, and did little to add production capacity or investments in the economy. This criticism appears to be supported by events in the subsequent years that have seen the growth of GDP fall from over 8 per cent level 2007–2008 to a sub 5.5 per cent level in 2012–2013. The tenets of the Fiscal Responsibility and Budget Management Act were given up during this expansionary phase. Subsequent budgets did little to correct the situation. The slowing down of GDP growth had its effect on government revenues, exacerbating the fiscal pressures. Fiscal deficit grew to 6.46 per cent of GDP in 2009–2010 and continued to be high at 5.75 per cent in the actual figures of 2011–2012. The budget estimates (BEs) of 2014–2015 show an attempt to reduce the deficit to 4.1 per cent of GDP. The absolute numbers of government borrowings remain substantial, and are budgeted to be over Rs. 540,000 crores in 2014–2015 BEs.

Subsidies in the energy sector are a significant contributor to the fiscal deficit. The central budget accounts for subsidies in the petroleum sector and the initiatives for non-conventional and renewable energy generation, while the state budgets have focussed on the subsidies for the power sector. Figure 3.3 shows the share of energy subsidies in centre's fiscal deficit from 2007 till 2012. Share of petroleum subsidies in the fiscal deficit from 2007 till 2014 is shown in Figure 3.4 (Expenditure Union Budget Documents, 2007–2014).

Fiscal deficit considerations are comparatively recent consideration in public finance and public accounts. In the early nineties, the International Monetary

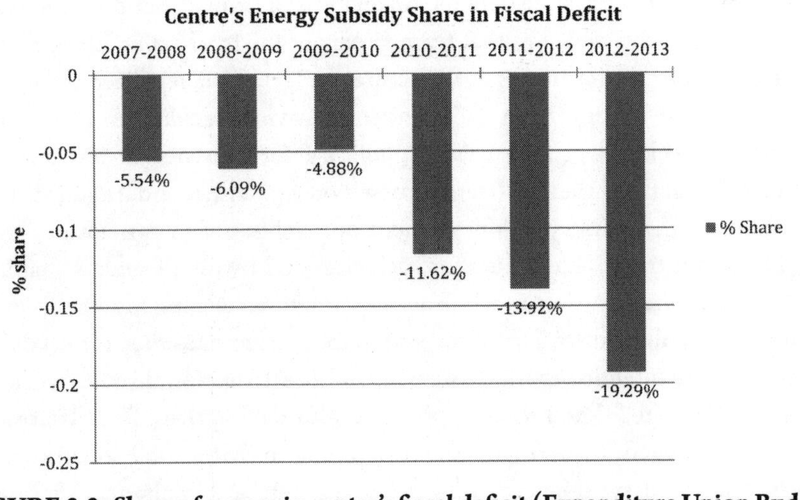


**FIGURE 3.3 Share of energy in centre's fiscal deficit (Expenditure Union Budget Documents, 2007–2014).**

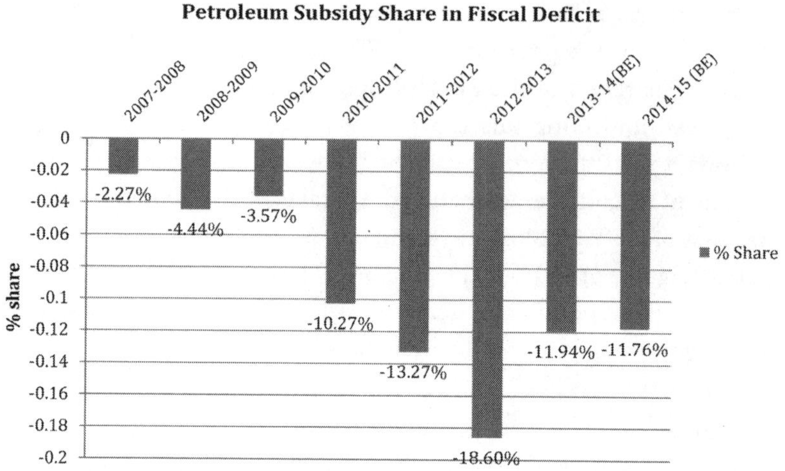


**FIGURE 3.4 Petroleum subsidy share in centre's fiscal deficit (Expenditure Union Budget Documents, 2007–2014).**

Fund (IMF), worried about the deteriorating finances of some Latin American countries, brought to the forefront consideration of fiscal deficits. The crisis of 1991 and the IMF support for India brought in this concept as an important parameter for measuring the health and soundness of public finances of the country. Until then, the concern had been primarily with revenue deficits. The initial concerns were shortage of funds for investments and capital expenditure, and the overhang of revenue deficits. An analysis of revenue deficits gave rise to concerns about the subsidies that formed part of the total expenditure budget. The three major subsidy items in the central budget, food, fertilizer and energy, have a political history. After independence, having decided on a socialistic pattern of development and a large public sector presence in industry and manufacturing, the earliest budgets focussed on agriculture and irrigation. Over two-thirds of the country was dependent on livelihoods in agriculture, and it was important to provide inputs for agriculture that would enable sustainable livelihoods in the farm sector, while at the same time keeping food grain prices under reasonable control for the urban sectors. Input subsidies for seeds and fertilizers were intended to modernize agriculture. Irrigation through wells and pump-sets required diesel to be supplied at affordable prices. Diesel subsidies would also benefit fishermen. States pitched in with rural electrification programmes and subsidies for power for agriculture. Simultaneously, public distribution systems (PDSs) provided subsidized cereals for the urban poor.

The complex web of subsidies was created within the first ten years after independence, and electoral politics has made unravelling of these extremely difficult. Therefore, the framework for our analysis lies much more in the realm of political economy than in public finance. The future of the subsidies would have to be examined against the context of developing political equations, and the damages to public finances weighed against the balance of electoral benefits.

India has historically subsidized energy in order to protect consumers from international price volatility and to provide energy access to the poor. The central budgets have subsidized the petroleum sector, while the state budgets have focussed on subsidies for electricity, most notably to the agriculture sector. Subsidies have included direct transfer of funds (grants, loans, loan guarantees), foregone government revenues as well as price support measures. Between producer subsidies and consumer subsidies, the central and state governments have preferred the latter, that is, to lower prices at which energy products are sold. This was driven by a political motive of reaching out to the consumers, who are larger in number than producers.[1] It is important to understand the evolution of these subsidies in order to arrive at the impact on the state and central deficits, and to examine ways in which it could be reduced.

There is also the distortion caused by taxation policies. Petroleum products are taxed heavily by the states, and in most of the states, it is the single largest contributor to state tax revenues. At the central level, there were (and continue to be) customs duties on import of crude oil as well as excise duties on petroleum products. Private companies regularly lobbied the government for an adequate arbitrage between the crude oil import rates and domestic taxes on products, to enable their refining margins to remain high. The historical development of taxes on petroleum products at the state as well as the central level merits a separate analysis. However, the taxation regime resulted in further distortion of pricing, with the subsidies at the central level being mopped up by higher taxes at the state level.

## Petroleum subsidies

Soon after Independence, the government introduced a cost-plus pricing formula based on import parity, which added up all cost elements such as ocean freight, import duties, and all other levies and charges. Oil companies were mandated by the government to surrender any extra realization on the sale of petroleum products based on import parity pricing and other agreed charge components. After the first oil shock of 1973–1974, the government decided to intervene aggressively to regulate prices of petroleum products, initially through a cost-plus pricing mechanism, and later through a system of administered prices. The administered pricing mechanism (APM) prescribed customer prices for the different petroleum products, based on periodic calculations. In 1974, government nationalized multinational oil companies Shell and Caltex operating in India, and secured a monopoly over refining and marketing of all petroleum products. Private-sector refineries came up in the nineties, but the pricing mechanism prevented any retail sales of petrol and diesel.

The three major oil-marketing companies (OMCs), Indian Oil, Bharat Petroleum and Hindustan Petroleum together operated the administered pricing account. The companies sourced oil from different sources, including bilateral agreements, and produced slightly different mixes of products at somewhat different productive refinery efficiencies. Retail prices of all products were fixed by the Ministry of Petroleum in consultation with the Oil Co-ordination Committee, which pooled together all the costs of production and logistics. The political executive would decide on whether the increases were too high or acceptable. There was a tendency to regard petrol as a rich man's fuel and allow market-based increases in prices, while tightly controlling prices of diesel and domestic cooking gas. Prices were seldom revised on a periodic basis, even though costs could vary based on imports of crude. An oil prices pool mechanism pooled together the over recoveries from the oil companies (the difference between the notified prices and the actual import parity costs) and it was argued that there would be a balance in the pool over price cycles, that would enable balancing of the over recoveries and the under recoveries, as also among the different OMCs. These mechanisms enabled the government to shield customer prices from the volatility of the second oil price shock in 1991–1992. Surpluses were held in an oil-pool account, while deficits were made good every year from the Union budget. However, the mechanism was cumbersome to administer, prices were ad hoc and non-transparent, and the oil pool account had several disputed claims from the OMCs pending settlement.

By 1997, the oil pool account was in substantial deficit, with the OMCs clamoring for compensation. The government decided to phase out the pricing mechanism between 1997 and 2002, and move to a market determined pricing mechanism. As a first step, prices of aviation turbine fuel and all the heavy distillates including furnace oil and naphtha were freed, and price control was limited to kerosene, liquefied petroleum gas (LPG), diesel and petrol. Prices of even the controlled commodities were revised substantially. In April 2002, it was decided to dismantle the APM completely, and the OMCs were free to fix market-based price of all products, other than LPG and kerosene. It was also decided that the subsidies for LPG and kerosene would be treated as explicit subsidies from the central budget, rather than through the oil pool account, which was dismantled. Between April 2002 and 2003, 23 price revisions were carried out on the prices of petrol and diesel. However, oil prices started rising in the international markets rapidly, and the OMCs were unable to pass on the full impact of these to the consumers.[2] There were little or no revisions of petrol, diesel, kerosene and LPG prices during 2004–2005.[3] Between 2004 and 2008, the prices of the Indian basket of crude increased by 348 per cent, and the prices of refined products at global hubs increased accordingly. However, these were not reflected in the pricing of products in India. The government of that time was reluctant to pass on the costs to the consumer. The burden of payments into the oil pool account ballooned during this period, and also the burden on public finances to pay for these subsidies. Hedging was not resorted due to capital controls – the rupee was not fully convertible, and hedging costs were usually very high.

During the years that the APM was in operation, stability in the revenues of the OMCs was achieved through the oil price pooling mechanism. During periods when the mechanism went into substantial deficit, the OMCs were permitted by the government to issue bonds in the market, which were guaranteed by the government. The bonds were issued in the market, and subscribed to by banks and funds, and had a secondary market as well. Government was thus saved from reflecting these liabilities on government account. Such off-market borrowings did not show up as liabilities in the government accounts, being shown on the balance sheets of the companies, and as oil prices were rising, commanded a good off take in the secondary market. To a substantial extent, there was no devolution of the bond liabilities on the government. This approach failed after 2007 as the non-adjustment of prices in the wake of sharp increases in international prices made it difficult for the OMCs to raise such a large debt on their balance sheets. However, when liabilities rose, and there was no market appetite for the bonds except at very high interest rates, which were unaffordable for the oil companies, this scheme failed. The approach of government guaranteed bonds was given up after 2008 in favour of more direct budget-based support to cover under recoveries by the petroleum sector undertakings. There was, however, one measure of cross subsidization. The Oil and Natural Gas Commission (ONGC) is a public sector undertaking enjoined with exploration and production of oil and natural gas. It has several operating fields as well as share in exploration blocks, both offshore as well as on shore. The production is sold to the state OMCs, at prices that are fixed by the government. During the years that the APM was in operation, ONGC production prices were fixed by the government, and surpluses diverted to the oil pool account, thus providing a cushion of funds for the marketing companies to draw from. In later years, after the APM was dismantled, the cross subsidization of under recoveries continued, with the ONGC output prices kept below the international basket prices. A levy was also charged in the budget, which went into the revenues of the government for meeting the oil subsidy expenditure.

A reluctance to allow consumer prices of petroleum products to rise combined with a growing gap between revenues and expenditure, have placed a heavy burden on public finances of the government on account of energy subsidies. The share of energy subsidies, represented predominantly by subsidies in petroleum and gas, grew steadily from 5.54 per cent in 2007–2008 to 19.29 per cent in 2012–2013. Figure 3.5 shows the total subsidies from centre for all forms of energy (Expenditure Union Budget Documents, 2007–2014).

During this period, there were three separate strategies adopted by the government to keep consumer prices of petrol, diesel, kerosene and LPG at levels that were considered politically acceptable to consumers. First, there was a gradual, and then a steep increase in budgetary support to the OMCs to compensate them for under recoveries. Figure 3.6 shows the under recoveries on sensitive petroleum products and compensation to oil companies by government (Petroleum Planning and Analysis Cell, 2012). Figure 3.7 shows

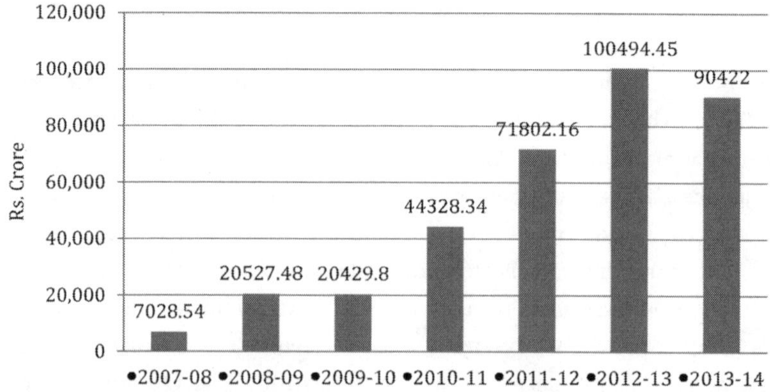


**FIGURE 3.5 Total subsidies from centre for all forms of energy.**

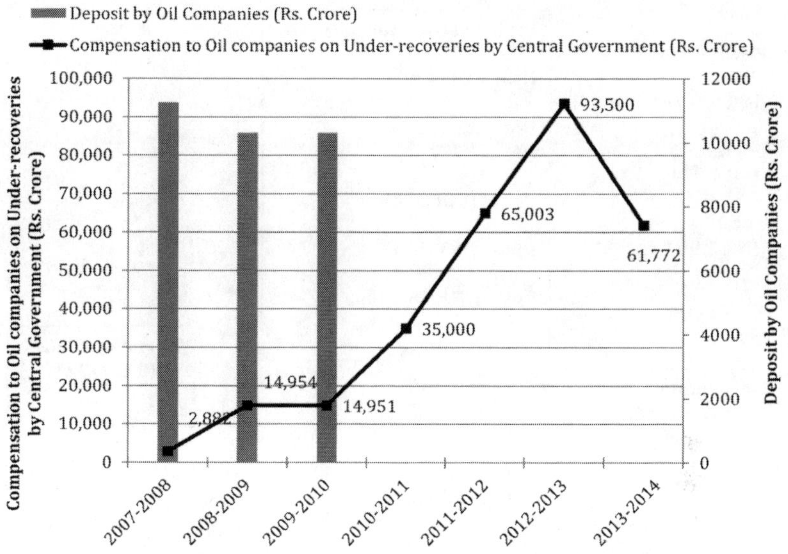


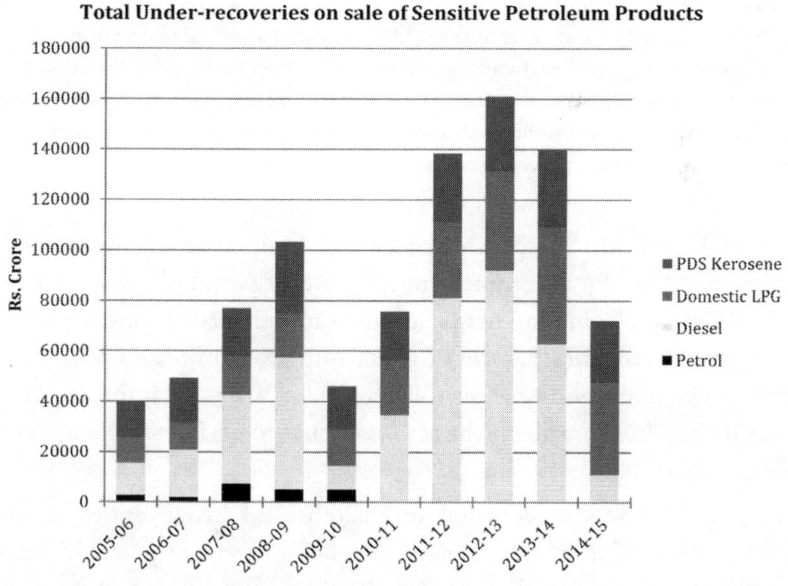


**FIGURE 3.6 (a) Under recoveries on sensitive products and compensation to oil companies. (b) Total under recoveries on sale of sensitive petroleum products. (Expenditure Union Budget Documents, 2007–2014).**

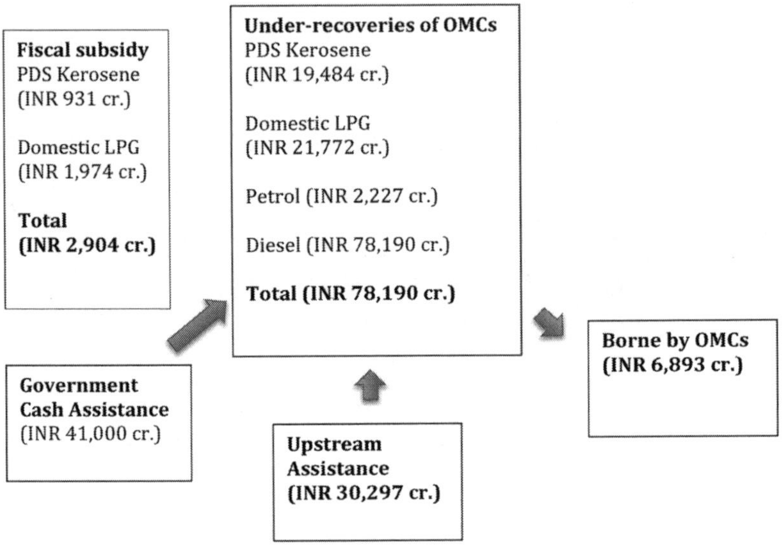


**FIGURE 3.7 Quantum of fiscal subsidies and under recoveries (2010–2011).**

*Source*: A Citizen's Guide to Energy Subsidies in India (2012) based on Ministry of Petroleum and Natural Gas.

*Note*: Three products PDS kerosene, domestic LPG and diesel were sold for less than international market prices. Government gave a fiscal subsidy for the first two. Even that covered only part of the under recovery (shortfall between the cost and selling price). To compensate government provided further ad-hoc cash assistance. Upstream oil producers also gave discounts to the OMCs referred to as upstream assistance.

a detailed breakdown of the under-recovery compensation mechanism and subsidies provided by government on the sale of petrol, domestic LPG and diesel (A Citizen's Guide to Energy Subsidies in India, 2012) and the variation of total under recoveries on sale of sensitive petroleum products since 2005 (Petroleum Planning and Analysis Cell, 2012). In 2010–2011, the fiscal cost of this was Rs. 41,000 crore due to the cash assistance to OMCs and Rs. 2,904 from the fiscal subsidy.

Second, there was a reduction in customs and excise duties to reduce production costs. In short, government revenues were given up to reduce impact on consumers. Table 3.1 shows the realization of excise and custom duties from crude oil and petroleum products to the government from 2004 till 2012 (Petroleum Planning and Analysis Cell, 2012)

**TABLE 3.1 Realization of excise and custom duties from crude oil and petroleum products**

| | Actual | Actual | Actual | Actual | Actual | Actual | Actual | Provisional |
|---|---|---|---|---|---|---|---|---|
| **Products** | **2004–2005** | **2005–2006** | **2006–2007** | **2007–2008** | **2008–2009** | **2009–2010** | **2010–2011** | **2011–2012** |
| A. Excise duties | | | | | | | | |
| Motor spirit | 13,792 | 17,554 | 18,303 | 20,102 | 21,075 | 24,809 | 26,771 | 28,795 |
| Kerosene oil | 1,273 | 212 | 236 | 241 | 281 | 223 | 283 | 351 |
| Refined diesel oil | 14,455 | 21,773 | 24,672 | 23,848 | 21,537 | 23,131 | 30,412 | 19,048 |
| Diesel oil (NES) | 1,246 | 505 | 389 | 306 | 288 | 188 | 240 | 247 |
| Furnace oil | 996 | 1,756 | 1,877 | 1,985 | 2,135 | 2,446 | 2,596 | 3,105 |
| Pol. products (NOS) | 3,711 | 4,623 | 4,919 | 6,313 | 6,840 | 5,822 | 6,488 | 11,435 |
| Petroleum dases | 2,424 | 319 | 454 | 570 | 595 | 705 | 896 | 1,372 |
| Cess on crude oil | 5,248 | 5,007 | 7,034 | 6,866 | 6,632 | 6,688 | 8,861 | 10,357 |
| Total (A) | 43,145 | 51,749 | 57,884 | 60,231 | 59,383 | 64,012 | 76,547 | 74,710 |
| B. Custom duties | | | | | | | | |
| Crude petroleum | 9,761 | 7,158 | 7,583 | 9,101 | 2,768 | 1,752 | 13,370 | 5,196 |
| Petroleum products | 3,489 | 4,236 | 6,426 | 9,041 | 8,406 | 6,003 | 12,912 | 15,323 |
| Total (B) | 13,250 | 11,394 | 14,009 | 18,142 | 11,174 | 7,755 | 26,282 | 20,519 |
| Grand total (A + B) | 56,395 | 63,143 | 71,893 | 78,373 | 70,557 | 71,766 | 102,829 | 95,229 |

*Note*: All values are in Rs. crore.

Recently, the central government has decided to allow a more market-based pricing mechanism. Pricing of petrol has been removed from government oversight, and since August 2012, prices of petrol have been increased 13 times. During FY2013, the government imposed a cap of nine cylinders per year on the sale of subsidized LPG and later authorized OMCs to raise diesel prices by Rs. 0.50 per litre per month till their losses are covered. By March 2013, state-owned OMCs were incurring under recoveries of 8.64 per litre on diesel and Rs. 439 per cylinder on LPG. Since, nearly 60 per cent of the OMCs' under recoveries are funded by the government, the phased deregulation is expected to help reduce the central government's fuel subsidy bill, estimated at 1 per cent of GDP in FY2013. Table 3.2 shows the revisions in retail selling prices of petrol, diesel, domestic LPG and PDS kerosene starting from August 2012 (Petroleum Prices, 2012).

**TABLE 3.2 Revisions in retail prices of petrol diesel PDS kerosene and domestic LPG after August 2012(Petroleum Prices, 2012)**

| Date of Revision | Petrol | Diesel | PDS Kerosene | Domestic LPG |
|---|---|---|---|---|
| 24.07.2012 | 68.48 | – | – | – |
| 01.08.2012 | 68.46 | 41.32 | – | – |
| 14.09.2012 | – | 46.95 | – | – |
| 07.10.2012 | – | – | – | 410.5 |
| 09.10.2012 | 67.9 | – | – | – |
| 03.10.2012 | – | – | 14.79 | – |
| 27.10.2012 | 68.19 | 47.15 | – | – |
| 16.11.2012 | 67.24 | – | – | – |
| 16.01 2013 | 67.56 | – | – | – |
| 18.01.2013 | 67.26 | 47.65 | – | – |
| 16.02.2013 | 69.06 | 48.16 | – | – |
| 02.03.2013 | 70.74 | – | – | – |
| 16.03.2013 | 68.34 | – | – | – |
| 23.03.2013 | – | 48.67 | – | – |
| 02.04.2013 | 67.29 | – | – | – |
| 16.04.2013 | 66.09 | – | – | – |
| 01.05.2013 | 63.09 | – | – | – |
| – | – | – | – | – |

| Date of Revision | Petrol | Diesel | PDS Kerosene | Domestic LPG |
|---|---|---|---|---|
| 01.04.15 | 60.49 | 49.71 | 15.24 | 621.00 |
| 02.04.15 | 60.00 | 48.50 | – | – |
| 16.04.15 | 59.20 | 47.20 | – | – |
| 01.05.15 | 63.16 | 49.57 | – | 616.00 |
| 16.05.15 | 66.29 | 52.28 | – | – |
| 01.06.15 | – | – | – | 626.50 |
| 16.06.15 | 66.93 | 50.93 | – | – |
| 01.07.15 | 66.62 | 50.22 | – | 608.50 |
| 16.07.15 | 66.90 | 49.72 | – | – |
| 01.08.15 | 64.47 | 46.12 | – | 585.00 |

*Note*: All values are in Rs. crore. Domestic LPG cylinder is 14.2 kg. Updated with PPPAC figures.

There has also been an attempt to limit subsidies on LPG. The initial suggestion was that, subsidies for each cardholder should be limited to six cylinders per year. There has been some outcry, and now the government is looking at making the subsidies eligible for nine cylinders a year, and also examining whether the subsidies could be directly passed on to the bank accounts of the beneficiaries (Interim Report of Task Force on Direct Transfer of Subsidies on Kerosene, LPG and Fertilizer).

The narration on subsidies for the petroleum sector would not be complete without a mention of the pricing of natural gas. There has been considerable distortion in the pricing mechanisms adopted for this product (Rangarajan, 2012). Natural gas was initially (in the eighties) considered an associative product to petroleum from the Bombay High fields owned by ONGC. Government policy at that time was to use this gas for the production of fertilizers, and, subsequently, for power generation. Since fertilizer prices were under government control, and pricing of power was regulated by the capacity to pay of the state power utilities, the early years saw a pricing mechanism for natural gas that provided for some cost plus returns, though not international market prices. Subsequently, the advent of small offshore production fields resulted in these operators being permitted to price their gas to private consumers close to market prices. After 2004, there has been an inflow of liquefied natural gas

(LNG), based on a long-term agreement with Qatar, for which the pricing is based on the costs of production plus a margin. Finally, government has decided on a pricing formula for the offshore D6 field owned and operated by Reliance Industries, where there has been a lot of discussion about the output as well as the pricing. It is important to note that none of these have been benchmarked to international gas prices, and therefore the gas market is a fragmented, differentially priced market. There have been no budgetary subsidies at the centre or the state level for natural gas, and hence a discussion on the impacts of these market price distortions is outside the purview of the current analysis.

The story of petroleum subsidies is characterized by reluctance on the part of the political executive to raise prices to market levels, fearing public outcry. After 2014, there has been an attempt to rationalise subsidies by the new NDA Government. Petroleum and Diesel prices are now based on market prices, and revised periodically by the OMCs. LPG subsidies are passed on directly to individual bank accounts, thus eliminating fictitious claims. Kerosene prices are also being revised, although they have not yet reached market parity. Except for cooking gas and kerosene, market parity in prices has been reached.[4]

## Subsidies in the coal sector

In the coal sector, indirect subsidies play an important role. After the nationalization of coal mines in 1973, prices of coal were administratively fixed. Capital expenditure was funded by government, and hence the prices were calculated on the basis of cost of production plus interest and depreciation, with a small return added on to it. An elaborate annual cost exercise was undertaken by Coal India Limited, which was then approved by the Ministry of Coal. The prices thus understated market costs of development of new mines as well as costs of logistics of transportation. While this enabled power producers to get coal at controlled prices, there was an element of subsidy built into the prices. Another measure was the freight equalization subsidy. The railways equalized freight rates for delivery of coal so that the distant power plants did not pay the full price for transportation. The theory was that dispersal of power stations was necessary in a large country like India, while coal production was limited to a few states. The freight equalization subsidy worked to equate freight rates with the nearer stations having to pay more to compensate. The net subsidy costs were borne by the railway budget.

There are no calculations about the under recoveries in coal prices from 1973 to about 2000 (when coal prices were freed up), nor about costs of freight equalization. Suffice it to say; these masked the true costs of power generation, and did not just true costs, but also the losses due to inefficiency and poor productivity.

## Subsidies in the power sector

The power or electricity sector has been dominated by state power utilities. Even prior to independence, power generation was in the hands of state electricity boards (SEBs), funded from the state budgets. There were some private franchisees that used to buy bulk power and distribute it in urban and industrial areas, but by the sixties, state governments had taken over all aspects of electricity generation, transmission and distribution. Funding for the state power utilities was directly from the state budgets, and the electricity boards were advanced loans in perpetuity from the state budgets. Debt servicing was the only return expected by the state governments, as there was no return on capital contemplated. In this approach, incremental capital for growth was provided through additional loans, and as the power utilities grew, they had a very large stock of state government debt with very little equity base.

This was not a major concern in the initial years, as consumption of electricity was limited to commercial and industrial undertakings, and to a few urban centres. In the post-independence, there was a strong move to provide electricity to the rural areas, both for irrigation as well as for households. Extension of distribution to rural areas required considerable investments in transmission and distribution as the villages were numerous and scattered. It was not possible to recover all the fixed costs from the consumers in any particular village, and the notion of rural electrification subsidies came into being from the First Five-Year Plan. These were considered capital outlays in the Five-Year Plans, funded as a support to the state plan outlays, and distributed from the state budgets. As they were considered plan capital outlays, the budget makers considered it benign development expenditure, and as they were more concerned with revenue deficits rather than fiscal deficits, there was not much concern over these costs. In the initial years, focus was on providing electric power for irrigation, and cost recovery was fairly efficient. It is true that there was considerable disparity in performance across states. States such as Punjab, Maharashtra, Gujarat, Tamil Nadu, Karnataka and Andhra Pradesh were at the forefront of this rural outreach. Other states such as West Bengal, Bihar, Orissa, Assam and Madhya Pradesh were late starters, and the rural networks did not come up even until the nineties. Figures 3.8 and 3.9 show the growth of installed generation capacity and rural electrification in India since 1947 (Central Electricity Authority, 2011).

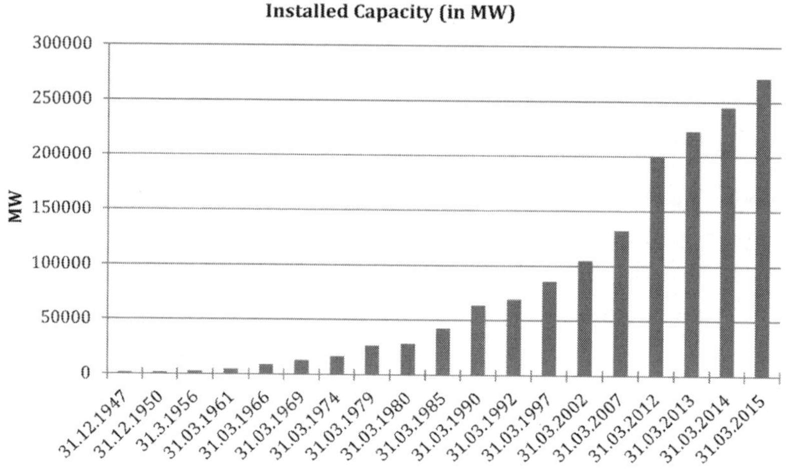


**FIGURE 3.8 Growth of installed generation capacity from 1947 to 2013 (Central Electricity Authority, 2013).**

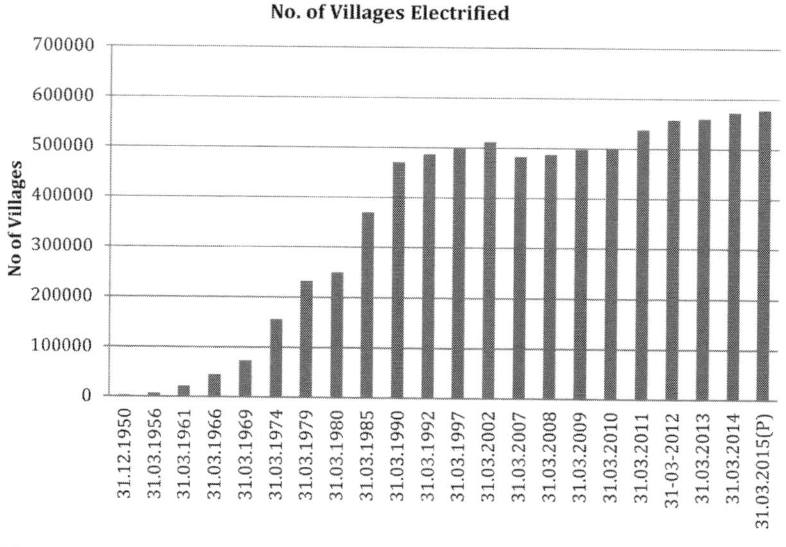


**FIGURE 3.9 Growth of rural village electrification from 1947 to 2013 (Central Electricity Authority, 2013).**

There was a parallel stream of developments that was being funded by the central government. During the First and Second Five-Year Plans, there was an emphasis on irrigation projects, and a number of Hydel-power stations were set up conjointly with irrigation projects. The Damodar Valley Corporation, the Bhakra-Nangal project, the Hirakud dam and power project are some examples.

These were set up as independent commercial entities that would sell power to the SEBs according to allocation patterns decided by the Central Ministry of Power. The advantage to the state public utilities was that the capital costs as well as the operating expenditures were borne by these units, and hence off budget for them.

In addition, the Nuclear Power Corporation was set, more or less as an experimental and research entity attempting to use different radioactive fuels for generation of electricity. The contribution of nuclear power to total power generation continues to be negligible.

The next stage of interventions happened in the early eighties. The social thrust of policies in the seventies had seen the nationalization of OMCs, all the private banking entities and the coal mining operations in the country. With such a stock of resources and capital in hand, the Government of India (GOI) decided to enter the power production and distribution arena. Several arguments were advanced in favour of this policy. First, there was a thrust on increasing power availability, in quality and quantity to reach all sections of the people. Second, the SEBs were not well run, and did not have the resources to undertake massive expansion of either generation or distribution. Finally, now that the government had nationalized coal production, input fuel costs were no longer market determined, but through administrative fiat. Therefore, it was possible to provide fuel at administered prices for power generation, thus keeping these costs under control. The establishment of the National Thermal Power Corporation (NTPC) was intended to serve this objective. Other entities set up around this time included the National Hydro Power Corporation (NHPC), the North Eastern Electric Power Corporation and the Neyveli Lignite Corporation (Narayan, 2012). As these undertakings were corporate entities with balance sheets of their own, they were structured to run as commercial undertakings, providing returns to the shareholder, the central government. Payments to these entities from the central budget were only for funding equity of these undertakings. These numbers did not enter the fiscal deficit figures in the budget, as they are in the nature of stock, rather than flow transfers of funds. Power produced was sold to the state utilities, and the distribution was left to the latter.[5] By the early nineties, state power utilities were already financially stressed. First, the recoveries from rural feeders were not adequate to meet costs. Second, there was a growing political move among most state governments to subsidize power costs to agriculture. Most state governments provide free power for irrigation and highly subsidized power for rural households. The World Bank suggested that there should be a reorganization of the sector, and that the state utilities should be unbundled into generation and distribution entities.[6] The suggestion that private sector should be involved in generation and that distribution and collection should be unbundled where possible created two entities (in some cases, three). State governments allocated fresh generation capacity to private players, often on a non-transparent basis. Most of these investors were rent seekers rather than entrepreneurs. In any case, without reforms in distribution and collection mechanisms, there was no way in which these projects could achieve financial closure. The entire nineties was a lost decade for power generation in India. The economic crisis of 1991–1992 resulted in a squeeze of capital availability for infrastructure including for power generation; and the unbundling exercise did not result in additions to fresh capacity. Interestingly, during 1997–1999 coal production exceeded demand. There was a sorry situation when there was adequate coal, transportation capacity, but no fresh generation coming up, and shortages of power everywhere.

The Electricity Act, 2003 was a serious attempt to set things right. Providing for private sector involvement through transparent bidding processes, and regulatory tariff fixation, the act has re-energized the sector, and the last decade has seen a revival in investments.[7]

It is clear from the above narrative that a mix of state and central policies, coupled with political expediency has led to the deterioration of the finances of the power sector in India. The burden of subsidies has been borne entirely by the state governments. Over the years up to 2003, the state power utilities ran up huge arrears of payments to central generation undertakings, quite apart from their inability to upgrade generation or distribution within their geography. There have been two attempts, one in 2003, and the other in 2012, to support the balance sheets of the state power utilities. In 2003, an amount of Rs. 25,000 crores was set apart by the Planning Commission for the subvention of state power dues to other generators. This was considered a one-time subvention. States agreed to deductions from plan allocations from the centre to the states for meeting dues of central generation undertakings, and this was pushed through over objections from the Reserve Bank of India in 2003. However, this relief proved temporary, as states have not been able to price power properly nor improve collections in the last decade.

Figure 3.10 presents the subsidies received by state power utilities and electricity departments across India. Even more than the petroleum sector, the financial condition of the electricity boards has a severe impact on the development agenda of the state. In Tamil Nadu, since 2012, power shut downs

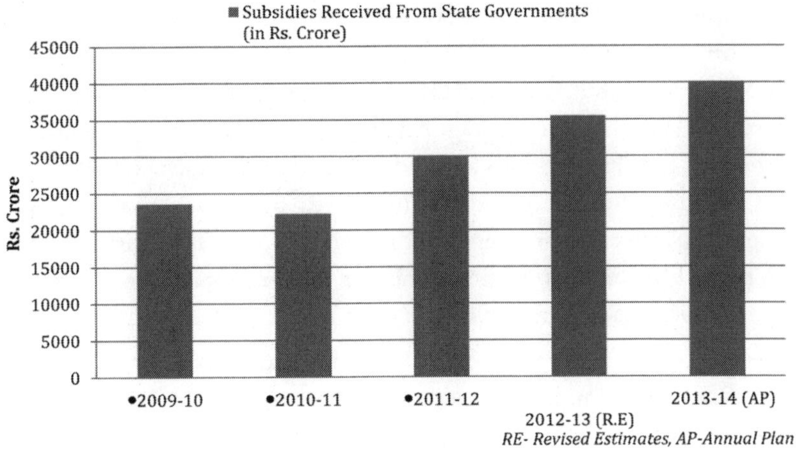


**FIGURE 3.10 Electricity subsidies received from state governments.**

*Note*: Annual Plan 2013–2014 on The Working of State Power Utilities & Electricity Departments, Planning Commission of India (n.d.).

of up to 2 hours in urban areas and over 8 hours in rural areas have become the norm. The loss to production and to gross state domestic product (GSDP) should be of the order of 2 per cent.

Electoral politics have made free supply of electricity to rural areas a plank for attracting votes, and it is unlikely that any regional party will step back from it. As state finances and state power utilities feel the financial stress of free power, they often resort to power cuts as a measure of reducing losses. When states opt for denying electricity to rural feeders rather than attempting to supply and charge, the entire generation, distribution and use framework get into disarray. A private power producer is no longer sure of-off take from the grid, and hence there are several power plants unable to operate at optimum capacity. The issue of power subsidies is politics and not economics, and there is little clarity how this can be ended.

## Renewable energy sector

There has been a Ministry for Renewable Energy at the GOI level since 1992. Initially, it focussed on wind-based generation. Policies created at the central level included tax concessions for import of equipment as well as advanced depreciation provisions for the investors, which provided them some income tax relief. However, policy as well as budgets did not take this sector seriously.

Solar power at that time was considered very expensive, and wind power installations were given investment and depreciation benefits. This encouraged private investment, but there was little regulation on efficiency of machines or productivity. With 100 per cent depreciation allowed and easy financing, several investors just put up windmills and did not worry too much about generation. Others persuaded the state power utilities to pick up the power, entering into power purchase agreements with them. Sometimes, this entailed new transmission lines and sub-stations, and the cost benefits of the entire exercise have never been made transparent.

Over the years, as power generation capacity started falling behind demand, wind power became an important source of augmentation. Never a base load power source, it was useful for managing peak loads for around four months in a year. States like Tamil Nadu encouraged the establishment of such stations, and now several states have done so. However, payment for the power generated suffers from the same problems as for other forms of electricity – there is no money to pay, as there is no will to charge market rates for power. Figure 3.11

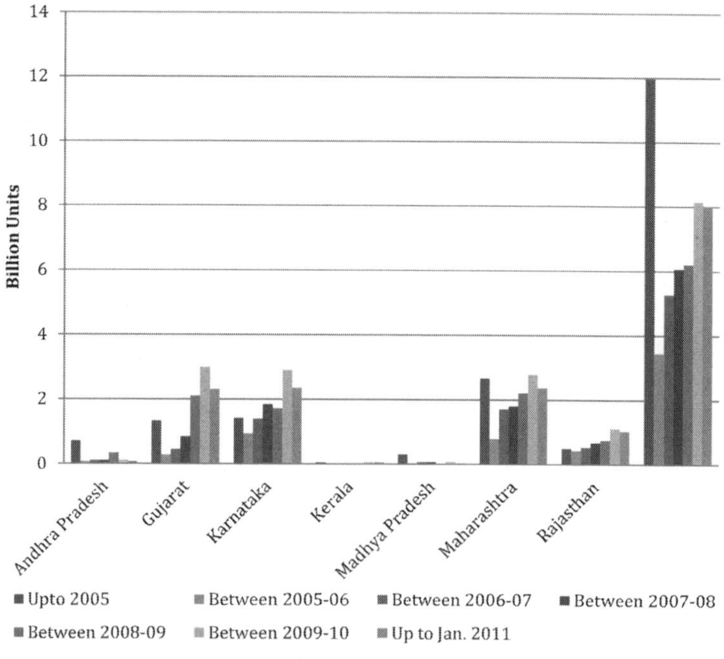


**FIGURE 3.11 State-wise cumulative wind generation data in BUs (as on 31.01.2011).**

shows the growth of wind generation in billion units (BUs) in certain states from 2005 till 2011 (Centre for Wind Energy Technology, 2012)

The fiscal impact of these concessions is difficult to measure, as the accounting of revenue foregone from tax concessions is being reported to the parliament only in the last few years. Even in this, there is no measurement of individual items, and hence figures for income tax foregone because of accelerated depreciation provisions, or customs and excise duties foregone for manufacture and imports are not available.[8] The central budget provides allocations for the Ministry of Renewable Energy, which is an indication of the budgetary burden for these operations.

Solar power is a later entrant. Only since 2005, there have been some ad hoc moves to encourage generation. Tariff policies have been muddled, and the growth in generation has been ad hoc. Since 2008, there has been a thrust on solar power as well. The policies have lacked clarity. Initially, there was an attempt to step up solar generation by 1,000 MW by providing a market-based pricing for the power. This power would be purchased by NTPC, which would then bundle it with all other power generated by it. In this approach, the subsidy burden would be borne by NTPC, which was permitted to spread it across all generation. GOI later came out with a plan of renewable energy certificates mandating all major consumers to use 15 per cent renewable energy, or to buy certificates from those who were generating renewable power. It was a good idea, but failure of the states to regulate and check this has led to the renewable energy certificates finding no market.

Subsequently, after 2010, there have been programmes with state specific subsidies for solar power. Most of these have focussed on capital subsidies for installing generation. State regulators are fixing tariffs, and though the tariffs are considerably higher than those for hydroelectric or thermal generation, it is not clear whether the capital subsidies as well as the additional tariffs would be adequate to compensate the investors and provide a reasonable rate of return. In order to provide a measure of compulsion, all state governments have mandated that bulk consumers should consume a certain percentage of their total electricity only from renewable sources. Such a mandate is part of central government policy, but it is yet unclear whether there are adequate governance mechanisms in all states to oversee its implementation or to ensure adherence.

The total generation from all renewable sources is yet a small (around 5 per cent) of the national generation capacity. There are a number of new initiatives coming up in different states, but the public finance impact of these will have to be seen only over time.

## Conclusions

In the entire energy sector, policy developments have led to market distortions. Whereas in the oil sector, the attempt has been to protect the consumers from the full impact of market determined prices, the power sector has witnessed selected subsidies for the rural consumers. The renewable energy sector, on the other hand, suffers from price distortions caused by input capital subsidies. The combination of all these distortions has had a significant and deleterious effect on the fiscal balance at the state as well as the central level. There have been some recent effects to correct the situation, both at the central and the state levels.

In the energy sector, the attempt to reduce subsidies is being done through consumer price adjustments. Petrol and diesel prices have been revised closer to market levels and pricing of petrol has been left to the OMCs. At the state level, several of the progressive states have attempted to revise tariffs to reflect more closely the costs of generation. The impact on the fiscal deficit is still quite significant. As long as India remains an energy importing country, depending on imported crude oil, coal and natural gas, such subsidies would weigh heavily not just on public finances, but also on the current account deficit.

Energy subsidies are closely linked to the political ideologies of the government in power. While at the state level, local politics prevent the full charge for power, petroleum subsidies are constrained by national politics. The new NDA government appears to be keen on removing subsidies, but there are no guarantees that subsequent governments will not roll back these decisions.

## Notes

1 Interestingly, government has chosen producer subsidies as a policy for the fertilizer sector, even though options for consumer subsidies were available. While it would be an interesting study to document how and why this came about, it lies beyond the scope of this chapter.

2 2004 was an election year, and the outgoing government as well as the new government was reluctant to face the odium of rapidly increasing petrol and diesel prices.

3 There was a change in government at this time – the incumbent government held price revisions for a year, and the new government was reluctant to adopt an unpopular measure.

4 There is a small gap in diesel prices, which would be bridged using a step-wise approach.

5 Central power utilities had normal pattern of supplying 40 per cent power to the state where they were located, and the balance to the other states in the regional grid, in proportion to their total generation and demand. This principle has been working satisfactorily since the seventies. Occasionally, the home state overdraws, putting the grid into difficulties. The interlinking of regional grids and the establishment of a national grid (almost complete) have eased up power flows across states. This has led to lower prices for traded power as well as efficiencies.

6 After a decade, the bank has admitted that these recommendations were inappropriate and not well thought out.

7 There are several policy-related problems even now, but are not relevant for this study.

8 An indirect measure of the impact of these subsidies on revenues arises from the fact that after government announced the withdrawal of these subsidies from 1 April 2013, several major wind turbine manufacturing firms, including Suzlon, the biggest of them all, have reported steep fall in orders and are in financial stress.

## References


A Citizen's Guide to Energy Subsidies in India. 2012. http://www.iisd.org/gsi/sites/default/files/ffs_india_czguide.pdf.

Annual Plan 2013-2014 on The Working of State Power Utilities & Electricity Departments, Planning Commission of India. (n.d.). Retrieved 2013. http://planningcommission.gov.in/reports/genrep/rep_arpower0306.pdf.

Central Electricity Authority. 2011. *Growth of Electricity Sector in India From 1947–2011.* http://powermin.nic.in/indian_electricity_scenario/pdf/Growth_of_Electricity_Sector_in_India_From_1947-2011.pdf.

Central Electricity Authority. 2013. *Growth of Electricity Sector in India From 1947-2013.* http://powermin.nic.in/indian_electricity_scenario/pdf/Growth_of_Electricity_Sector_in_India_From_1947-2011.pdf.

Centre for Wind Energy Technology. 2012. Retrieved 2013. http://www.inwea.org/aboutwindenergy.htm.

Expenditure Union Budget Documents. 2007–2013. Retrieved 2013. http://finmin.nic.in/; http://indiabudget.nic.in/budget.asp; http://finmin.nic.in/the_ministry/dept_expenditure/index.asp.

Expenditure Union Budget Documents. 2007–2014. Retrieved 2014. http://finmin.nic.in/; http://indiabudget.nic.in/budget.asp; http://finmin.nic.in/the_ministry/dept_expenditure/index.asp.

Ministry of Finance. n.d. *Interim Report of Task Force on Direct Transfer of Subsidies on Kerosene, LPG and Fertilizer.* http://finmin.nic.in/reports/Interim_report_Task_Force_DTS.pdf.

Ministry of Finance. n.d. Retrieved 2013. http://finmin.nic.in/.

Minsitry of Petroleum and Natural Gas. 2012. *A Citizen's Guide to Energy Subsidies in India.* International Institute for Sustainable Development, TERI and PPAC. New Delhi: Ministry of Petroleum and Natural Gas.

Narayan, S. 2012. 'National Thermal Power Corporation: Power in Public Enterprises.' In *The Political Economy of State-Owned Enterprises in China and India*, 151–76. Palgrave Macmillan South Yarra, Australia. https://books.google.co.in/books?id=PsHrj-XmEiIC&printsec=frontcover&source=gbs_ge_summary_r&cad=0#v=onepage&q&f=false.

Petroleum Planning and Analysis Cell. 2012. Retrieved 2013. http://ppac.org.in/WriteReadData/userfiles/file/PS_2_b_UR_on_SensitiveProducts(H).xls.

Petroleum Prices. 2012. Petroleum Planning and Analysis Cell. Retrieved 2013. http://www.reuters.com/article/2013/04/30/india-fuel-prices-idUSL3N0DH3EX20130430; http://164.100.47.134/intranet/Petroleumprices.pdf.

Rangarajan, C. 2012. *Report on Gas Pricing.* http://eac.gov.in/pressrel/press_psc0201.pdf

4

# Fiscal Implications of Food Security in India

## A Critical Review

**N. R. Bhanumurthy and Ruth Kattumuri**

## Introduction

The Global Hunger Index (GHI), prepared by IFPRI, ranks India as 55 among 76 countries based on data for 2014, which is an improvement from its rank in 2013. While improvements have been significant in the last decade (India has seen the sharpest decrease in its Hunger Index compared to any other country), the country's situation is still categorized as 'serious' and further improvements are needed. In comparison with its South Asian neighbours, India ranks lower than Sri Lanka and Nepal (39 and 44 ranks, respectively) and only slightly higher than Bangladesh and Pakistan, which are jointly ranked at 57 (IFPRI, 2015).

This trend is similar when one looks at other related indicators such as severely underweight children under five years, child mortality, undernourishment, stunted children, wasting and other nutrition measures. According to IFPRI (2015), 30.7 per cent of children below five years in India are underweight, which is an improvement from 44.8 per cent in 1993–1997. Underweight children under the age of five are 12.8 per cent in Bhutan, 21.6 per cent in Sri Lanka, 29.1 per cent in Nepal, 31.6 per cent in Pakistan and 36.8 per cent in Bangladesh.

At the all India level the trends seem to be encouraging although further improvements are necessary, the trends at the state level are divergent and discouraging. According to the Ministry of Women and Child Development and UNICEF (2015), it was found that while at the all India level 29 per cent of children below five years are underweight, at the state level, this ranges from 14 per cent in Manipur to as high as 42 per cent in Jharkhand (Figure 4.1). States

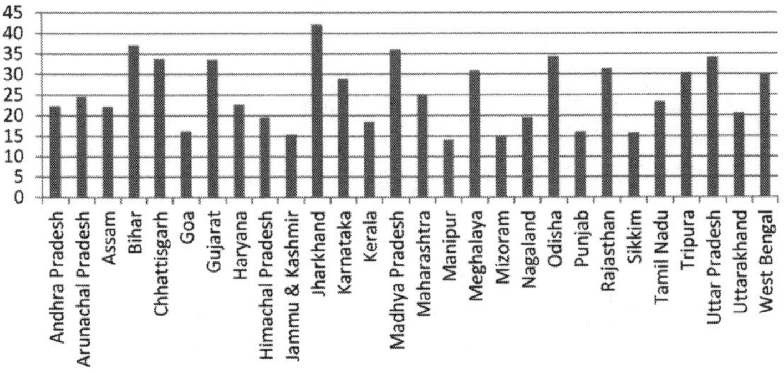


**FIGURE 4.1 Underweight children below five years (in %).**

*Note*: All India figure is at 29 per cent
*Source*: Rapid Survey on Children, 2013–2014 (2015).

such as Bihar, Gujarat, Madhya Pradesh, Meghalaya, Odisha, Rajasthan, Uttar Pradesh and West Bengal have higher rates of underweight children compared to the all India average. In the case of stunting also, while all India rate is around 39 per cent, states such as Assam, Bihar, Chhattisgarh, Gujarat, Rajasthan, Madhya Pradesh and Uttar Pradesh have a higher proportion with Uttar Pradesh having 51 per cent of children with stunting. Kerala has the lowest stunting rate of 20 per cent.

From the previous discussion, it is evident that India is among highly food insecure nations in the world with large divergence between states. Hence, there is a need for the government to address the serious issue of food insecurity and high levels of under-nutrition in the country. In this chapter, an attempt has been made to understand the existing linkage between public policy (in terms of government interventions) as well as its outcomes. This chapter attempts to review some policy interventions in India and in some neighbouring countries. This study also tries to discuss the National Food Security Act (NFSA), its implementation as well as its fiscal implications in India.

## Concept of food security

The concept of food security, which evolved initially as an assurance of food in terms of nutrition to the entire population of the country (or a region), has now expanded as a social, cultural and political context in addition to its economic concept. It also includes issues of food availability, affordability and public delivery systems, which have become crucial factors for ensuring overall food security in a region. Maxwell and Frankenberger (1992), while discussing various definitions of food security, broadly suggest that food security is nothing but 'secure access at all times to enough food'. This broad explanation is applicable to all the regions over time, at the same time there are variations within a region, for instance, 'enough' can be evaluated differently in rural and urban Indian context.

FAO's World Food Summit (1996) defines, 'Food security, at the individual, household, national, regional and global levels [is achieved] when all people, at all times, have physical and economic access to sufficient, safe and nutritious food to meet their dietary needs and food preferences for an active and healthy life'. This definition was refined in 'The State of Food Insecurity, 2001' as 'Food security [is] a situation that exists when all people, at all times, have physical, social and economic access to sufficient, safe and nutritious food that meets their dietary needs and food preferences for an active and healthy life'. As the definition suggest, this has three components: Food availability: sufficient quantities of food available on a consistent basis; Food access: having sufficient resources to obtain appropriate foods for a nutritious diet; and Food consumption: appropriate use based on knowledge of basic nutrition and care, as well as adequate water and sanitation. Food security, as suggested by Koc et al. (1999), consistes of availability, accessibility, acceptability and adequacy. However, in implementation of universal food security program, there are different concepts that are adopted in different regions and different times. It also depends on five important questions: coverage, timing, implementation, quantity and finally quality.

## Fiscal policy and food security in India

Before we look at NFSA, it is necessary to place India's public policy in perspective, especially from the fiscal policy point of view. As discussed earlier, there is a clear improvement in most food security indicators at the all India level. While IFPRI attributes this to the end of 'data drought' in India regarding hunger indicators, the improvements can also be attributed to initiatives that have been instituted in the last decade at national level as well as in all states. These are in addition to the Public Distribution System (PDS) and the Integrated Child Development Services (ICDS) (Kattumuri, 2011). The fiscal cost of food-related programmes is categorized as food subsidy in the centre and state government budgets. Before implementation of NFSA, there were two types of subsidies – consumer subsidy and buffer subsidy. Consumer subsidy includes subsidies provided through Food Corporation of India (FCI) to families above poverty line (APL) and below poverty line (BPL), Antyodaya Anna Yojana (AAY), Mid-day meal schemes (MDMSs), exports, defence, and open market sale (OMS). Over the years, there has been an increase in food subsidy across all the programmes. Figure 4.2 presents food subsidy (in both centre and states) as a ratio of gross domestic product (GDP), which clearly shows that it has increased from 0.47 per cent in 1995–1996 to 0.9 per cent by 2013–2014, with a peak in 2002–2003 when the food subsidy bill increased to 1 per cent of GDP. The Fiscal Responsibility and Budget Management Act-2003 (FRBM) at the central level and medium-term fiscal policy (MTFPs) as well as Finance Commission (FC) conditionalities at the state level seems to have brought down the subsidy bill until 2007–2008. However, the global financial crisis followed by large fiscal stimulus measures have led to fiscal slippage as evident in food and total subsidies (Figure 4.2). Such trends are also reflected in the case of total government subsidies (including fuel and fertilizer subsidy). There has been a sharp increase from 1.6 per cent in 2007–2008 to 2.6 per cent in 2008–2009, especially due to sharp increase in the international oil prices. Food subsidy comprises nearly 40 per cent of total subsidy.

By 2011–2012, both food and total subsidy had reached high levels and led to threats of downgrading India's credit rating. Following such high levels of subsidy and the fiscal dominance in the post-global crisis period, Indian economy experienced a long period of higher inflation. This has resulted in contractionary monetary policy leading to sharp fall in investment rate,

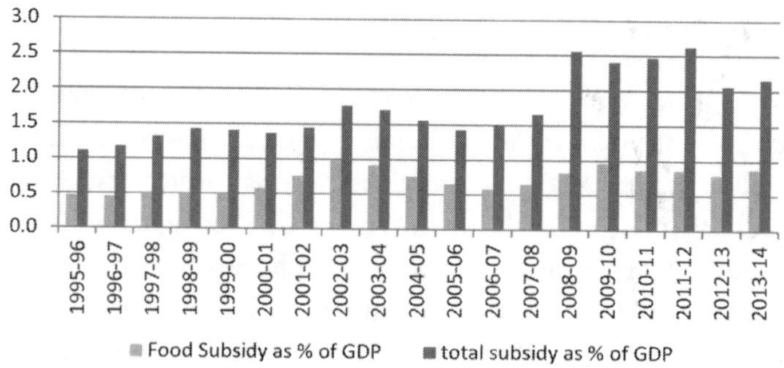


**FIGURE 4.2 Trends in food subsidy and total subsidy (centre + states) (as % of GDP).**

*Source*: Authors' calculation based on Indian Public Finance Statistics, GOI.

especially private investments, and, consequently, growth deceleration. This has forced the re-working of the fiscal consolidation road map that was suggested by the 13th Finance Commission. One of the main targets in the revamped fiscal consolidation road map was to bring down the total subsidy bill to below 2 per cent and is largely through reduction in food subsidy. Further, the extent of off-budget liabilities due to higher food subsidy are also cause for serious concern.

Figure 4.3 shows the trends in the extent of subsidy released by the government to the actual subsidy incurred in a year. The difference between the two is the under recovery in expenditures. The stock of under recovery is also presented in this figure. It is clear that since 2001–2002, the government has never fully compensated FCI (the institution that implements a large part of the food subsidy programme) as the share of compensation was much lower than 100 per cent, and in recent years this was as low as 60 per cent. The accumulated under recovery under the food subsidy bill had reached a high of Rs. 1.1 lakh crore (close to 1 per cent of GDP) by 2013–2014. Although this under recovery has not been financed by the government and allowed FCI to float bonds, servicing these bonds could put additional pressure on the revenue deficit, which could be increasing every year. Addressing this issue becomes crucial in the process of achieving fiscal targets. India being a country with a large proportion of poor and vulnerable people, some level of social protection (especially, food and nutrition security) is necessary and unavoidable and could require higher subsidies. But, what is crucial is regular assessment of these social protection measures

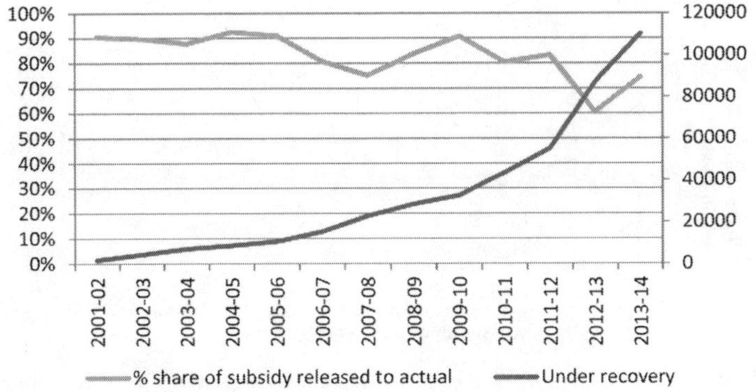


**FIGURE 4.3 Trends in under recovery in food subsidy.**

*Source*: Authors' calculation based on FCI data.

in terms of the overall development outcomes. This chapter also highlights inadequacies in the overall design, implementation and quantification of subsidy, which is discussed in subsequent sections.

What is the impact of food expenditure on the developmental outcomes? In other words, it is necessary to analyse the impact of fiscal policy interventions on food security and nutrition in India. This could bring out the efficiency of public expenditures in terms of design and implementation of various government schemes. As shown in Figure 4.4, it is clear that higher the nutrition expenditures (percapita expenditure on nutrition by each state, lower the severely under weight children (below 5 years) in the states in the year 2012–2013. The outcomes vary across the states with Kerala, Goa, Tamil Nadu, Punjab and Andhra Pradesh (AP) having less than 6 per cent while states such as Bihar, Gujarat, Rajasthan, Uttar Pradesh, Odisha and few other smaller states having over 10 per cent severe underweight children. One major reason for these variations could be the extent of public expenditure on nutrition at the state level.

As shown in Figure 4.5, there is a wide divergence in the percapita nutrition expenditures at the state level. In 2012–2013, both AP and Tamil Nadu spent over Rs. 300 percapita while states having high proportion of underweight children (in double-digit) such as Bihar, UP and West Bengal spent less than half of the expenditure in better performing states. In states such as Gujarat and Rajasthan, while the expenditures are high the outcomes are poor, which requires further investigation. It is also interesting to see that in states such as Kerala and Uttarakhand, the percapita expenditures are almost negligible as

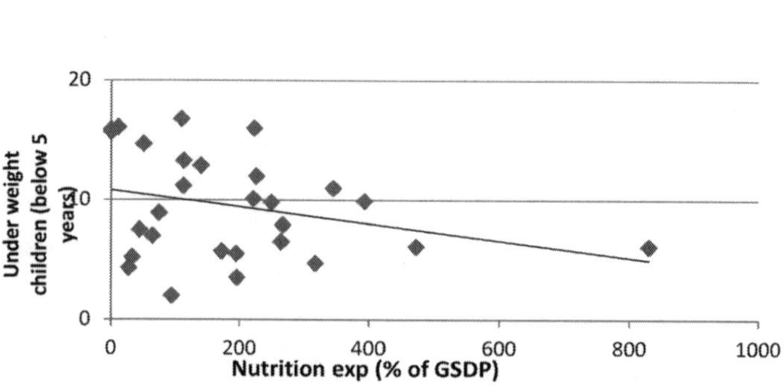


**FIGURE 4.4 Link between food expenditure and nutrition levels among children.**

*Source*: Based on data from MOSPI and UNICEF (2014).

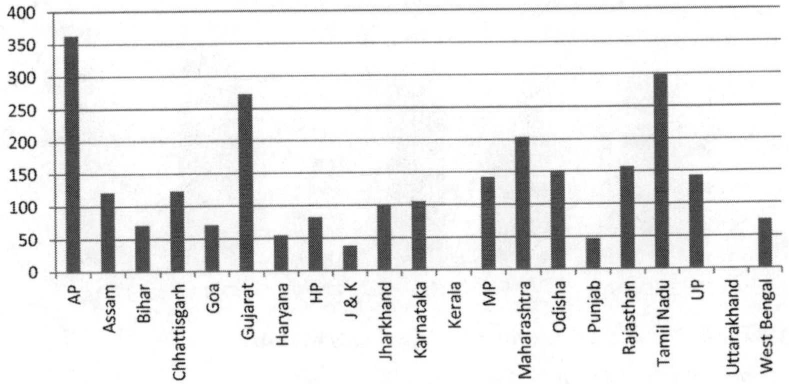


**FIGURE 4.5 Divergences in percapita nutrition expenditures across the states (in Rs.).**

*Source*: Based on UNICEF report (2014).

nutrition levels in these states are high; this enhances available resources for other developmental priorities in these states.

From the previous discussion, what is intriguing is why India has one of the lowest percapita calorie intake in spite of all the public policy interventions, we discuss some details regarding this in later sections. Percapita calorie intake in India is currently at 2,233 for rural areas and 2,206 for urban areas in 2011–2012 (Figure 4.6). While this shows significant increases, it is still below the ideal of 2,400 calorie that had been suggested by the erstwhile Planning Commission. This norm was also used for estimating the incidence of poor in the country, which indicates a close relationship between food security and extent of poverty. It may be noted that the increasing trend in calorie intake is associated with declining trend in poverty incidence in India between 2004–2005 and 2011–2012. As shown by the nutritional expenditures across states (Figure 4.5), similar divergences are also found in the percapita calorie consumption at the state level. The agricultural rich states such as Punjab, Haryana and AP had highest calorie consumption while Gujarat and Tamil Nadu had below average consumption in rural areas. Same pattern is found in urban areas as well.

Despite the above trends in expenditures and nutritional intake, India is still categorized as 'slow or almost off-track' in achieving Target-2 of the first Millennium Development Goal (MDG-1) which was to 'halve, between 1990 and 2015, the proportion of people who suffer from hunger' (see Ministry of

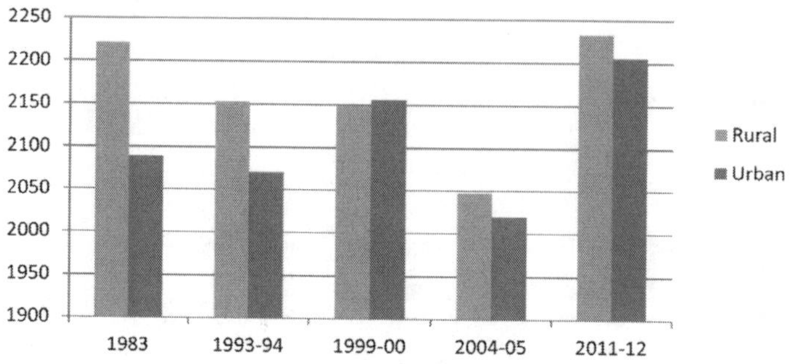


**FIGURE 4.6 Per capita calorie intake (in kcal) in India.**

*Source*: Nutritional Intake in India, 2011–2012, 68th Round, NSSO.

Statistics and Programme Implementation [MOSPI], 2015). As malnutrition, especially among women and children, has large social consequence across generations, several measures were initiated in the past decade, which are discussed in later sections. Despite these initiatives, the outcomes still appear to be sub-optimal. This led to the movement of Right to Food as a fundamental right. Following representations and discussions, the government has enacted NFSA-2013 in order to ensure food for all. The following section presents a brief discussion on food security policies that are adopted in other countries, especially among South Asian countries.

## Food security policies in some countries

As previously discussed, food security refers to physical and economic access to sufficient, safe and nutritious food for all individuals at all times. Based on Food and Agriculture Organization (FAO) assessment, in the last two decades countries within South Asia have made significant progress towards alleviating hunger and food insecurity. The Rapid Survey on Children MWCD (2015) report suggests that India has made significant progress in bringing down malnutrition among children below five years. However, it is still a long way for India to bring this ratio to below 5 per cent from its current level of over 30 per cent.

Literature suggests that there are some common policies that are identified for ensuring food security (South Asia policies are largely reviewed from Wickramasinghe, 2014). These are (1) Improving agricultural productivity and production systems; (2) Enhancing agricultural R&D, dissemination and sharing (especially early warning systems); (3) Managing food security risks and vulnerabilities; and (4) Introducing safety nets. The following is a brief overview of various food security policies adopted by some South Asian countries. Knowledge sharing between neighbouring countries could provide important learning of best practices.

## *Bangladesh*

Bangladesh adopted 'The National Food Policy Plan of Action 2008–2015' (PoA-2008) with the objective of: providing adequate and stable supply of safe and nutritious food through increasing production, managing food stocks, strengthening market linkages, and managing vulnerability; increasing access to food by better managing disasters, enhancing market participation of women and disabled people, and supporting food processing; and providing adequate nutrition for all individuals (especially vulnerable). In addition to this Food Policy, Bangladesh has a few safety net programmes such as vulnerable group feeding (VGF), test relief (TR), food vulnerable group development (VGD), open market sales (OMSs), gratuitous relief (GR) – Food Assistance in Chittagong Hill Tracts Area, and Food For Work (FFW) programme. Some estimates suggest that food security programmes in Bangladesh cost around 1.2 per cent of GDP (see Rahman, Choudhury and Ali, 2011). However, to substantially reduce food insecurity in the country (for instance to bring children underweight below five years from the current 36.8 per cent to the global norm of below 5 per cent), the country may need to spend much more.

## *Bhutan*

Among South Asian countries, Bhutan has the lowest number of children underweight below five years, at 12.8 per cent (in 2010). However, the Government of Bhutan has been undertaking various measures to bring the indicator to below 5 per cent. The country has adopted the Food and Nutrition Security Policy of the Kingdom of Bhutan 2014 (FNSP-2014) that tries to cover all aspects of food security that are discussed in the previous section titled 'Fiscal policy and food security in India'. Bhutan focuses on increased domestic production; enhancing the distribution of imported food through markets; maintaining a national food security reserve (buffer stock policy) under the Food Corporation of Bhutan (FCB) comprising of rice, oil and sugar; and the promotion of commercial market and FCB distribution system. Bhutan also has some policies that help in managing shocks in food prices (especially through imports) and narrowing regional variations in nutrition levels across the country.

### Maldives

In Maldives, with 17.8 per cent of children below five years being underweight in 2009, the country has a long term Agricultural Development Master Plan 2006–2020 (ADMP-2006) that provides guidelines for both food security policy and agricultural development. In the country with the constraints of very less cultivable land and shortage of agricultural labourers, the Master Plan focuses on six key aspects: (1) promotion of garden farming for household consumption; (2) commercialization of agriculture by collaborating with resorts; (3) leasing out selected islands for farming on commercial basis; (4) promotion of value addition for generating higher employment and improving purchasing power; (5) adoption of sustainable technological options; and (6) ensuring a regional balance of agricultural development and gender equity.

### Nepal

The Global Hunger Report ranks Nepal at 44th position with nearly 29.1 per cent of children below five years being underweight in 2014. This shows a decline from 39.8 per cent in 2007 at the same time there has not been much decline in the proportion of undernourished people. While the decline in underweight children was largely due to National Nutrition Action Plan in 2007 that includes inter-sectoral strategy, however, that strategy alone was not sufficient to bring down overall hunger index. For this Nepal has initiated the Nepal Agriculture and Food Security Country Investment Plan (AFSP-2010) (GoN, 2010) that had multiple objectives. Under the plan, the objectives are: making high quality seeds available to farmers on continuous basis; enhancing agricultural productivity; and direct and targeted interventions to enhance food and nutrient intake by vulnerable populations.

### Pakistan

Pakistan appears to face major challenge in terms of hunger and malnutrition. In 2013, there were 17.2 per cent undernourished people, 31.6 per cent of children below five years were underweight, and under-5 mortality was 10.1 per cent.

To address this, Pakistan had a few regional level programmes such as the Special Programme for Food Security (SPFS), supported by FAO that was subsequently scaled up and covered 100 villages under the Crop Maximization Programme (CMP-I). This was further expanded to cover over 1,000 villages under CMP-II. Pakistan Agricultural Storage and Supply Corporation (PASSCO) is one such programme aimed at stock management. A formal price support system was first introduced in 1960s by fixing wheat price, which was later extended to other crops. The Benazir Income Support Programme (BISP), a large-scale safety net programme offers support services to low-income people, but its outreach and depth of coverage has been limited.

## *Sri Lanka*

Within South Asia, Sri Lanka has achieved considereable progress in terms of achieving MDG goals. The prevalence of underweight in children under five years is currently at 21.1 per cent while the under-five mortality is at 1 per cent. However, undernourished population in 2013 was around 23 per cent, highest compared to all other countries in the sub-continent. Two major policy initiatives in Sri Lanka for food security are the Sri Lanka National Agricultural Policy (NAP-SL) (GoSL, 2014) and the National Nutrition Policy of Sri Lanka 2010 (NNP-2010) (GoSL, 2010). These programmes give high priority to enhance agricultural sector output. Sri Lanka is also one of the highest exporters of agricultural products. The other programmes focused on enhancing food security are national campaign for encouraging the production of indigenous food crops under *Api Wawamu-Rata Nagamu* (Let us grow – develop the country) programme. Further there are other special programmes targeting priority sectors such as water and soil conservation, Northern agricultural development, crop forecasting, dry zone livelihood support, and national agricultural research. The country has also launched Samurdhi (prosperity) in accordance with the SAARC Charter for elimination of poverty. This is a social safety net programme that provides a monthly allowance for low-income households along with scheme for encouraging savings in the formal banking sector that allows households the possibility for using it as collateral for securing microcredit.

In addition to these South Asian countries, among the emerging market economies, Brazil has also undertaken one of the most successful programme of *Fome Zero* (Zero Hunger) in 2003. With this, the country could bring down

GHI to below 5 per cent. This has brought down the undernourished population to 6.9 per cent, underweight children under five years at 2.1 per cent and under five mortality to 1.4 per cent. The Zero Hunger strategy has four aspects: improving food access (Bolsa Familia), family agriculture, income generation strategy and civil society participation (Chmielewska and Souza, 2011).

In addition to this programme, Brazil has also made Right to Food as a fundamental right within its constitution. These initiatives in Brazil, which resulted in better food security indicators, provide indications of best practices for other countries to adopt.

India has been facing declines in food production as well as yields. This could be due to many structural factors (such as land, energy, infrastructure, irrigation, marketing and credit) that have been discussed extensively in the context of sustained high double-digit inflation in food prices. India's malnourishment levels are high, consequently hampering the growth of women and children. Similar to countries discussed earlier, India has also adopted several programmes to ensure food security through improving availability, access and absorption of nutrition. Some of these measures are discussed in the following section.

## Review of food security policies in India

Similar to Brazil, India also adopted Right to Food as a fundamental right in the constitution and has enacted NFSA (2013). While the Act and its fiscal implications are discussed in the following section, here, we discuss other public programmes that are aimed at alleviating poverty and hunger under three aspects: availability, access and absorption.

### *On availability*

In the process of globalization, one sector that has not received enough support is agriculture. Low growth of food production results in increases in prices. This decline is attributed to decline in public capital expenditure in the agriculture sector as well as to other structural issues such as fall in allocations for power, rural roads, agricultural marketing, agro-based research, limited financial access and so on. These constraints would have also reduced farm productivity across the country. Together with this, lack of crop diversification and deceleration in agricultural allied activities also could have resulted in productivity decline. While some of these activities fall under the purview of sub-national governments, overall there seems to be inadequate investment in the agriculture sector and resulted in decline in per capita food availability. To encourage production and improve productivity, the government has brought in two important policies: Minimum Support Prices (MSP) and Buffer Stock policy.

MSP and Procurement: Providing minimum assured prices, which is largely based on cost of production, for some major agricultural items would ensure farmers of minimum return that might encourage to increase investments and, hence, production. This would also protect consumers' interest by ensuring reasonable and expected prices of some food items. The Commission for Agricultural Cost and Prices (CACP) at present recommends prices for 24 important crops in advance, much before the sowing session. The recent trends in increase in MSP suggest that off-late, MSP has increased significantly and some attribute these increases to the high food inflation that India experienced between 2009 and 2013.

Buffer stock policy: The importance of building up a buffer stock of food grains like rice and wheat is to ensure food security to the country from large variation in food grain output from unforeseen events such as droughts or calamities, or any other supply shocks. This buffer stocks are also used for providing food through Targeted Public Distribution System (TPDS) for people below the Poverty Line and also helps in stabilizing the retail market prices from demand-supply mismatch. As of 2015, the government has more than 60 million tonnes of food grains, which is nearly three times more than the buffer stock norm of 21.41 million tonnes suggested for the FCI. The challenges due to lack of storage facilities and wastage of food grains also require to be addressed.

The other important aspect here is the role of weather forecasting. The precision of weather forecasts in India have seen improvements in recent years, which could help farmers in mitigating the risks by timing their sowing sessions. However, it is important to ensure these forecasts are communicated well and accessible to all farmers.

## *On access*

Under access, India has one of the oldest and largest food distribution network system of Targeted Public Distribution System (TPDS), which is a system for ensuring food security particularly to Below Poverty Line (BPL) families. This system ensures availability of essential commodities such as rice, wheat, edible oils, pulses, sugar, and kerosene to the consumers through fair price shops (FPS). At present India has nearly 4.5 lakh such shops that are ensuring distribution of essential commodities to BPL families. However, there have been certain drawbacks to the TPDS system. While there were steps to reform the TPDS system through involvement of panchayats and Self Help Groups (SHGs), recent studies suggest that PDS system has not been effective enough for ensuring food security for all in the country.

### Antyodaya Anna Yojana

In the year 2000, the Central Government initiated a scheme called Antyodaya Anna Yojana (AAY) to target ten million poorest of the poor families among the BPL families. Under the scheme each family would be provided with 35 kilograms of rice and wheat at Rs. 3 and Rs. 2 per kg respectively. As the scheme was successful in the first phase, this has been further augmented by ten million more families by 2004.

## *On nutrition*

To improve the nutrition levels especially among children, India has initiated two major schemes: Integrated Child Development Services (ICDS) for early child care and the Mid-Day Meal scheme for school going children. Both these schemes have become best practices at the global level.

## *Integrated child development services*

The Integrated Child Development Services (ICDS) was launched on 2nd October 1975 to ensure overall development of children up to the age of six years while having special focus on children upto two years. The scheme also covered expectant mothers. This scheme is a package of six important services that covers health as well as nutrition of children as well as expectant mothers. The services that are provided under the scheme are health check-ups, immunization, referral services, supplementary feeding, non-formal pre-school education, and health & nutrition education. While this program is one of the world's largest programs for early child care, some evaluation studies have shown that the impact on child health and nutrition were limited.

## Mid-day meal scheme

The Mid-Day Meal Scheme (MDMS), which was implemented first in the state of Tamil Nadu, has been implemented at the primary level across the country from September 2004. While the scheme was initially introduced to improve the school enrollment as well as the retention levels, it has also focused on improving nutrition levels among school children. However the scheme has been facing problems regarding its implementation as well as in its design. To improve the Scheme, in 2009, the government has changed the food norms to maintain the nutrition balance and also brought in changes in implementation. In addition, some state governments have brought in convergence with other schemes such as NRLM (National Rural Livelihood Mission) under which women SHGs were given responsibility of managing the meal. Convergence with MGNREGS in encouraging kitchen gardens as well as maintaining hygiene was also undertaken by some states. School level committees with parent representatives were also introduced to improve the implementation of the scheme. The 11th Plan also provided many suggestions to improve the governance structure of the scheme (see Dev & Sharma, 2010 for more details). All these changes are expected to improve the overall implementation of the scheme.

## Social security through MGNREGS

In India, at the moment there are no conditional cash transfers in the form of social security measure as in countries such as Brazil that could ensure consumption smoothing. In 2006, India initiated the Mahatma Gandhi National Rural Employment Guarantee Scheme (MGNREGS) in an effort to ensure 'Right to Employment'. This is a demand driven programme that aims to ensure livelihood security in rural areas by providing at least 100 days of wage employment in a financial year to one person in every household. Labour-intensive activities such as creation of rural infrastructure are carried out under this scheme. Apart from providing economic security and creating rural assets, MGNREGS is also meant to help in protecting the environment, empowering rural women, reducing rural–urban migration and fostering social equity. As per the government statistics, since its inception in 2006, around Rs. 1.1 lakh crores has been spent as wages to rural households and 12 billion person-days of employment has been generated.

From the above discussion, one can note that India historically has several policies that aim at food security. However, despite these policies food insecurity and malnutrition still remain at high and unacceptable levels. A holistic and coordinated approach towards better provisioning of food through improved storage and delivery systems may be required. Social mobilization and community participation are also required for ensuring food security within households. Along with these, policies that help in crop diversification and improved research & technology are also needed. Access to credit, technology and infrastructure are essential for furthering the reach of food security policies to needy people.

## NFSA, 2013: What are the macro-fiscal impacts?

In spite of the various public policy initiatives in India, the outcomes in terms of various food security indicators, although improved, are still below par and categorized as 'serious'. Consequently, Right to Food has been made a fundamental right and the NFSA was signed in 2013. This section briefly discusses the provisions of this Act and the coverage and costs of implementing the Act are discussed in the following section.

The Government of India notified the NFSA, on 10th September 2013 with an aim *to provide adequate quantity of quality food at a subsidized and affordable price to all its citizens.* The Act aims to cover 75 per cent of rural population and 50 per cent of urban population for food security and thereby covering nearly two thirds of the population under TPDS. The eligible households for these schemes are sub-divided into two categories:

1. Households covered under the existing AAY
2. Priority households (identified in accordance with the state governments guidelines)

Under NFSA, each households covered by AAY are entitled to get 35 kg of food grains per month and those belonging to priority households are provided with

5 kg of food grains per month. In terms of cost, beneficiaries of PDS are entitled to get food grains at the prices of Rs. 3 per kg for rice, Rs. 2 per kg for wheat and Rs. 1 per kg for coarse grains. Every pregnant women and lactating mothers (except those who are working regularly in central or state government or public undertaking and getting similar benefits through other sources) will get free meals during pregnancy and for six months after child birth. They are also entitled to get maternity benefit of a one-off payment of not less than Rs. 6,000. School going children upto the age of 14 years are eligible to get free nutritious meals. In case of non-supply of food grains, the beneficiaries will get a food security allowance from the respective state government. The Act identified the following provisions to help with its implementation:

1. Developing a mechanism to identify eligible households.
2. Reforming TPDS.
3. Empowering women through providing ration cards to eldest women above 18 years of age in each household.
4. Setting up of grievance redressal system at the district and state levels.
5. Obliging every state government to constitute a State Food Commission for the purpose of monitoring and review of implementation of the Act.

In order to help and support administration, if the state decides to set up State Food Commission exclusively for implementation of these policies, the central government will provide one-time financial assistance for non-building assets (including furniture, office equipment and computers) although no assistance will be provided for any construction activity or any recurring expenses. Currently, Haryana, Delhi, Himachal Pradesh, Rajasthan, Punjab, Karnataka, Chhattisgarh, Uttrakhand, Maharashtra and Meghalaya have set up State Food Commissions.

## Review of some existing estimates on fiscal implications of NFSA

The most important aspect regarding NFSA that was debated extensively is the coverage and cost of its implementation. Here, we briefly discuss various aspects of the Act and the fiscal implications as projected by some existing studies.

An Expert Committee (EC) was set up under the chairmanship of Dr C. Rangarajan, which examined the implications of the proposals of the National Advisory Council (NAC), which had cleared the draft National Food Security Bill (NFSB), and the recommendations of the Ministry of Rural Development (MoRD) to replace the existing BPL survey with a socio-economic survey. The recommendations of the EC pertained to – food grain entitlement, subsidy implications, reform of the PDS, and identification of beneficiaries (GoI, 2011).

## Food grain entitlement

As estimated by the EC, the total food grain requirement to meet NAC recommendations covering 72 per cent of the population in the first phase and 75 per cent in the final phase is 68.76 million tonnes and 73.98 million tonnes, respectively. Based on past trends, the EC projects that the government would be able to procure about 30 per cent of the total production in a given year. Based on past experiences of production of food grains, the likely procurement works out to be 56.35 million tonnes for phase I and 57.61 million tonnes for the final phase. This implies a shortfall of about 12 million tonnes for phase I and 16 million tonnes for the final phase.

As opposed to the idea of accepting NAC's recommendations of 7 kg per capita entitlement to 'priority' households and 2 kg for the 'general households', the EC suggested a more pragmatic option of restricting the assured delivery of food grains at Rs. 2 per kg for wheat and Rs. 3 per kg for rice, to the really needy households, with the entitled population being defined as the percentage of population below the official Tendulkar poverty line plus 10 per cent of BPL population to capture some of the households at the margin. Forty six per cent of rural and 28 per cent of urban population constitute the entitled category for food security programmes. The committee estimated total food grain requirement for the entitled population to be 50.96 million tonnes in the year 2011 (first phase) and 51.93 million tonnes in the year 2014 (final phase) based on the requirements for buffer stocks and other welfare programmes such as the MDMS, ICDS and other public distribution schemes. For the remaining households, that is, the non-entitled population, the distribution could be done at an issue price equal to the MSP. Further, the committee called for a reduction in coverage of the entitled population by anchoring it to the official poverty line, citing procurement difficulties and shortages.

## Subsidy implications

The EC concluded that the total subsidy outgo is expected to be much higher than NAC projections when the population estimates were revised based on October 2011 and 2013 figures for phase 1 and final phase, respectively, and assuming 100 per cent off-take. Additionally, given the current procurement and storage capacity, significant increase of procurement, warehousing and supply chain operations scale-up implementation costs. Further, as the entitlements have a legal bearing, procurement may have to be scaled up through large increases in the MSP or imports, leading to higher fiscal burden. Other components such as the cost of carrying buffer stock and the increase in economic cost over time could also inflate the subsidy outgo. Supplying subsidized grain to the non-entitled households at MSP which are lower than the economic cost of grain, would magnify the subsidy bill.

## PDS and alternative distribution mechanism

The EC recommended reforming PDS by undertaking a comprehensive computerization of PDS network from the allocation of grain to tracking of food grain bags using barcode from FCI godowns to FPSs and until final delivery to the targeted beneficiary. The EC also suggested introduction of smart cards for beneficiaries, whereby food subsidy may be directly transferred to beneficiaries on presentation of their smart cards or food coupons, thereby attempting to plug leakages and improving efficiency.

## Identification of beneficiaries

Identification of beneficiaries has been the most contentious issue. The committee emphasized the need for accuracy and broad uniformity of approach in this regard. It proposed that a socio-economic survey should be undertaken for identifying beneficiaries.

Given these recommendations, many independent researchers have looked into the implementation and cost implications of NFSA. The study by Kotwal, Milind and Bharat (2012) highlighted the large-scale inefficiencies in the functioning of existing PDS, leading to high leakages, diversions and wastages, with a significant part of the allotment ending up in the open market. The study estimated that in 2004–2005, about 70 per cent of the poor were excluded from the benefits of PDS and were left with no option but to buy grain in the open market. The authors proposed cash transfers policy rather than in-kind transfers as suggested in NFSA. The study cites examples of successful reforms to PDS in the states of Chhattisgarh and Tamil Nadu, with near universal coverage and information technology being used to trace every shipment of foodgrains so that diversions could be detected. The study also highlighted the role of community participation in curbing local corruption, through the system of social audits.

A study by Ramaswami and Murugkar (2013) suggested that food subsidy through PDS constitutes high fiscal cost to the government. The study estimates food subsidy cost of about 1 per cent of GDP and about 8.25 per cent of the non-plan expenditure budget of the central government. It estimates that the existing food subsidy bill would increase by about 50 per cent for implementation of NFSA. The same study also considered the issue of 'coverage' and suggested that the more easily identifiable group of the 'non-poor' be identified and excluded from any subsidy and all others be given equal allocations of the designated subsidy. It also opines that most serious political problem in implementing NFSA might be the strong opposition from the state governments on account of loss of autonomy in the food policy.

Gulati et al. (2012), published by the Commission for Agricultural Costs and Prices (CACP), highlight some critical challenges for implementation of NFSA. It mentions the centralized procurement model that the bill seeks to impose even though past experiences have shown such models to be unsustainable. On the other hand, decentralized procurement system introduced in 1997–1998 under which states were invited to assist in the procurement and distribution of foodgrains under TPDS had been quite successful in Madhya Pradesh and Chhattisgarh. The study also discusses operational and financial challenges for implementation of NFSA, that requires large-scale procurement and distribution infrastructure, over and above the expenditure on direct food subsidy, entailing high financial burden on an already burdened fiscal system. It estimates the food subsidy bill in the coming years to escalate due to lower central issue price of grain, a significant rise in the number of entitled beneficiaries and the need to keep raising the MSP to cover the rising costs of production as well as provide incentives to farmers to increase production. Apart from the growing food subsidy bill, enormous additional expenditure would be imperative to support NFSA by enhancing production, storage and marketing infrastructure, procurement and distribution set up, the entire envisaged paraphernalia for adequate administrative set up, additional manpower for effective implementation of the Act, expenditure on welfare schemes and so on. The study estimates a total financial expenditure of around Rs. 682,163 crore over a three-year period, with roughly Rs. 2.3 lakh crore a year.

There are other apprehensions that Gulati et al. (2012) highlight. One of them is the likely shift of resource allocation more towards subsidies rather than investments, which might prove to be detrimental for long-term growth in agricultural production and productivity. Further, massive government intervention in procurement and policing would crowd out the private sector from the food grains sector. Increased focus on foodgrains could reverse the movement of Indian agriculture from high value commodities to foodgrains, thereby forcing the agricultural sector in a low equilibrium trap, besides generating inflationary pressures on food prices.

Mishra (2013) tried to examine the financial consequences of NFSA. The study estimated that the food subsidy cost of implementing the Act, assuming a total coverage of 75 per cent of rural and 50 per cent of the urban population with an entitlement of 5 kg per person per month of food grains at issue prices of Rs. 2 and 3 per kg for wheat and rice, respectively, to be Rs. 124,502 crores for 2013–2014.

## Incremental costs

Mishra (2013) also calculated 'incremental' food subsidy over and above the existing TPDS at roughly, Rs. 24,000 crores, equivalent to 0.2 per cent of GDP. Further, there would have been significant incremental expenditures in addition to the food subsidy. These include setting up and running of appropriate infrastructure, for instance, State Food Commissions and District Grievance Redressal Offices (DGROs); expenditures on intra-state transportation of food grains; and cash benefits to pregnant and lactating women. Mishra suggested that a range of other expenditures stated in the bill need to be included, for example, costs to be incurred for a new system for identification of beneficiaries. The total incremental fiscal cost of implementing the NFSA over and above the existing TPDS (including the quantifiable expenditures in addition to the food subsidy) was thus estimated for 2013–2014 at Rs. 44,711 crores. In addition to the incremental costs under the baseline scenario, additional costs of 'grandfathering' of existing beneficiaries and subsidizing BPLs who were misclassified were included, the total incremental costs of implementing NFSA over the TPDS was estimated to range from Rs. 44,711 to Rs. 76,486 crores in 2013–2014. Further, if the cost of procuring additional food grains according to historical norms was added, the incremental costs were estimated to reach Rs. 81,411 crores, that is, about 0.7 per cent of GDP.

Bhalla (2013a) estimated that the NFSB would cost nearly 3 per cent of GDP in the first year of implementation. Using data from the National Sample Survey Consumer Expenditure Survey for 2011–2012, the study concluded that taking into account the proportional increase in coverage from 45 per cent to 67 per cent, the increase in average PDS consumption from 2.1 kg per person to 5 kg per person and proportional increase in subsidies per kg, the total food subsidy expenditure would amount to Rs. 314,000 crores, that is, about 3 per cent of GDP.

Ramaswami, Murugkar and Kotwal (2013) asserted that NFSB would raise the subsidy burden by 18 per cent. They pointed out that Bhalla (2013b) made an arithmetic error by not properly adjusting for the base population. Ramaswami, Murugkar and Kotwal (2013) emphasized that the average consumption refers to what the households received and not what the government supplies and it is the difference between the two that constitutes leakages in PDS. This chapter acknowledges that while the supply of grain per entitled person under NFSA has decreased from 7.9 to 5 kg, the coverage has increased from 44.5 to 67 per cent. The authors reiterate that the major concern of NFSA should be to ensure that leakages are curtailed and full benefits are provided to beneficiary households. They reiterate that the debate should be centred upon the minimization of costs by judicious use of cash transfers and other policies.

Based on the above debate of the estimates, the government brought in a policy that it is willing to take responsibility for implementation, irrespective of the size of the bill. The adjustments that are made in budget allocation are shown in Table 4.1.

In the 2015–2016 Union Budget, the central government allocated a sum of Rs. 95,827 crores for implementation of NFSA. This allocation subsumes the allocations that were made under BPL/APL and additional to 2014–2015, when NFSA was implemented only partially. However, the overall additional food subsidy allocated in 2015–2016 is about Rs. 26,000 crores, which after adjusting

**TABLE 4.1 Changes in the pattern of Central Government allocations**

| Sl. No. | Scheme | 2014–2015(RE) | | 2015–2016(BE) | |
|---|---|---|---|---|---|
| A | Consumer Subsidy | | | | |
| | NFSA | 29,588 | | 95,827 | |
| | Other than NFSA | 686 | | 2,025 | |
| | APL | 12,870 | | – | |
| | APL Additional | 4,243 | | – | |
| | BPL | 16,830 | | – | |
| | BPL Additional | 6,044 | | – | |
| | AAY | 11,881 | | 17,990 | |
| | Mid-Day Meal (MDM) | 4,799 | | 5,262 | |
| | Defence | −19 | | −7 | |
| | Open Market Sale | 2,865 | | 3,763 | |
| | Export | 14 | | – | |
| | Others | 4,593 | | 5,014 | |
| | Total Consumer Subsidy | | 94,394 | | 111,884 |
| B | Buffer Subsidy | | 8,082 | | 6,850 |
| | Food Subsidy incurred during the year | | 102,476 | | 118,734 |
| | Less: Deductions pending audit certificate | | 5,124 | | 5,937 |
| | Net Food Subsidy | | 97,352 | | 112,797 |
| C | Arrears for earlier year (on furnishing audit cert) | | 45,633 | | 56,109 |
| | Total Food Subsidy to be claimed | | 142,985 | | 168,906 |

*Source*: http://fciweb.nic.in/articles/view/327.

for the growth trend (a norm for increasing allocation every year), the additional food subsidy due to NFSA is not substantial. As discussed earlier, NFSA is currently implemented only in eleven states and these budgets are manageable. However, when the Act is implemented universally, the fiscal implications might be higher.

## Integration of NFSA with social protection programmes

As discussed in the earlier section, the additional fiscal implication of universal implementation of NFSA according to existing studies could range from 0.5 to 2 per cent of GDP depending upon the methodology that was used. In addition to fiscal implications, there were other microstructural concerns that have been raised by existing studies in terms of implementation such as identification of beneficiaries, plugging leakages (which are a major concern in such schemes) and creating institutional capacity in all states.

In the broader context, there is an overall effort to reduce subsidy programmes across food, fuel and fertilizers, as many studies have suggested that as a result of leakages, the existing subsidies do not reach the actual beneficiary. There are efforts to enhance use of technology to transfer benefits directly through *Aadhaar*-based platform (direct benefit transfer [DBT]) in order to reduce leakage and ensure that eligible beneficiaries receive the subsidies. The initial assessment of using such platforms has been successful (in particular, transferring liquefied petroleum gas [LPG] subsidy through DBT, which is also called PAHAL). There are estimates that suggest that the savings from using DBT could be around 25 per cent of current expenditures. However, some studies (especially done by International Institute of Sustainable Development [IISD], Geneva, 2015) suggest that the savings might not be substantial. It may be noted that the discrepancy between these studies could be due to sharp decline in the under recovery in the petroleum sector due to fall in the international oil prices. What is more important is that the benefits have been channelled through formal financial structures. In other words, even if the savings might not be substantial through using DBT, the fact remains that DBT could help significantly in reducing leakages. Following from some initial success, the government is progressing to implement DBT system for food security as well from 2016-2017. Shanta Kumar Committee on PDS has suggested that there is a diversion of foodgrains of about 47 per cent from the PDS system. It will be a major success if effective implementation of NFSA through DBT, could succeed in reducing these diversions and leakages even by half. Thereby, the additional fiscal implication of implementing NFSA could be negligible. Here, we reiterate that subsidy per se may not be a major issue, as it is inefficient administration and leakages that results in unintended and unwanted consequences on growth and welfare.

Other ways to reduce the fiscal burden is to co-ordinate, integrate and subsume NFSA with other social welfare schemes, especially the anti-poverty programmes. Some existing schemes could be overlapping with NFSA in terms of their objectives. The recent Shivraj Chouhan Committee on reforming Centrally Sponsored Schemes submitted to NITI Aayog, suggested reduction of the number of schemes to 27, which could include only the flagship programmes while shifting all other social protection schemes to the states, which may be funded from the increased devolution funds as recommended by the 14th FC. Thereby, the responsibility rests with state governments to avoid duplication of benefits from schemes for reducing poverty and malnutrition at the state level.

Other discussions pertaining to effective implementation of NFSA are to be considered. Basu (2011), while arguing against distribution of food grains at subsidized prices, suggested that, based on the success in other countries such as Brazil, PDS could be replaced with either providing food coupons or by cash transfers to beneficiaries' bank accounts. The argument here being that the beneficiary may be allowed to use cash benefit for other nutritional items instead of being forced to consume rice or wheat. At the same time it is essential to ensure that they have market access to suitable alternatives. Such policies could also help limit leakages in implementing the scheme. While distribution of food coupons could require large institutional capacity similar to PDS, the DBT system, once it is established after overcoming challenges of setting up, could be extremely effective in improving public delivery mechanism while also reducing leakages.

## Way forward

With persistent high rates of undernourished people in the country, it is imperative for India to continue to implement food security policies and programmes. Hence, implementing NFSA by central and state governments in India is essential. As many studies have suggested, the fiscal implications for the exchequer are expected to be considerable. However, the fiscal burden could be mitigated through use of information technology (DBT) and by developing formal financial systems and procedures and improving administrative capability. Additionally, these mitigation policies would be helpful for minimising leakages, which is a major challenge for many social protection programmes in India. Further, co-ordination and integration of implementation of NFSA together with other social security programmes will enable efficient public delivery mechanisms and ensure fiscal feasibility and sustainability.

Regular monitoring is also essential to improve performance of NFSA and evaluate its sustainability based on the needs and priorities at any given time for inclusion, growth and development of the people and the country.

## References


Basu, Kaushik. 2011. 'India's Foodgrain Policy: An Economic Theoretic Perspective.' *Economic and Political Weekly* 46(4), January 29.

Bhalla, Surjit. 2013a. 'Manmonia's FSB: 3% of GDP.' *The Indian Express*, July 6. http://www.indianexpress.com/news/manmonias-fsb-3--of-gdp/1138195/.

——— 2013b. 'Rotting Food, Rotten Arguments.' *The Indian Express*, September 4. http://www.indianexpress.com/news/rotting-food-rotten-arguments/1164123/.

Chmielewska, Danuta and Darana Souza. 2011. *The Food Security Policy Context in Brazil.* Country Study no.22. Brazil: IPC of Inclusive Growth.

Dev, S. M. and A. N. Sharma. 2010. *Food Security in India: Performance, Challenges and Policies.* New Delhi: Institute for Human Development, Oxfam Working Paper.

Food and Agriculture Organisation - World Food Summit (1996). 'Rome Declaration on World Food Security and World Food Summit Plan of Action', 13-17 November 1996. Available at: www.fao.org/wfs/. Accessed January 20, 2011.

Government of India. 2011. *The National Food Security Bill.* Department of Food and Public Distribution, Government of India. Available at: http://fcamin.nic.in/dfpd_html/Draft_National_Food_Security_Bill.pdf. Accessed February 12, 2012.

Government of Nepal. 2010. *Nepal Agriculture and Food Security Country Investment Plan (AFSP-2010).* Kathmandu, Nepal.

Government of Sri Lanka. 2010. National Nutrition Policy of Sri Lanka. https://extranet.who.int/nutrition/gina/sites/default/files/LKA%202010%20Sri%20Lanka%20National%20Nutrition%20Policy-English_0.pdf. Accessed January 12, 2016.

——— 2014. Sri Lanka National Agricultural Policy. http://www.agrimin.gov.lk/web/images/docs/1252389643AgPolicy4.pdf. Accessed January 12, 2016.

Gulati, Ashok, T. Jyoti Gujral, Nandakumar, Surbhi Jain, Sourabh Anand, Siddharth Rath and Piyush Joshi. 2012. *National Food Security Bill: Challenges and Options.* Discussion Paper No. 2. New Delhi: Commission for Agricultural Costs and Prices.

IFPRI. 2015. *Global Hunger Index.* Report by International Food Policy Research Institute. http://www.ifpri.org/topic/global-hunger-index.

Jha, Praveen. 2013. 'Securing Food for All Is It Really Difficult to Afford?' *Economic and Political Weekly*, January 26.

Joshi, P. K. 2013. *National Food Security Bill and Need for a Stronger Implementation Strategy*. New Delhi: Governance Knowledge Centre. http://indiagovernance.gov.in/thinkpiece/?thinkpiece=5.

Kattumuri, Ruth. 2011. *Food Security and the Targeted Public Distribution System in India*. Asia Research Centre Working Paper 38. http://www.lse.ac.uk/asiaResearchCentre/_files/ARCWP38-Kattumuri.pdf.

Koc, M., R. MacRae, Mougeot, L. J. A. and J. Welsh, eds. 1999. *For Hunger-Proof Cities: Sustainable Urban Food Systems*. Ottawa: IDRC.

Kotwal, Ashok, Milind Murugkar and Bharat Ramaswami. 2012. 'The Political Economy of Food Subsidy in India.' *The Copenhagen Journal of Asian Studies* 30(2).

Maxwell, S. and T. Frankenberger. 1992. *Household Food Security: Concepts, Indicators, Measurements: A Technical Review*. Rome, Italy: IFAD/UNICEF.

Ministry of Statistics and Programme Implementation. 2015. Millennium Development Goals: India Country Report, 2015. Available at

Ministry of Women and Child Development (2015). Rapid Survey on Children 2013-14. wcd.nic.in/acts/rapid-survey-children-rsoc-2013-14. Accessed January 15, 2016.

Mishra, Prachi. 2013. *The National Food Security Bill (NFSB) Incremental Financial and Distributional Implications: 2013-14 to 2015-16*. http://southasia.ifpri.info/files/2013/05/NFSB2.pdf.

Rahman, Z. H., L. A. Choudhury and K. S. Ali. 2011. *Social Safety Nets in Bangladesh: Review of Issues and Analytical Inventory*. Volume 1. Dhaka: Power and Participation Research Centre and UNDP.

Ramaswami, B. and M. Murugkar. 2013. *Food Policy Reforms: A Rapid Tour of Possibilities*. Manila, Philippines: Asian Development Bank.

Ramaswami, B., Milind Murugkar and Ashok Kotwal. 2013. 'Correct Costs of the Food Security Bill.' *The Financial Express*, September 2. http://www.financialexpress.com/news/correct-costs-of-the-food-security-bill/1156251/0.

UNICEF 2015. The State of the World's Children. Available at: www.unicef.org/publications/files/sowc_2015.

Wickramasinghe, U. 2014. *Realizing Sustainable Food Security in the Post-2015 Development Era: South Asia's Progress, Challenges and Opportunities*. Development Papers 1402. New Delhi: ESCAP-SSWA.

5

# Land and Food Acts

## Trading Economic Pragmatism for Political Gain

**Amitendu Palit***

## Introduction

The early 1990s marked the beginning of an economic transition in India. The state began withdrawing from the various key spaces it occupied in production with new regulations encouraging allocation of resources on market-driven principles. The policies continued through the 1990s and into the first decade of the next century.

As the country went into the 14th elections to the Lok Sabha (the Lower House of the Indian Parliament) in April–May 2004, there were no significant expectations of these policies changing under the next government. Expectations of market-friendly policies continuing became stronger with the victory of the Congress-led United Progressive Alliance (UPA) given that the Congress, and the new Prime Minister Manmohan Singh, was the harbinger of economic reforms in India.

Over time, however, these beliefs changed as the Congress and the UPA were found pursuing an economic programme hesitant to sanction greater freedom to market-based regulations in product and factor markets; on the contrary, the UPA increasingly, and particularly in its second tenure from May 2009 onwards, began pursuing policies that while not undoing the framework put in place by earlier economic reforms, tried balancing the thrust on markets by forcefully emphasizing greater role of the state in expanding economic entitlements of individuals and households and guaranteeing rights to such entitlements.

* Amitendu Palit is Senior Research Fellow and Research Lead (Trade and Economic Policy) at the Institute of South Asian Studies (ISAS) in the National University of Singapore. He can be reached at isasap@nus.edu.sg and Amitendu@gmail.com. Usual disclaimers apply.

In the monsoon session of the Parliament in 2013, the UPA government enacted two major legislations. The first one prescribed a new framework for acquiring land and compensating the landowners and replaced the Land Acquisition Act (LAA) of 1894. The second was an Act entitling three-fourth of the rural population and half of the urban population to the receipt of subsidized food grains. Both the Acts were significant in their economic and political impacts. While they were in sync with the UPA's agenda of inclusive growth and a rights-based economic approach, they have been criticized on two grounds: first, for increasing production and fiscal costs in the national economy, and second, for being pushed as populist legislations for securing political gains.

The Bharatiya Janata Party (BJP)-led National Democratic Alliance (NDA) has taken up the land legislation for amendment after its victory in the 16th general elections to the Lower House in April–May 2014. Interestingly, the BJP, as the main opposition in the Parliament, had eventually supported the passage of both legislations in 2013. In this respect, the BJP's desire to not send politically 'incorrect' signals a few months before the general elections, marks its overlooking of economic pragmatism for greater political mileage.

This paper studies the political economy impacting the two legislations, from the perspectives of dominant influences shaping their growth, within the incumbent UPA government. It argues that the timing of the enactment of the two legislations and their frameworks cannot escape the criticism of having sacrificed economic pragmatism for political benefits. Both legislations have arguably created additional obstacles in ushering in fiscal discipline at a time when it is an imperative for the Indian economy.

## Land acquisition and compensation

Acquisition of land in India came under the purview of a new legislation – the *Right to Fair Compensation and Transparency in Land Acquisition, Rehabilitation and Resettlement Act, 2013* – from 26 September 2013. The introduction of the Act marked the culmination of a long period of controversy over the process of land acquisition during the tenure of the UPA government from May 2004 to May 2012. While the Act obviously does not put to an end the discussions and debates surrounding land acquisition in the country, it signifies a historical milestone by replacing the LAA of 1894, which had governed the process of acquisition in the country since the colonial times and for more than six decades in independent India. The new Act is also significant in pulling in both acquisition of land and rehabilitation and resettlement (R&R) of the displaced population within a uniform legislative framework.

The evolution of the new Act has been connected to the striking changes in circumstances that led to its conceptualisation and implementation during the UPA government's term in office. The shifting circumstances reflect the complex and intriguing political economy surrounding land acquisition in India. The complicated political economy was evident from the variable postures of the government on the bills introduced in the Parliament at different points in time for amending the LAA of 1894. These postures and the slants of the legislations also point to the sharp rifts within the government on the issue, which further mirror the complex political economy through the influences of different stakeholders and associated perceptions of the government and the legislature.

The LAA of 1894 enabled the Indian state to exercise 'eminent domain'[1] for acquiring private land in 'public purpose'. The Indian state is not an exception in this regard. Similar legislations empower various national governments across the world to acquire land, particularly for constructing large-scale projects aiming to supply public goods and infrastructure facilities. The central and state governments in India have used the law time and again to acquire land for constructing railways, irrigation projects, and other facilities deemed as producers of public goods and meant for non-exclusive public consumption. These acquisitions hardly generated controversies, primarily because dispossession from private property and its expropriation by the state was assumed a virtuous exercise in terms of the socio-economic welfare it could generate through enhanced supply of public goods, which, arguably, from a Pareto-efficiency[2] perspective was a preferable outcome notwithstanding the loss of welfare of private property owners.

The welfare notion came under serious criticism during the first tenure of the UPA government. The trigger was the introduction of the Special Economic Zone (SEZ) Act in 2005. It is important to note that SEZs were not new to India. Indeed, it established the third SEZ in the world, and Asia's first, in as early as 1965 through the Kandla Export Processing Zone (EPZ). Subsequently, several other EPZs came up in India before the SEZ Act of 2005.[3] Most of these SEZs were owned and developed by the central government and different state governments. A few were developed by the private sector too such as the Mahindra apparel, IT and auto SEZs and the Nokia SEZ in Tamil Nadu, and the Wipro SEZ in West Bengal. The new SEZ policy of the UPA government envisaged a much greater role of the private sector and extended generous fiscal incentives to private developers for building SEZs. The fiscal generosity generated considerable criticism over whether India's public finances were indeed at a stage where the country could afford to forego revenues for abetting private investments in industrial growth.[4] These criticisms reflected concerns over the revenue loss noted for India's early state-promoted SEZs that came up before the SEZ Act of 2005.[5]

As the policy took off, there was a rush among private investors, including foreign investors, to submit proposals for SEZs in different parts of the country. The rush was accompanied by intense controversy over various aspects of the policy. From the fiscal consolidation perspective, concerns were expressed over the revenue outgo on SEZs at a time when the country had begun reducing revenue and fiscal deficits in a time-bound manner within the framework of the Fiscal Responsibility and Budget Management Act (FRBMA) of 2003.[6] The fiercest controversy, however, was on the process of acquiring land for developing SEZs and the role of the state in doing so. The prevailing opinion was that of the state misusing the 'public purpose' clause in the LAA of 1894 for acquiring land on behalf of private industry. The state's exercise of eminent domain in the context of acquiring land for private SEZs underlined the sharp polarisation of views on the role of state in land acquisition (Palit, 2012). While information asymmetry between industry and landowners is taken as an important ground for advocating proactive state intervention (Bardhan, 2011), a relatively 'hands off' approach limiting state participation to specific projects for supplying public goods has gained currency among political parties given the substantive political sensitivities associated with acquisition.[7]

The SEZ policy was introduced at a time when the Indian economy was riding its highest growth trajectory. Beginning from 2003 to 2008, the economy picked up momentum to record annual gross domestic product (GDP) growth in the range of 8–9 per cent, except in 2004–2005, when it grew by 7 per cent. Coming at a time of high economic growth contributed by a series of market-friendly measures encouraging greater investment in the economy and accelerating growth in manufacturing output and exports, SEZs were visualized as instruments for propelling export-led growth through private enterprise and investment. The vision reflected the prominence of a market-friendly approach in economic strategy aiming to maximize growth. Land acquisition came up as a stumbling block in the vision. The criticism of the state for expropriating land for private developers through the LAA of 1894 by justifying such acquisition on the ground of the land being used in projects likely to generate benefits for the public[8] assumed the state acting as broker for maximizing private profits. The criticism extended to describing such acts as far-removed from the objective of enhancing social welfare and being pervasive applications of the authority of eminent domain.

The UPA's victory in the 2004 general elections to the Indian Parliament was largely credited to its emphasis on 'inclusive' growth, underpinning the redistributive and qualitative aspects of economic growth, rather than its rate. Whether this was a vision produced by the political necessity to counter the incumbent BJP-led NDA government's conspicuous accent on high economic growth and the high-pitched 'India Shining' campaign, or a result of the Congress party's genuine conviction on following an economic development strategy focussing on redistribution of wealth and resources through a larger role of the state in guaranteeing individual and community-based economic rights for maximizing social welfare, is difficult to identify. The Congress and the UPA government clearly did not lack 'champions' of market-friendly policies with several architects of India's economic reforms in the 1990s, led by the Prime Minister Manmohan Singh, holding key economic portfolios in the UPA government. These included, among others, Finance Minister P. Chidambaram and Deputy Chairman of the Planning Commission Montek Singh Ahluwalia, both known for their pro-market economic views.

It is noteworthy that the market-friendly views within the UPA co-existed with alternative rights-based quasi-socialist orientations, both within the Congress Party, as well as its coalition partners at different points in time, such as the Left parties during the first tenure of the UPA and the Trinamool Congress (TMC) on the second occasion. Within the Congress, the alternative 'inclusive' agenda arguably had the most influential backing from the UPA chairperson and President of the Congress Party, Sonia Gandhi. The National Advisory Council (NAC) headed by Sonia Gandhi was responsible for articulating the frameworks for several rights-based initiatives the UPA subsequently legislated, including the Right to Information (RTI) Act, the Forest Rights Act and the Land Act.

The rift between the market and rights-based ideologies widened into an almost unbridgeable chasm over the decade long tenure of the UPA. It had a striking manifestation in the UPA government's handling of the issue of land acquisition. It would perhaps not be erroneous to conclude that the controversy created over the state's role in acquiring land for private industry, as experienced through the SEZ policy, was the first flashpoint between the two ideologies.

Acquisition of land for use by private developers was notionally antithetical to the centrist-left posture of the UPA. Following the victory in the 2004 general elections, the work programme of the UPA was developed in close consultation between the senior leaders of the Congress and the Communist Party of India (Marxist) (CPI (M)). Other external supporters – the Samajwadi Party (SP) and the Bahujan Samaj Party (BSP) – both parties with centre-left postures and drawing support from the economically and socially weaker sections along with religious minorities, also endorsed the programme. Given such ideological posturing, announcement of a SEZ policy that encouraged real-estate developers to submit proposals and seek approvals of state governments in securing private land was somewhat unexpected from the UPA; it was suggestive of contradictions existing not only within the UPA and its constituents and the Congress Party, but also within the Left parties.

Despite its sharp critique of some of the neo-liberal policies of the Congress and the UPA, the leading Left party, the CPI (M) suffered considerable loss of political credibility after the incumbent Left government in Bengal used the LAA of 1894 to acquire private and mostly agricultural land for building the Indonesian Salim group promoted SEZ at Nandigram in the East Midnapore district of West Bengal. The acquisition led to large-scale protests and agitations resulting in loss of several human lives and bloodshed in what was probably the most violent consequence of forcible land acquisition in India. The agitation at Nandigram, followed by similar developments at Singur in the Hooghly district of West Bengal over acquisition of farming land for constructing an automobile manufacturing facility by the Tata Group, and protests over land acquisition for the Korean steel giant Posco's SEZ at Jagatsinghpur in Orissa, forced the UPA to proceed on amendments of the LAA of 1894.

The various stages in the replacement of the LAA of 1894 with the new Act of September 2013 included introduction of two separate bills in the Parliament for amending the LAA of 1894 and providing guidelines on R&R of affected people in 2007; further introduction of a revised Land Acquisition, Resettlement and Rehabilitation (LARR) bill of 2011 clubbing both acquisition and R&R; and examination of the latter by the Parliamentary Standing Committee of the Ministry of Rural Development followed by examination by a Group of Ministers (GoMs). The two bills introduced in 2007 subsequently lapsed, as both Houses of the Parliament within May

2009, or the first five years of the UPA in office, failed to approve them. The two bills were clubbed together into the LARR bill of 2011 with additional qualifications and amendments; after much debate and deliberation the bill was finally approved as the Right to Fair Compensation and Transparency in Land Acquisition, Rehabilitation and Resettlement Act of 2013, replacing the LAA of 1894.

The new Act does not prohibit acquisition of land by the state for private industry on 'public purpose'. It makes it mandatory to obtain the prior consent of at least 80 per cent of the landowners for projects to be executed by private industry; and 70 per cent in the instances of 'public–private partnership' (PPP).[9] It does not stipulate prior consent for acquisition for projects that would be entirely owned and managed by the state thereby protecting the scope of employment of eminent domain. At the same time, it also refrains from removing the ambiguities in defining 'public purpose', which was a major criticism of the LAA of 1894.

What, however, it does is make the cost of acquisition exceptionally steep by factoring in the cost of R&R within the cost of acquisition. The Act is a peculiar legislation where the government's supposed 'accommodation' of private industry has been attempted to be balanced by extracting heavy prices from it for acquiring land by paying higher compensation at pre-determined rates. Such thinking has been influenced by the view that original landowners are deprived of the benefits of future appreciation in the value of the land – an expected development once the land is dedicated to industrial or infrastructure use.[10]

The emphasis and purpose of the Act is comprehensible from the political thinking within the UPA that influenced the legislation. The UPA was returned to office in May 2009 with a stronger verdict. The outcome was largely attributed to the electorate's appreciation of the inclusive growth policies, particularly the rights-based programmes like the Mahatma Gandhi National Rural Employment Guarantee Act (MGNREGA) providing hundred days secure employment to rural households, preserving the rights of forest-based communities for local produce and the RTI Act. The rights-based work agenda, as a result, intensified during the second term of the UPA with the onus on transfer of economic power and resources to marginal sections of the society. The policy of direct cash transfer of subsidies to beneficiaries, the promulgation of the food security legislation discussed later, and the new Land Act, were seen as instruments enabling such transfer.

The overwhelming emphasis on compensation in the new Land Act to the tune of four times the market value of acquired land in rural areas and twice in urban areas,[11] and application of the land acquisition award in past cases with retrospective effect, highlights the intention to convey a strong message to the rural households on the UPA's commitment to their cause. A similar signal was also sought to be conveyed to the scheduled caste and tribes (SC and ST), traditional constituencies of the Congress, by making the R&R compensation 'sweeter' for affected SC and ST families. It is indeed not surprising that the Congress Vice President Rahul Gandhi had participated actively in agitations against the incumbent state government in the state of Uttar Pradesh (UP) over acquisition of farming land and had promised enactment of a pro-farmer land acquisition legislation.[12]

Taken together with the food security legislation, the new Land Act represents a conscious and sweeping attempt to expand the scope of economic entitlement for certain sections of the society, which the UPA, and particularly the Congress, would have hoped to have fetched dividends in the general elections for 2014. Interestingly, the main opposition party BJP was also seen supporting the passage of the LARR Bill in Parliament and praising the Rural Development Minister Jairam Ramesh for his efforts in implementing the bill in what, probably, was a carefully thought-out strategy for avoiding an anti-farmer image eight months before the general elections.[13]

## Food security

The support of the BJP was also forthcoming in the passage of another landmark legislation in the monsoon session of the Parliament in 2013. The approval of the National Food Security Bill 2013 by both Houses of the Parliament and its enactment as the National Food Security Act of 2013 on 10 September 2013 was significant for a variety of reasons. As mentioned earlier, taken together with the new Land Act, the Rural Employment Guarantee Act, and the Forest Rights Act, the Food Security Act represented the UPA government's efforts to empower citizens, particularly the poor and rural populations by entitling them to economic rights. While the Land Act conceives empowerment in terms of a fixed and pre-determined formula for compensating landowners in acquisition of land for projects involving private industries, the Food Security Act legalizes empowerment through access to food at subsidized prices.

The UPA has been variously criticized for passing these legislations a few months before the general elections; the consent of the BJP on both also indicated the erosion of political capital it envisaged from opposing the legislations in the Parliament. Indeed, it is interesting to note how the two major national political parties in India – the Congress and the BJP – perceived the political impacts of the rights-based economic legislations introduced in India over the last few years, and their almost similar calculations of political benefits from these, notwithstanding the BJP's being critical of the legislations at various points in time. For the Land and Food Acts, as well as the Rural Employment Act implemented earlier, constituencies that would benefit from their introductions were deemed critical by both parties. This is probably why the BJP, despite having different views on certain aspects of the legal frameworks of the two legislations and keen on imparting them a more distinct 'BJP' stamp,[14] never opposed them fundamentally.

Unlike the commitment to rural employment, which found a specific mention in the common minimum programme (CMP) adopted by the Congress and other members of the UPA in May 2004, the articulation on food security was less distinct: 'The UPA will work out, in the next three months, a comprehensive medium-term strategy for food and nutrition security. The objective will be to move towards universal food security over time, if found feasible'.[15] Incidentally, land acquisition did not find any mention in the CMP of the UPA, understandably so, as it was hardly an issue at the time when the UPA assumed office.

The Congress government's initial emphasis in enhancing food security was on making the public distribution system (PDS) more efficient through a targeted focus on beneficiaries, particularly poor families, and among these the poorest households, who have been receiving subsidized food grains under the Antodaya Anna Yojana (AAY).[16] The Food Security Act of 2013 expands the scope of the targeted PDS by making a much larger section of the country legally entitled for receiving subsidized food grains. It does so by identifying large numbers of new below-poverty-line (BPL) and above-poverty-line (APL) families as beneficiaries under the subsidized food scheme. With the coverage of the programme expected to include around 75 per cent of the rural population and 50 per cent of the urban population, the legislation, while not being a conceptual novelty and essentially an expanded edition of the targeted PDS, can significantly enhance the welfare of the economically marginal sections of the population (Palit, 2013). And this is precisely where the politics of the Act kicks in.

The CMP of the UPA identified its key constituencies: farmers, farm labour, workers (particularly unorganized), SC, ST and other backward castes (OBCs), and religious minorities.[17] Over its two tenures, the UPA was particularly conscious of safeguarding the interests of these constituencies and ensuring their greater participation in economic growth by increasing their entitlements and legally empowering them to the entitlements. The Food Security Act has been an important achievement in this regard. While the UPA stopped short of bringing in a legislation embracing universal food security, India's Food Security Act, by its sheer scale and coverage is one of the largest in the world. The spread of the Act to around two-third of the country's population has obviously been motivated by the desire to engulf as much and as many of the UPA's core constituencies as possible. Indeed, the eligibility criteria for receipt of subsidized food grain under the Act is likely to exclude the urban middle class, which was clearly a less important constituency for the UPA. The Act also gives special priority to women by making the eldest women in eligible families the custodian for holding biometric food security ration cards as well as taking special care of the needs of pregnant women and lactating mothers.[18] This could have been influenced by the criticism of the UPA government's inability to prevent the rising incidence of intolerance against women in the country.

While the coverage of the Food Security Act of 2013 extends to several key constituencies of the UPA, the latter are also important support bases for other political parties. This was responsible for the food security bill going through largely unopposed in the Parliament, as like the Land Act, no party wished to block its passage and convey wrong signals to key constituencies. Neither the BJP, nor the SP and the BSP, were seen as obstructionist forces. However, parties were keen on influencing the contents of the Act for satisfying their respective niche constituencies. The SP, for example, insisted on introducing amendments like changing the definition of BPL for including more poor households and ensuring guaranteed prices to farmers on their produce.[19] Similarly, the BJP also sought amendments while clarifying that it would not oppose it.[20] The apparent realisation on part of the other political parties was that while they could not afford to antagonize key constituencies by opposing the bill, they could aim to leave their own 'imprints' on the legislation by proposing amendments accommodating interests of their own specific constituencies.

## Bearing the burden

Both the Land Act and the Food Security Act, as discussed, have aimed to increase the entitlements of individuals and households coming under their purview by legally empowering them to enhanced entitlements. In this respect, both Acts are consistent with the political and economic ideologies of the UPA government that manifested through the programme of 'inclusive' growth based on a left-of-the-centre vision. Both legislations furthered the objective of 'rights-based' economic development in the country, as opposed to a relatively more market-friendly approach, and have, at least partially and in the near term, led to the state playing a much greater role in managing the supply side of the Indian economy.

Certain implications of the approach guiding the implementation of the Acts have been unfortunate. From a business perspective, as well as from the fiscal viewpoint, the land and food legislations imply higher cost. Payment of compensations on acquisition amounting to four times the market value of land in rural areas, and two times in urban areas, makes the cost of land for industry rather onerous. The view that the Act has actually set back the growth of manufacturing and infrastructure and is likely to discourage investment was expressed by influential opinions within the UPA itself.[21] In an unusually candid admission, Amitabh Kant, Secretary of the Department of Industrial Policy & Promotion (DIPP), Ministry of Industry criticized the Act for being excessively bureaucratic and time consuming due to the various new processes it recommended, such as social impact assessment (SIA) and obtaining consent of at least 70 per cent of the affected households. What is noticeable is that such consent is not required for acquisition for projects that would be entirely owned and developed by the government; indeed, such a requirement puts the onus of infrastructure development almost entirely on the government since even for PPPs where the ownership of land 'continues to vest with the government',[22] the consent and compensation requirements are arduous. The implication sends wrong signals at a time when the thrust of infrastructure development in major projects like the Delhi–Mumbai Industrial Corridor (DMIC) is through PPPs.

The NDA government has proposed amendments to the land legislation passed by the UPA. In doing so, it has tried to balance conflicting interests. The process of acquisition has been made simpler by removing mandatory consent and SIA conditions for land being acquired for projects relating to national security, defence, rural infrastructure (including electrification), industrial corridors and affordable housing for the poor, including PPP projects. These changes are expected to remove hurdles faced by major infrastructure projects and encourage greater private investments in PPP ventures.

Along with these amendments, which have been criticized as 'anti-farmer', the NDA has tried to minimize controversy and political damage by extending the provisions of compensation and R&R to several other central legislations (e.g. Mines Act of 1885, Atomic Energy Act of 1962, the Railways Act of 1989, the Electricity Act of 2003 etc.).[23] Due to lack of majority in the Upper House (Rajya Sabha) of the Parliament, the government has not been successful in implementing the amendments till now. While the bill containing the amendments is being reviewed by a Joint Committee of the Parliament, the government has been trying to facilitate the amendments through an ordinance which has been re-promulgated thrice till June 2015.[24]

The various negative opinions on the current Land Act, other than highlighting the disappointment over the low or negligible priority of the UPA government to improving investor climate and attracting more investment by reducing land costs, also reflect the prevalence of views within the executive that were at sharp variance with those guiding the framing of the new Land Act. The polarisation among the decision makers has been evident at various stages of the debate and maturing of the new Land Act. The difficulties that the NDA government continues to face in changing the provisions of the Land Act reflect the persistence of the polarization across the executive and the political community. The predicament also reveals the price that the BJP and the NDA are paying for their political opportunism in the past.

If the current land acquisition law that makes cost of land-intensive development from an industry perspective excessively high continues to prevail, it might actually lead to greater demand of fiscal incentives from industry and developers for undertaking new projects, for compensating the higher cost of land they henceforth will have to bear (Palit, 2014). This might pry open a fresh cycle of tax sops that would entail further deviation from the path of fiscal consolidation.

With the cost of acquisition now fixed at levels far higher than what market prices entail under several circumstances, fiscal burdens of states in implementing infrastructure projects would sharply increase. This is evident from the high prices paid by the UP government in purchasing land from farmers for the Agra–Lucknow expressway project through mutual agreement.[25] Such high prices would be distinct disincentives for industry if states plan to implement similar projects through the PPP mode. There are also other possible adverse fiscal implications for states that can arise from land markets stagnating and land transactions freezing as a result of the prevailing political complications over the Land Act, given that stamp duties paid on land sales continue to be major sources of revenue for Indian states.

The Food Security Act and its ambitious target of providing subsidized food grain to around two-third of the Indian population could be yet another fiscally unsustainable proposition.[26] Indeed, it is actually surprising that the UPA government decided to go ahead and implement the national food security bill at a time when the fiscal health of the country was rather precarious (Palit, 2013). The indifference to the adverse impact on fiscal health reflected the intention of the government to push through a significantly politically popular welfare measure without taking note of the Indian state's ability to sustain the measure.

The Act has already roused the concern of the international community over the impact that it can make on global food prices if India 'dumps' subsidized wheat and rice in the global market from the large pool of public food stocks it is expected to build up under the Act. Indeed, it is rather puzzling as to why a measure, fiscally damaging and globally unpalatable given the rules of multilateral trade at the World Trade Organization (WTO), was not implemented after more careful consideration of its implications. This is where, again, the timing of the passage of Food Act, seven months before the general elections, can hardly escape attention.

However spirited a defense, the UPA government puts up for the Land Act and the Food Security Act by justifying them as its flagship schemes and outcomes of an inclusive rights-based development agenda, the adverse fiscal and business implications of both and the hurriedness with which they were passed in the monsoon session of Parliament during August–September 2013, underline sacrifice of economic pragmatism in favour of short-term political dividends. They also vindicate the marginalisation of pro-market economic positions within the government by what might appear well meaning, but are essentially unsustainable posturing on populist rights-based actions. On the other hand, however hard the NDA government tries to undo what was done with its support in the Parliament, it cannot avoid the costs of political compulsions it succumbed to, along with the UPA, in securing impending electoral gains.

## Notes

1 Eminent domain is the authority of the state to acquire private property without the owner's consent.

2 Following the celebrated work of Italian economist Vilfredo Pareto in the early twentieth century, a Pareto-efficient situation would typically be a condition of distribution of goods and resources where at least one individual is better off after the distribution, and none is worse off. The act and implications of acquiring land do not qualify as typically Pareto-efficient given that the dispossessed private property owners might be worse off post-allocation, which would depend on the compensations they receive. From a collective normative perspective, greater provision of public goods and concomitant increase in economic welfare are likely to exceed the individual 'worse-offs' and make the situation Pareto improvement given that there are hardly any other alternative distributions qualifying for strong satisfaction of the Pareto improvement criteria.

3 Apart from Kandla, the other zones include Santacruz Electronic Export Processing Zone (SEEPZ) SEZ in Mumbai, Maharashtra: Noida SEZ in UP; Madras Export Processing Zone (MEPZ) SEZ in Chennai, Tamil Nadu; Cochin SEZ in Cochin, Kerala; Falta SEZ in Falta, West Bengal; and Visakhapatnam SEZ in Visakhapatnam, Andhra Pradesh. While all these zones were created as export processing enclaves, they were subsequently notified as SEZs. http://www.sezindia.nic.in/writereaddata/pdf/ListofoperationalSEZs.pdf (Accessed on 15 April 2014). State government promoted zones were functioning in Madhya Pradesh, Gujarat, Rajasthan, Uttar Pradesh and West Bengal.

4 See Palit and Bhattacharjee (2008), Chapter 6, pages 126–130 for a detailed description of the fiscal incentives offered to developers and units in SEZs and the criticism encountered by their award.

5 See Tantri (2015) for a resource-cost-based analysis of revenue loss from India's early SEZs.

6 Enacted on 26 August 2003, the FRBMA required the central government to eliminate revenue deficit by 31 March 2008 and specify annual targets for reduction of fiscal and revenue deficit. See Sections 4(1) and 4(2)(a) of the FRBMA for greater details on the principles of fiscal management. http://finmin.nic.in/law/frbmact2003.pdf (Accessed on 15 April 2014).

7 This, for example, has been the view of the Mamata Banerjee-led TMC government in the state of West Bengal. The TMC obtained significant political capital from the violence witnessed in Nandigram and Singur over acquisition, which, inter alia, was responsible for it ousting the Left Front Government in state assembly elections in 2011. 'Mamata Banerjee firm on no land acquisition stand',

*IBNLive*, 13 February 2013; http://ibnlive.in.com/news/mamata-banerjee-firm-on-no-land-acquisition-stand/372487-3-231.html (Accessed on 17 April 2014).

8 An amendment to the LAA of 1894 introduced in 1962 justified acquisition of land by the state for private businesses if the final objective of the acquisition was to develop projects 'likely' to be beneficial for public. See Palit (2012) for various amendments to the employment of 'public purpose' in LAA of 1894.

9 Section 2(2)[b]{i}, {ii}, Chapter 1, page 2–3, 'Right to Fair Compensation and Transparency in Land Acquisition, Rehabilitation and Resettlement Act, 2013', 26 September 2013; http://indiacode.nic.in/acts-in-pdf/302013.pdf (Accessed on 9 April 2014).

10 Distinguished experts like M. S. Swaminathan have argued that the LAA of 1894's prevention of courts from taking into account the rise in the value of the acquired land from the use it will be put to, is an anti-farmer provision. The impact of the limitation is on landowners approaching courts for benefitting from the appreciation in value of land from its future use. See Palit and Bhattacharjee (2008), Chapter 6.

11 Cash compensation based on market value of land has been criticized on the ground of it not reflecting the owner's true valuation of land in imperfect land markets like those in India. See Ghatak and Ghosh (2011) for a detailed critique.

12 'Rahul Gandhi promises pro-farmer land acquisition bill', *DNA*, 7 July 2011; http://www.dnaindia.com/india/report-rahul-gandhi-promises-pro-farmer-land-acquisition-bill-1563356 (Accessed on 18 April 2014).

13 'Land Acquisition Bill passed in Lok Sabha, Rahul Gandhi says he is "quite happy"', *NDTV*; http://www.ndtv.com/article/cheat-sheet/land-acquisition-bill-passed-in-lok-sabha-rahul-gandhi-says-he-is-quite-happy-412021 (Accessed on 18 April 2014).

14 'Narendra Modi rues absence of 'BJP' imprint on food security bill', *The Indian Express*, 30 August 2013; http://archive.indianexpress.com/news/narendra-modi-rues-absence-of-bjp-imprint-on-food-security-bill/1162059/ (Accessed on 19 April 2014).

15 As mentioned in the text of the CMP released by the UPA; 'UPA government to adhere to six basic principles of governance', *The Hindu*, 28 May 2004; http://www.hindu.com/2004/05/28/stories/2004052807371200.htm (Accessed on 19 April 2014).

16 Households under the AAY are currently entitled to 35 kg of rice and wheat at subsidized rates of Rs. 3 and Rs. 2 per kg; the non-AAY BPL households are entitled to the same amount but at rates of Rs. 5.65 and Rs. 4.15 for rice and wheat, respectively. The APL households receive food grain on the basis of availability and at higher prices (Palit, 2013).

17 As in 13 above.

18 Sections 4(a) and (b) and 13 (1) and 13 (2) of the National Food Security Act 2013, Ministry of Law and Justice, Government of India; http://indiacode.nic.in/acts-in-pdf/202013.pdf (Accessed on 19 April 2014).

19 'Samajbadi Party to back food bill if amendments suggested are accepted', *Business Line*, 12 August 2013; http://www.thehindubusinessline.com/news/politics/samajwadi-party-to-back-food-bill-if-amendments-suggested-are-accepted/article5015170.ece (Accessed on 19 April 2014).

20 'BJP will not oppose passage of food security bill in Parliament', *Business Line*, 6 July 2013; http://www.thehindubusinessline.com/news/politics/bjp-will-not-oppose-passage-of-food-security-bill-in-parliament/article4888427.ece?ref=relatedNews (Accessed on 19 April 2014).

21 'Industry Ministry Secretary for rejig of land acquisition law', *Business Standard*, 19 April 2014; http://www.business-standard.com/article/economy-policy/dipp-secy-denounces-new-land-acquisition-law-114041800844_1.html (Accessed on 20 April 2014).

22 As in 8 earlier; Section 2(2)(a).

23 'Decoded: What changes has the Narendra Modi government made in the Land Acquisition ordinance', *DNA*, 22 March 2015; http://www.dnaindia.com/india/report-decoded-what-changes-has-the-narendra-modi-government-made-in-the-land-acquisition-ordinance-2048240 (Accessed on 31 May 2015).

24 'Land ordinance repromulgated 3rd time despite opp protest', *Financial Express*, 31 May 2015; http://www.financialexpress.com/article/economy/land-ordinance-repromulgated-3rd-time-despite-opp-protest/78439/ (Accessed on 31 May 2015).

25 For speedy and dispute-free acquisition of land, the UP government decided to purchase land from owners at mutually agreed prices that were four times, and two times, the prevailing circle rates, in rural and urban areas. 'India's longest e-way tells a story of land acquisition feat', *The Times of India*, 28 May 2015; http://timesofindia.indiatimes.com/india/Indias-longest-e-way-tells-a-story-of-land-acquisition-feat/articleshow/47451496.cms (Accessed on 31 May 2015).

26 Most estimates on the cost of implementing the Food Security Act point to its unaffordability. See Sinha (2013) for more details.

## References

Bardhan, P. 2011. 'The Real Issues Behind Land Acquisition.' *The Hindu*, August 1. Accessed March 17, 2014. http://www.thehindu.com/todays-paper/tp-opinion/article194362.ece.

Ghatak, M and P. Ghosh. 2011. 'The Land Acquisition Bill: A Critique and a Proposal.' *Economic and Political Weekly*, 46(41), 8 October. Mumbai, India.

Palit, Amitendu. 2012. 'The Land Acquisition, Resettlement and Rehabilitation (LARR) Bill 2011: Providing Solutions or Raising Questions?.' *Journal of Emerging Knowledge on Emerging Markets* 4. Accessed April 5, 2014. http://digitalcommons.kennesaw.edu/cgi/viewcontent.cgi?article=1092&context=jekem.

——— 2013. 'India's Food Security Bill: Grave Digger or Game Changer?.' *ISAS Insights* 226. Accessed April 19, 2014. http://www.isas.nus.edu.sg/Attachments/PublisherAttachment/ISAS_Insights__226_-_India's_Food_Security_Bill__Grave_Digger_or_Game_Changer_04092013163457.pdf.

——— 2014. 'India's SEZs: Victims of Ideology.' *Northwestern Journal of International Law and Business* 34. Accessed April 20, 2014. http://scholarlycommons.law.northwestern.edu/njilb/vol34/iss4/1.

Palit, Amitendu and Subhomoy Bhattacharjee. 2008. *Special Economic Zones in India: Myths and Realities*. London and New York: Anthem Press.

Sinha, D. 2013. 'Cost of Implementing the National Food Security Act.' *Economic and Political Weekly*, 48(39), 28 September. Mumbai, India.

Tantri, M. L. 2015. 'Fiscal Implications of Special Economic Zones (SEZs) Expansion in India: A Resource Cost Approach,' *Journal of International Commerce, Economics and Policy* 6 (1). Accessed May 31, 2015. doi:10.1142/S1793993315500064.

# 6

# A Separate Debt Management Office in India

**Charan Singh***

## Introduction

In recent years, after the global crisis, the issue of separation of monetary policy, fiscal policy and debt management has re-emerged. In many countries, during the period of crisis, scope of fiscal policy was expanded and debt to gross domestic product (GDP) ratios increased significantly. Consequently, debt management, in general, became difficult and coordination between monetary and debt management assumed significance.

Historically, the debt crises of 1982 and the Asian Crisis of 1997 had led many countries to assign priority to public debt management and then, a number of countries chose to separate debt from monetary management. As developments in the government securities market became more sophisticated, a different institutional structure was considered to be better suited to achieve different monetary policy and debt management objectives. In normal economic circumstances, the central bank operates at the short end of the market, and debt management on the long end to minimize cost of raising resources, but in times of crisis, the operations can become blurred. A separation in responsibilities was considered a better solution that reduces the risk of policy conflicts in the central bank actions. Once the financial markets had developed, the role of the central bank in sustaining the markets was considered minimal. Therefore, in many of the Organization for Economic Cooperation and Development (OECD) countries, separation of debt and monetary management had been undertaken in the 1990s.

* RBI Chair Professor of Economics, IIM Bangalore. Views are personal. The author wishes to thank Debaleena Dutta and Jafar Baig for research assistance.

This chapter discusses the basics of debt management and its separation insection 'Some basics of debt management'. Traditional viewpoints about separation of debt management, central banks' independence, and coordination between debt management, monetary and fiscal policy, are presented in section 'Separate debt management office: A traditional view'. After 2008, the traditional view on separation of debt and monetary management has been challenged by a few central bankers. This debate is presented in section 'Separate DMO: Post-crisis debate'. Indian debt management practices, role of Reserve Bank of India (RBI) and the debate about separation of debt management in India are discussed in section 'Debt management in India'. Finally, conclusions are presented in last section.

## Some basics of debt management

The main objective of debt management is to minimize the cost of borrowings over the medium to long run, consistent with a prudent degree of risk. To achieve this minimisation of cost, promotion and development of efficient primary and secondary market for government securities are also important complementary objectives for debt management. Hence, public debt management can be explained as the process of executing a strategy for managing the government's debt – to raise the required amount of borrowings, pursue cost/risk objectives, and also meet any other goal that the government might have set (International Monetary Fund and World Bank, 2003). This may be expressed as a numerical target for the stock composition of the debt referred to as the strategic benchmark. The policy instrument is medium- to long-term debt, and the composition is managed through new debt issuance, as well as changing the composition of existing debt through swaps, debt buybacks and exchange offers (Togo, 2007).

## Separate debt management office: A traditional view

There was a growing consensus among practitioners to treat debt management as a separate policy instrument from monetary policy until 2008. A number of countries with liberalized financial markets and high levels of government debt sought to adopt professional debt management techniques to save cost and to provide policy signals to the market (Giovannini, 1997). The benefits of separation of the two functions were basically conditional upon the level of financial development as argued by Blommestein and Turner (2012). The trend started with New Zealand in the 1980s, with the government recognizing the need for proper policy assignment and accountability framework for debt management to meet the fiscal targets set in the adopted Fiscal Responsibility Act. In Europe, several countries that were heavily indebted in the late 1980s and early 1990s such as Belgium, France, Ireland and Portugal, decentralized debt management to varying extents, in order to reduce the variability of debt service cost that could jeopardize the targets set by the growth and stabilization pact. In the United Kingdom, debt management responsibilities were taken out of the Bank of England in order to remove the perception of conflict of interest in conducting debt management and monetary operations (Togo, 2007).

A number of countries have chosen to open a separate debt management office (DMO) to have a more focussed debt management policy (Table 6.1). The location of the DMO is important and will depend on a number of considerations. The dispersal of debt management functions within different layers of government can lead to lack of coherent debt management policy and overall risk assessment, and therefore higher operational risk. Some OECD countries have opted for an autonomous DMO to improve operational efficiency (Austria, Finland, Ireland, Portugal, Sweden, Germany, Hungary and United Kingdom) while others, seeking a balance between public policy and financial management, have a separate office but operating under the Ministry of Finance (Australia, Belgium, Canada, France, Netherlands, New Zealand, Poland and United States). In Denmark, debt management is undertaken by a privately owned central bank (OECD, 2002). In the case of developing countries, Currie, Dethier and Togo (2003) argue that the separate office can be initially placed under the Ministry of Finance while Kalderen (1997) suggests that separate office may be unsuitable for overall policy effectiveness of debt management.

On the basis of the experience of OECD countries, Cassard and Folkerts-Landau (1997) conclude that several reasons emerge that justify the separation of debt management – to preserve the integrity and independence of the central bank, to shield debt management from political interference, to ensure transparency and accountability, and to improve debt management by

**TABLE 6.1 Location of debt management office in select countries**

| Country | Location of DMO | Scope of Debt Management | | | Advisory Board |
|---|---|---|---|---|---|
| | | Cash | Debt | Contingent | |
| 1. Australia | Separate agency under Treasury since 1999 | Yes | Yes | No | Yes |
| 2. Brazil | Debt office under Treasury since 1988 | Yes | Yes | No | No |
| 3. Colombia | Debt office under Treasury since 1991 | No | Yes | Yes | Yes |
| 4. Denmark | Debt office in Central bank | Yes | Yes | Yes | No |
| 5. France | Separate agency under Treasury since 2001 | Yes | Yes | No | Yes |
| 6. Germany | Separate agency under Treasury since 2001 | Yes | Yes | No | No |
| 7. Ireland | Separate agency under Treasury since 1991 | Yes | Yes | No | Yes |
| 8. Italy | Debt agency under Treasury – 1997 | Yes | Yes | No | No |
| 9. Mexico | Separate office in Treasury | No | Yes | Yes | No |
| 10. New Zealand | Separate office under Treasury since 1988 | Yes | Yes | Yes | Yes |
| 11. Poland | Debt office within Treasury since 1994 | No | Yes | Yes | No |
| 12. Portugal | Separate debt office under Treasury since 1996 | Yes | Yes | Yes | Yes |
| 13. Sweden | Separate debt office under Treasury since 1789 | No | Yes | Yes | Yes |
| 14. United Kingdom | Separate debt office under Treasury since 1997 | Yes | Yes | No | Yes |
| 15. United States | Debt office within Treasury | Yes | Yes | No | No |
| 16. South Africa | DMO within Treasury | Yes | Yes | Yes | No |

*Source*: Singh (2005).

entrusting it to portfolio managers with expertise in modern risk management techniques. The separation of debt and monetary management positively affects expectations as it explicitly indicates to the market and credit rating agencies that monetary policy is independent of debt management.[1]

A separation of debt and monetary management is expected to resolve the conflict between different economic policies of the government. The classic conflict between monetary and debt management policy relates to the fixation of interest rates.[2] The conflict between fiscal policy and debt management relates to the choice of keeping debt servicing costs low over the short term or over the medium-long term.

In case the central bank conducts debt management policy, conflicting objectives may emerge. Should liquidity be tightened based on monetary conditions prevailing in the economy or should it be relaxed to ensure success of market borrowing programme of the government? Another area of concern could be interest rates which are of prime importance to the central bank. The government will like to borrow at low costs while the central bank will consider monetary and financial stability more important. The central bank may be tempted to manipulate financial markets to reduce the interest rates at which government debt is issued (Cassard and Folkerts-Landau, 1997). Goodhart (2010) argues that liquidity management is integral to the management of systemic stability and essential for the operation of a central bank but why should the central bank, set the official interest rates? Again, central bankers have not taken adequate cognizance of financial conditions and monetary developments while fixing interest rates, according to Goodhart. Taylor (1998) argues that the Accord between the Federal Reserve and the Treasury in 1951, which emancipated the Fed from assisting the Treasury in borrowings at low rates of interest, helped the Fed to focus on interest rates. Even if a separate department within the central bank conducts debt management, the market will still perceive that the debt management decisions are influenced by inside information on interest rates.

## *Central bank independence*

The other factor of separation of debt from monetary management was the argument of independence of a central bank. In the years until 2008, because of the great moderation and Volcker's victory over inflation in the 1980s,[3] substantial evidence had been advanced in theoretical and empirical literature to support the political and economic independence of the central bank (Grilli, Masciandaro and Tabellini, 1991a). In support of central bank independence, Kydland and Prescott (1977), Barro and Gordon (1983a and 1983b), Burdekin and Laney (1988), Eschweiler and Bordo (1993) and Grilli, Masciandaro and Tabellini (1991b) argue that more independent central banks successfully reduce the rate of inflation, while Alesina and Summers (1993) conclude that such independence has no impact on real economic performance. Wagner (1998) argues that making a central bank independent lowers the expectations pertaining to inflation of the private sector that determine wage and price contracts, and thereby also the expectations that impact the exchange rates.

## Need for coordination

In each country, the economic situation, including the state of domestic financial markets and the degree of central bank independence, would play an important role in determining the range of activities to be handled by the debt manager and the level of coordination that is necessary. Monetary policy and debt management clearly have to be complementary to each other but debt management should not be considered a tool of monetary management nor should monetary policy be considered the objective of debt management (Bank of England, 1995). In the case of the Economic and Monetary Union (EMU), monetary policy is operated by the European Central Bank (ECB) while national authorities conduct debt management. The sharing of adequate information between Treasuries, national central banks and the ECB is a norm, and ensured for the purpose of liquidity management.

In the case of developing countries, coordination between fiscal, monetary and debt management functions is considered even more crucial, where financial markets are under-developed, and forecasts of government revenues and expenditure are inaccurate. The issuance of government securities by a separate debt office needs to be closely coordinated with the open market operations undertaken by the central bank to ensure appropriate liquidity conditions in the market.

Therefore, the role of the central bank in public debt management, though separated, would continue to be crucial. As an issuing agency of government securities, the central bank organizes rules and procedures for selling and delivering securities and for collecting payments for the government. As a fiscal agent, the central bank makes and receives payments, including interest payments and servicing of principal. As adviser to the government and to the debt manager, it could provide policy inputs on the design of the debt programme, mix of debt instruments and maturity profile of debt stock. These inputs will be useful in providing stability to the overall debt programme, facilitating smooth functioning of the market, and providing a stable environment for the conduct of monetary policy.

## Separate DMO: Post-crisis debate

In view of the financial crisis, in recent years, there has been a rethink on the issue of separation of debt from monetary management because of the following factors:

1. A sharp increase in government deficit and debt, because of the fiscal stimulus, in many countries (Table 6.2).
2. The use of unconventional monetary policy in advanced countries involving large scale purchase of government securities of varying maturities.

**TABLE 6.2 General government gross debt**

| Country/Year | 2006 | 2008 | 2010 | 2012 |
|---|---|---|---|---|
| France | 64.1 | 68.2 | 82.3 | 90.3 |
| Germany | 67.9 | 66.8 | 82.5 | 82 |
| Greece | 107.5 | 112.5 | 147.9 | 158.5 |
| Iceland | 30.1 | 70.4 | 90.6 | 99.1 |
| Ireland | 24.6 | 44.5 | 92.2 | 117.1 |
| Japan | 186 | 191.8 | 216 | 237.9 |
| Netherlands | 47.4 | 58.5 | 63.1 | 71.7 |
| Portugal | 63.7 | 71.6 | 93.2 | 123 |
| Singapore | 86.4 | 96.3 | 99.3 | 111 |
| Slovenia | 26.4 | 22 | 38.6 | 52.6 |
| Spain | 39.7 | 40.2 | 61.3 | 84.1 |
| United Kingdom | 43 | 52.2 | 79.4 | 90.3 |
| United States | 66.1 | 75.5 | 98.2 | 106.5 |

3. Imposition of new liquidity requirements resulting in higher demand of government securities.
4. Increase in foreign ownership of government debt.

According to the conventional mandate, central banks were expected to operate in the bills market or short end of the market while debt managers were expected to operate in the long end of the same government securities market. In the post-crisis period, the boundary between debt management and monetary policy became blurred mainly because of fiscal domination and unconventional monetary policy. The flotations of bonds by the debt manager, given the uncertainty, were of shorter maturity and not long-term bonds. This blurring of role also created confusion in the role of the central bank and debt manager (Committee on the Global Financial System, 2011).

Thus, the thrust of the recent debate is that under difficult macroeconomic situation, the lines between debt and monetary policy become blurred and hence the two functions should be brought under the same agency. In the United Kingdom, there is an active discussion on the subject but not in the United States where the two functions had been separated in 1951. Goodhart (2012) argues that under quantitative easing, there is a possibility that the policy of the debt management can negate the policy pursued by the central bank. When the debt ratios increase, as in the case of United Kingdom or Greece, the short-term interest rates also become a matter of concern to the Ministry of Finance. Obviously, then the monetary policy and debt management have to be closely coordinated. Therefore, according to Goodhart (2012) separation between debt management and monetary policy is not desired as the existing arrangements are already under stress. The minutes of the US Treasury Borrowing Advisory Committee had also hinted at some tensions according to Blommestein and Turner (2012). Earlier, Goodhart (2010) argued that the central banks should be encouraged to revert to their role of managing national debt because with rising debt levels, debt management cannot be treated as a routine function which can be delegated to a separate independent institution. On the other hand, the Study Group (SG) commissioned by the Committee on the Global Financial System (Chairman: Paul Fisher, 2011), after an extensive research, observed that there was little evidence that existing arrangements' for operational independence of sovereign debt management and monetary policy have created material problems.

Recent experience shows that there is a need for close communication and coordination among the relevant agencies managing monetary policy and debt management, as stressed by SG. This conclusion was also consistent with the Stockholm Principles, International Monetary Fund (2010), which stated that 'communication among debt managers and monetary, fiscal and financial regulatory authorities should be promoted, given greater interlinkages across objectives, yet with each agency maintaining independence and accountability for its respective role'.[4]

Another important change is concurrently occurring in the monetary policy objectives, internationally. While theoretical arguments can be made to justify recent departures from policy, the reality is that in the post-crisis world, objectives of the central bank are no longer limited to price stability. The dilution of the central bank independence is because of the multiple objectives being entrusted on monetary policy such as pursuit of GDP growth, job creation and financial stability.[5] Further, the need to establish priorities when there are trade-offs, clearly requires political decisions, which cannot be made by unelected officials alone. Moreover, by pushing interest rates towards zero, the current policy of quantitative easing has strong, often regressive, income effects which cannot be implemented without political patronage. Hence, the emerging consensus, in the post-crisis period is that central banks' decision making should be subject to political control (Blejer, 2013).

According to Goodhart (2010), the separation of debt and monetary management in England took place when debt operations became simpler and standardized, falling into a routine pattern. But given the crisis, debt management can no longer be considered as routine and delegated to a separate and independent body. But, the above argument by Goodhart is contrary to following reasons explained by Bank of England (1995) for separating debt management from the monetary policy – (1) Monetary policy decisions should be seen as separate from debt management policy; (2) To ensure that, DMO did not have advance access to other policy decisions; (3)To avoid possible conflicts which could undermine the achievement of debt management objective of minimizing the cost of government financing and (4) To create a clearer allocation of the responsibilities for debt management and monetary policy.[6]

There are other important developments which have been largely ignored. The separation of debt management from monetary management in the United States and OECD, provided transparency to the rescue operations launched by many governments in the face of global crisis. Independence of operations and objectives, and close coordination between different agencies lent credibility to the government policies.

## Debt management in India

In India, presently public debt management is divided between the central and state governments, and the RBI. The RBI manages the market borrowing programme of central and state governments while external debt is managed directly by the central government. The RBI acts as the debt manager for marketable internal debt, for the central government as an obligation and for the state governments by an agreement, under the RBI Act, 1934. RBI decides about the maturity pattern, calendar of borrowings, instrument design and other related issues in consultation with the central government (International Monetary Fund and World Bank, 2003).[7]

### *Dimensions of public debt in India*

The public debt of the country has been declining since 2000–2001 and was estimated at 66 per cent of GDP at end March 2013 (Table 6.3).

The major components of domestic debt are internal debt, small savings, provident funds, and reserve funds and deposits (Table 6.4). The Constitution of India provides for the option of placing a limit on the internal debt, both at the centre and the states, but no such limit has been imposed so far. Internal debt, the most prominent component of domestic debt, consists of

**TABLE 6.3 Public debt of the government**

| | As Per Cent to the Total | | | As Per Cent of GDP | | |
|---|---|---|---|---|---|---|
| Year | External Debt | Domestic Debt | Public Debt | External Debt | Domestic Debt | Public Debt |
| 1980–1981 | 18.8 | 81.2 | 100 | 9 | 38.9 | 47.9 |
| 1990–1991 | 16.4 | 83.6 | 100 | 11.3 | 57.5 | 68.9 |
| 2000–2001 | 11.8 | 88.2 | 100 | 8.7 | 64.9 | 73.7 |
| 2010–2011 | 5.5 | 94.5 | 100 | 3.6 | 61.9 | 65.5 |
| 2011–2012 | 5.5 | 94.5 | 100 | 3.6 | 61.9 | 65.5 |
| 2012–2013 | 5 | 95 | 100 | 3.3 | 62.7 | 66 |

*Source*: RBI.

**TABLE 6.4 Components of domestic debt of the government (as per cent of total)**

| Year | Internal Debt | Small Savings Deposits and Provident Funds | Reserve Funds and Deposits and Other Accounts | Domestic Debt |
|---|---|---|---|---|
| 1980–1981 | 60.6 | 22.6 | 16.8 | 100 |
| 1990–1991 | 51.3 | 23.3 | 25.4 | 100 |
| 2000–2001 | 67.4 | 13 | 19.6 | 100 |
| 2010–2011 | 70.7 | 16.6 | 12.7 | 100 |
| 2011–2012 | 73.5 | 15.2 | 11.2 | 100 |
| 2012–2013 | 75.9 | 14.1 | 10 | 100 |

*Source*: RBI.

markets loans, Treasury bills and other bonds issued by the central and state governments.

Since the start of planning in India in 1951, the amount of market loans mobilized annually has been rising rapidly.

While formulating the borrowing programme for the year, the government and the RBI take into account a number of considerations such as the central and state loans maturing for redemption during the year, an estimate of available resources (based amongst others, on the growth in deposits with the banks, premium income of insurance companies and accretion to provident funds) and absorptive capacity of the market.

The amount of outstanding market loans has increased from Rs. 16 billion in 1952 to Rs. 862 billion in 1991 and Rs. 39,048 billion in 2013. In general, the share of central government, in total outstanding amount, is significantly large but varies over time, depending on annual market borrowings. Illustratively, net annual borrowings by the centre were Rs. 80 billion in 1990–1991 which rose to Rs. 4,929 billion in 2012–2013 while in comparison, that by the states rose from Rs. 26 billion to Rs. 1,130 billion over the same period. In the case of ownership of market loans, the share of commercial banks, insurance and provident funds has changed significantly over the years.

The government also offers a variety of small savings schemes to meet the varying needs of different groups of small investors. In respect of each scheme, statutory rules are framed by the central government indicating various details including the rate of interest and the maturity period.[8] Small saving instruments can be classified under the following three heads: postal deposits, savings certificates and public provident fund (PPF), with PPF being a small component. Illustratively, of the outstanding amount of small savings of Rs. 6,066 billion, at end March 2012, PPF through post offices accounted for a small amount of Rs. 360 billion only.

The ownership pattern of small savings is not available, though some ad-hoc surveys have been undertaken.[9] In fact, there is lack of comprehensive analysis of the liabilities of the central and state government and their distributional aspects, which impedes informed decision regarding domestic borrowing.

## *Important role of the RBI*

The key role in management of internal debt is played by the RBI which could conflict with its pursuit of the objectives of monetary policy. The RBI is the regulator and supervisor of the financial system, including banks, and also of the money, government securities and foreign exchange markets. The RBI has to balance the needs of the markets (manage liquidity), government requirements (fiscal requirements), balance sheet of the banks (asset prices and interest rate movements) and general price level (growth of money supply).

In the RBI, the Department of Internal Debt Management (DIDM), set up in April 1992, undertakes the work relating to government securities, Treasury bills and cash management. DIDM is organized essentially as a separate DMO with the essential units – primary market (borrowing and cash management of both central and state), policy and research, dealing room, MIS and regulation (of primary dealers). The actual receipts of bids and settlement functions are undertaken at various offices of the RBI specially public debt offices (PDOs) across the country. The PDOs of RBI, located in various parts of the country also manage registry and depository functions, including the book entry form of ownership. The Department of Government and Bank Accounts (DGBAs) maintain the accounts of both the governments – central and state, on a daily basis. On external debt, Department of External Investment and Operations (DEIOs) in RBI works as a front office along with MOF. The function of cash management of the central and state governments is also performed by DIDM and DGBA in RBI. The managerial structure of public debt management is presented in Table 6.5.

**TABLE 6.5 Management of public debt in India**

| Major Items | Appropriated By | Managed By | Amount | Fixation Authority for/Determination of Maturity | Interest Rate |
|---|---|---|---|---|---|
| *1* | *2* | *3* | *4* | *5* | *6* |
| Market Loans | Centre | MOF, RBI | MOF | MOF, RBI | Market |
| | State | DOF, RBI | MOF | DOF, RBI | RBI, Market |
| Market Bonds | Centre | RM, MOF, RBI | RM, MOF | RM | RM, MOF, RBI |
| | State | RD, DOF, RBI | RD, DOF | RD | RD |
| Treasury bills | Centre | MOF, RBI | MOF, RBI | MOF, RBI | Market |
| WMA | Centre | MOF, RBI | MOF, RBI | MOF, RBI | RBI |
| | State | DOF, RBI | RBI | RBI | RBI |
| Loans from Bk and FI | State | DOF | RD | RD | RD, DOF |
| Small Savings | State | MOF, DOF | MOF, DOF | MOF | MOF |
| Provident Funds | Centre | MOL, MOF | MOL, MOF | MOL | MOL |
| | State | MOL, DOF | DOF | MOL | MOL |
| Reserve Funds/ Deposits | Centre | RM, MOF | RM | RM | RM |
| | State | RD, DOF | RD | RD | RD |
| External Debt | Centre | MOF, RBI | MOF | MOF | MOF |
| Contingent Liabilities | Centre | RM, MOF | RM | RM | RM |
| | State | RD, DOF | RD | RD | RD |

*Note*: MOF: Ministry of Finance; DOF: Department of Finance; MOL: Ministry of Labour; RM: Respective Ministry; RD: Respective Department; Bk: Banks; FI: Financial Institutions.

*Source*: Author's compilation.

## Coordination between RBI, government and markets

To coordinate the activities of debt management with fiscal authorities, various committees function in RBI. The Cash and Debt Management Committee, consisting of officials from the MOF and RBI meets regularly to discuss the operational details of market borrowings for the central government. The issues pertaining to the state governments are discussed in a semi-annual meeting with the officials from MOF, DOF and RBI. The Technical Committee on Money and Government Securities, consisting of representatives from market, academia, government, banks, and RBI, meets regularly and advises the RBI on development and regulation of the government securities market.

## Fiscal responsibility legislations

Financial Responsibility and Budget Management Act 2003 (FRBMA) was brought into force effective 5 July 2004. On the recommendations of the 12th Finance Commission (FC) and 13th FC, even states have some form of fiscal legislation (Table 6.6).

## Need for a separation of debt and monetary management

In India, the separation of debt would provide the RBI with necessary independence in monetary management and an environment to pursue an inflation target, if assigned by the government.[10] The separation of debt management would provide focus to the task of asset-liability management of government liabilities, undertake risk analysis and also help to prioritize government expenditure through higher awareness of interest costs. The need for setting up a specialized framework on public debt management which will take a comprehensive view of the liabilities of government, and establish the strategy for low-cost financing in the long run has been advocated by various expert committees since late 1990s (Table 6.7).

In India, an important watershed in the institutional arrangements of debt management was the setting up of the middle office in the Ministry of Finance in 2008, to formulate debt management strategy for the central government. Again the Union Budget 2011–2012 had stated that the government was in the process of setting up an independent DMO in the Ministry of Finance. The DMO was

**TABLE 6.6 Fiscal responsibility legislation for states**

| | | Original Documents | | | Targets as Per 13th FC |
|---|---|---|---|---|---|
| Year | State | RD by March 31 | GFD as Per Cent of GSDP as on March 31 | Debt as Per Cent of GSDP as on March 31 | Percentage of GSDP by 2015 |
| 2002 | Karnataka | Nil; 2006 | 3; 2006 | 25; 2015 | 25.2 |
| 2003 | Kerala | Nil; 2009 | 3; 2008 | – | 29.8 |
| | Tamil Nadu | Nil; 2009 | 3; 2008 | – | 25.2 |
| | Punjab | Nil; 2009 | 3; 2008 | – | 38.7 |
| 2004 | Uttar Pradesh | Nil;2009 | 3; 2009 | 25; 2018 | 41.9 |
| 2005 | Andhra Pradesh | Nil; 2009 | 3 | 35; 2010 | 27.6 |
| | Assam | Nil; 2010 | 3; 2010 | 45; 2010 | 28.5 |
| | Chhattisgarh | Nil; 2009 | 3; 2009 | – | 23.9 |
| | Gujarat | Nil; 2008 | 3; 2009 | 30; 2008 | 27.1; 2012 |
| | Haryana | Nil; 2009 | 3; 2010 | 28; 2010 | 22.9 |
| | Himachal Pradesh | Nil; 2009 | – | – | 40.1 |
| | Madhya Pradesh | Nil; 2009 | 4; 2010 | 40 | 35.3 |
| | Maharashtra | Nil; 2009 | 3; 2009 | – | 25.3 |
| | Manipur | Nil; 2010 | 3 | – | 54.3 |
| | Tripura | – | 3; 2010 | 40; 2010 | 43.8 |
| | Uttarakhand | Nil; 2009 | 3; 2009 | 25; 2015 | 43.8 |
| | Odisha | Nil; 2009 | 3; 2009 | Debt stock limited to 300 per cent of total revenue receipt; 2008 | 29.5 |
| | Rajasthan | Nil; 2009 | 3 | Debt should not exceed twice consolidated fund receipt. | 36.5 |

(*continued*)

**TABLE 6.6 Fiscal responsibility legislation for states (*continued*)**

| | | Original Documents | | | Targets as Per 13th FC |
|---|---|---|---|---|---|
| Year | State | RD by March 31 | GFD as Per Cent of GSDP as on March 31 | Debt as Per Cent of GSDP as on March 31 | Percentage of GSDP by 2015 |
| 2006 | Arunachal Pradesh | Nil; 2009 | 3; 2010 | – | 50.1 |
| | Bihar | Nil; 2008 | 3; 2008 | – | 41.6 |
| | Goa | Nil; 2009 | 3; 2009 | 30; 2009 | – |
| | Jammu & Kashmir | – | – | 55; 2010 | 49.3 |
| | Meghalaya | Nil | 3 | 28 | 31.7 |
| | Mizoram | Nil; 2009 | 3; 2009 | Debt should not exceed twice consolidated fund receipts. | 74.8 |
| | Nagaland | Nil | 3; 2009 | 40; 2010 | 52.3 |
| 2007 | Jharkhand | Nil; 2009 | 3; 2009 | Debt stock limited to 300 per cent of total revenue receipt. | 26.9 |
| 2010 | Sikkim | – | 3; 2014. | – | 55.9 |
| | West Bengal | Nil; 2015 | 3; 2015 | 34.3; 2015. | 34.3 |

*Notes*: RD: revenue deficit; GFD: gross fiscal deficit; GSDP: gross state domestic product.
*Source*: Various FRBM Acts of States.

entrusted with the responsibilities of piloting the evolution of legal, governance and comprehensive risk management framework suitable for independent debt office, formulation of strategies regarding long-term debt management and annual debt issuance; and maintaining centralized database on government liabilities and dissemination of debt-related information to public. Similarly, the Union Budget for 2012–2013 proposed to move the Public Debt Management Agency (PDMA) Bill in the Parliament.

However, an important re-think in the whole process was required because the RBI was not convinced that the separation would be useful for the financial

**TABLE 6.7 Timeline: Separation of Debt Management**

| Year | Source | Recommendations |
|---|---|---|
| 1997 | Report of the Committee on Capital Account Convertibility (Chairman: Dr S. S. Tarapore) | Setting up of an Office of the Public Debt (OPD) |
| 1997 | A working group on Separation of Debt Management from Monetary Management (Chairman: M. Narasimham) | Separate DMO as a company under the Indian Companies Act |
| 2000 | The Advisory Group on Transparency in Monetary and Financial Policies | Independent DMO, in a phased manner |
| 2001 | The RBI Annual Report 2000–2001 | Separate DMO |
| 2001 | The Internal Expert Group on the Need for a Middle Office for Public Debt Management (Chairman: A. Virmani) | Establishing an autonomous PDO |
| 2004 | The Report on the Ministry of Finance for Twenty-First Century (Chairman: Vijay Kelkar) | National Treasury Management Agency |
| 2004 | The Fiscal Responsibility and Budget Management (FRBM) Act | Prohibits the Reserve Bank from participating in the primary market for Central Government securities with effect from April 2006 |
| 2006 | Fuller Capital Account Convertibility (Chairman: S. S. Tarapore) | Set up of Office of Public Debt outside RBI |
| 2007 | The Union Budget 2007–2008 | Establishment of a DMO in the government |
| 2008 | The High Level Committee on Financial Sector Reforms (Chairman: Raghuram Rajan) | Structural change of public debt management, such that it minimizes financial repression and generates a vibrant bond market. Set up independent DMO |
| 2008 | Internal Working Group on Debt Management (Chairman: Jahangir Aziz) | Establishing a DMO |
| 2009 | Committee on Financial Sector Assessment (Chairman: Rakesh Mohan) | Setting up DMO |

*(continued)*

**TABLE 6.7 Timeline: Separation of Debt Management (*continued*)**

| Year | Source | Recommendations |
|---|---|---|
| 2012 | Report of the Working Group on Debt Management Office (Chairman: Govind Rao) | Independent DMO |
| 2012 | The Financial Sector Legislative Reforms Commission Approach Paper | Separation of debt management with specialized investment banking capability for public debt management |
| 2013 | The Financial Sector Legislative Reforms Commission (Chairman: B. N. Srikrishna) | Specialized framework to analyse comprehensive structure of liabilities of the government, and strategizing minimal cost techniques for raising and servicing public debt over the long term within an acceptable level of risk |

*Source*: Various Reports, GoI and RBI.

markets. The proposed argument was that in the post-crisis period there has been an increased need for close coordination between monetary policy, financial stability and debt management. Debt management, according to Khan (2012), was a difficult exercise in a developing country and was not simply raising resources from the market. The size and dynamics of government borrowing has a wider influence on interest rate movements, and liquidity and credit growth. Therefore, focus only on the cost factors may not be an appropriate way to manage debt. He also argued that policy co-ordination may not be operationally effective especially, if the fiscal deficit was high. According to Subbarao (2011), despite a large borrowing programme, the RBI was able to complete successfully market borrowings in a cost efficient manner and with the long average maturity of ten years, amongst the longest maturity profiles in the world. Merely shifting the debt management to a different agency in an uncertain environment and with large size of deficit would not help as the pressure on the central bank would continue to ensure government borrowing at low cost. The remedy is fiscal consolidation and not separation of debt management, according to him. Also, significant capital flows require close co-ordination between debt management and monetary policy, especially when sterilisation through government bonds has to be undertaken by the central bank. According to Mohan (2003), given the federal structure of India, debt management of the state governments is difficult. In the case of state governments, a substantial amount of deficit financing is through government borrowings. In view of the size of the borrowings by the state and central government, it is necessary to harmonize the annual borrowing programme of the government, and a separation from the central bank would make such harmonisation difficult.

There are also other views as to why the two functions should not be separated.[11] These can be summarized as follows:

1. High level of fiscal deficit and over all government debt to GDP ratio.
2. Conflict of interest between debt manager and the government's role as an owner of public sector banks.
3. Debt and monetary management roles, management of government debt, regulation of banks and monetary policy will be interlinked.
4. Difficulty in harmonising the operations of debt issue redemptions, Statutory Liquidity Ratio (SLR) maintenance and Market Stabilization Scheme.
5. Existing expertise is exclusively available in the RBI.
6. Inappropriateness of state debt management by a central government entity.

Task force on PDMA was set up on 30 September 2014 by the Government of India (GOI) and expected to submit a report within a year. The taskforce was expected to develop a road map for an independent PDMA. The terms of reference of the taskforce include reviewing international best practices; develop organization design for PDMA, generate process manuals and prepare a plan for transition from current debt management system to the PDMA. The taskforce also undertook designing the reporting mechanism and the release of datasets to be analysed by independent researchers.[12]

## A discussion on the views against separation

A separate DMO will help to consolidate all debt-related activities of the government in one office. At present, various schemes operate, some under the GOI and few under states, many of which are independently managed by different governments. There are no economies of scale being explored and little interaction or synchronization of activities occurs between these offices and their practices.

Further, the argument that because the central government has an ownership share in public sector banks, debt management should not be placed under the same government needs further analysis. If the central bank regulates and supervises the government securities market then in a similar vein it can be argued that there is a conflict between regulation/supervision and participation in the market, as the RBI participates in the government securities markets as a dealer/trader too. Similarly, as the central bank is a regulator and supervisor of commercial banks there could emerge a conflict of interest to strengthen the balance sheet of commercial banks, therefore RBI may prescribe higher stipulations of holding government bonds. The central bank could also use its influence over the regulated entities to subscribe to flotations that it manages on behalf of the government. Goodhart (2010) goes further and questions the necessity of entrusting the role of setting interest rate on central banks which already manage the essential role of liquidity management and financial stability in the country. The argument is weak on the issue of conflict emerging due to ownership pattern on select institutions in the financial sector, mainly public sector banks because of following reasons – (1) RBI had a share in State Bank of India (SBI) for many years, and that never diluted the RBI's supervision or regulation of SBI; (2) The share of ownership of the government in public sector banks, has been declining over the years and is expected to decline even further; (3) The government, even if not the owner, is finally responsible for the operations of the commercial banks, as demonstrated by the recent financial crisis in many countries in the United States and Europe; (4)The share of public sector banks in holding of government securities has been declining in recent years while the share of non-public sector banks has been rising and (5) There are different techniques to ensure an arms length's distance between ownership of public sector banks and administration of separate DMO, most important being public dissemination of information.

Finally despite the ownership, performance of public sector banks, in terms of NPAs or return on assets, are not significantly different when compared with other banks operating in India. Even if there is a separate department with the requisite 'firewall' conducting debt management, within the central bank, the markets will still suspect the influence of inside information on interest rates. This 'joint family approach' does not augur well for transparency in management of debt and monetary policy formulation. And when the central bank is balancing different objectives of debt and monetary management, accountability is difficult to fix. In practise and performance, the movement of various interest rates of government securities was substantially lower than the average lending rate of commercial banks,[13] which could be interpreted rather negatively by the markets, despite the fact that central government borrowings were being raised in auction (Figure 6.1). In contrast, market borrowings in a difficult financial market have been raising as also weighted average maturity but not the yield curve (Figure 6.2).[14]

Data on lending rates relate to either prime lending rate (PLR) or benchmark prime lending rate (BPLR) or base rate, as the case may be for the relevant year. BPLR system effective November 2003 was replaced by the base rate system effective from 1 July 2010.

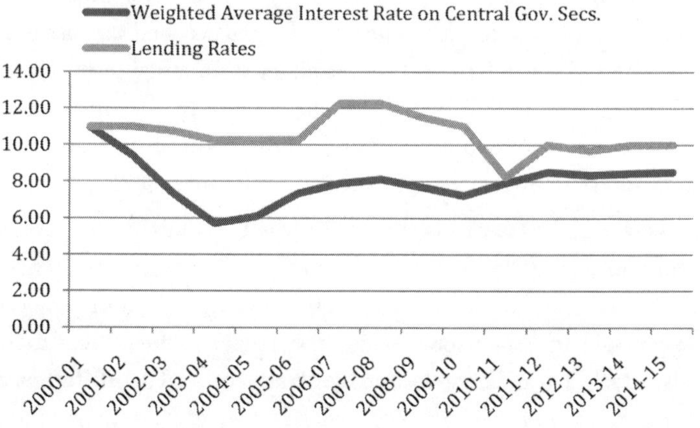


**FIGURE 6.1 Trends in select interest rates.**

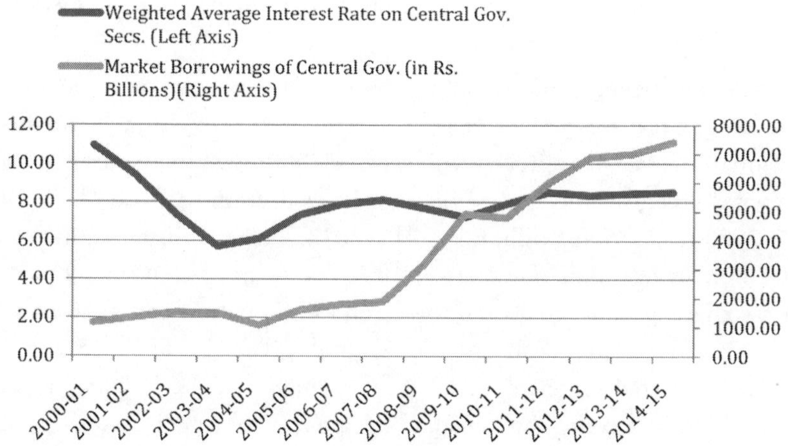


**FIGURE 6.2 Interest rates and market borrowings of central government.**

*Source*: RBI.

A separate DMO also ensures that there are alternative views of the economic situation of the markets and the economy, and not just that unique view which has been formed by the central bank through its trading desk and market intelligence. The debt manager has to carefully understand the pulse of the market and the economy through constant interaction, in the financial markets. Through proper coordination between the central bank and debt manager, a better view of the financial markets and the economy can be formed.

The arguments against the separation like difficulty in harmonising the operations, could basically be resolved by better coordination between various agencies, similar to the type of informal as well as institutionalized coordination between the RBI and the Ministry of Finance. A separated agency has an advantage that it will bring in transparency in the operations of debt management. It will also help in focussing on the communication policy as well as dissemination of debt-related information to the market.

On the issue of lack of expertise to manage the DMO, as in other countries, the government could consider hiring experts, temporarily or permanently, that are available in the RBI or from rest of the world. Incidentally, it may be considered that in the central bank, in absence of any specialized cadre of debt management recruits, the staff is transferrable and generally moved to different desks. In contrast, in a proposed DMO, the staff will be completely dedicated to activities of debt management and gain specialization and expertise on the job. On a long-term basis, certification courses to ensure specialized training to individuals in the DMO could be initiated in leading educational and management institutions in the country.

Finally, the benefits of separating debt from monetary management are significantly large. First, given that fiscal deficits are large and that debts are substantial, a focussed approach will be useful. In the last six years, government borrowings (centre and states) have increased from Rs. 1,657 billion in 2007–2008 to Rs. 6,811 billion in 2012–2013. Such a substantial increase of annual borrowings of market loans from 3.6 per cent of GDP to 7.2 per cent, over a six-year period would require careful examination and analysis which a specialized institution can provide. Second, given the focussed approach, specifically tailored schemes for different segments of the population can be simulated. Illustratively, the outstanding amount of small savings schemes like Senior Citizen Scheme and PPF have increased from Rs. 436 billion in 2007–2008 to Rs. 628 billion in 2011–2012 but the ownership pattern remains unknown because of which, it becomes difficult to tailor social security schemes for the elderly in terms of interest rates and maturity. This also applies to other social security schemes which result in increasing liabilities of the government. Third, an autonomous DMO would imply an annual statutory report and consequent public scrutiny, and dissemination of information. This would ensure that the government does not take undue advantage of being the owners of public sector banks and does not practise fiscal profligacy by access to easy borrowing at low rates of interest.

## Conclusion

The objective of debt management, as generally defined, is raising resources from the market at the minimum cost while containing the risks. In contrast, the objective of monetary policy in India is to maintain a judicious balance between price stability, economic growth and financial stability. Thus, the objective of debt management is subsumed in the overall objectives of monetary policy in India, if the two functions are not separated.

To implement the specifically focussed debt management strategy, and choosing to separate debt from monetary management, governments seek to emphasize the role assigned to debt management, to preserve the integrity and independence of their central banks, to shield debt management from political interference, and to ensure transparency and accountability in public borrowing. Hence, the choice of separating debt from monetary management by many countries while ensuring that their activities are coordinated.

The overall conclusion from recent research is that there is an extensive interaction between debt management, monetary policy and financial policy in mutually reinforcing or conflicting ways. Such interactions become intense during strained macroeconomic policy conditions and therefore there is a need for close coordination between the three organs of economic policy.

Since the budget speech of 2007–2008, the Finance Minister had proposed to set up an autonomous DMO. Many developments have occurred since then except the DMO. Earlier, since 1997, various groups of experts set up by the RBI and the GOI had consistently suggested hiving of debt management function from the RBI to an independent entity.

The middle office has been up in the Ministry of Finance but the hiving-off has not been undertaken. The reasons offered for the reluctance, are that the global circumstances are not conducive in terms of volatile capital flows and need for intervention/sterilisation; deficits and debt levels are still high; staff of the proposed DMO may not have the requisite skills; and there could be a conflict between the role of government as a debt manager and owner of public sector banks.

On the other hand, the paper argues that separation of debt management will help to establish transparency, and assign specific responsibility and accountability on the debt manager. This could lead to an integrated and more professional management of all government liabilities, currently dispersed in different offices, with a focussed mandate to operate on sound economic and commercial principles. The strategy could ensure that resources are available to the government at competitive market rates of interest prompting expenditure prioritization and fiscal discipline in budget making.

## Notes

1 In case the two are not separated, then debt management policy eventually becomes subservient to the monetary policy as the monetary authorities attempt to use debt instruments to strengthen monetary policy signals and to enhance the credibility of the central bank.

2 In the literature on transparency and independence of a central bank, the relationship between government and monetary management is an important consideration (Dincer and Eichengreen, 2013).

3 Fed Reserve's victory (Under Paul Volcker) over inflation in the United States was institutionalized in legislation and practices that granted central bank greater autonomy and, in some cases, formal independence from long-standing political constraints. Now many central banks could be trusted to do the right thing, and they delivered (El-Erian, 2013; International Monetary Fund, 2010).

4 Stockholm Principles (2010) were promulgated by debt managers and central bankers from 33 advanced and emerging market economies.

5 Initially, central-bank independence was based on two main arguments which no longer apply because of multiple objectives being assigned to a central bank – First, politicians can exploit expansionary monetary policy's positive short-run effects at election time, without regard for its long-run inflationary consequences. Second, central banks have a clear comparative advantage in dealing with monetary issues, and can therefore be trusted to pursue their targets independently.

6 In fact, this was a key factor in shaping the new arrangement.

7 Thorat, Singh and Das (2003).

8 However, there is a unique small saving scheme run by the government of Kerala.

9 The ownership pattern of small savings is not available but on the basis of a survey undertaken in Uttar Pradesh in 2000–2001, it can be concluded that industrial

labourers top in terms of aggregate investments in small savings schemes followed by traders and government employees. In terms of invested amount, traders show the maximum investment followed by the government employees. Kisan Vikas Patra and post office time deposits are the most popular instrument amongst farmers. Amongst the government employees and self-employed persons, National Saving Certificates and Public Provident Fund are the most popular instruments. In 2011, the Report of the Committee to Review National Small Savings Fund observed that there appears to be an urban bias in ownership of social security schemes. Of the outstanding amount in PPF, 87 per cent is from urban and metropolitan areas, according to the Report.

10 The government and RBI agreed to set a consumer inflation target of 4 per cent, with a band of plus or minus 2 per cent points, from the financial year ending in March 2017 (Reuters, Mon Mar 2, 2015) http://in.reuters.com/article/2015/03/02/india-rbi-idINKBN0LY0B320150302.

11 The reasons offered by the Committee on Financial Sector Assessment (GOI and RBI, 2009).

12 PDMA was proposed in the Finance Bill, 2015. As a corollary of the decision to create a PDMA, the RBI or the Central Bank in India was given the task of inflation targeting under a monetary policy framework agreement. However, the creation of PDMA was put on hold due to the difference of opinion on the matter and the relevant clauses were dropped from the Finance Bill, 2015 while the latter was passed (http://www.arthapedia.in/index.php?title=Public_Debt_Management_Agency_(PDMA)).

13 Data on lending rates sourced from RBI and relate to five major public sector banks up to 2003–2004. For other years, data relate to five major banks.

14 Kumar and Kumar (2012) attempted to verify the interest rate conflict, underlying the idea of separation of debt management, empirically and conclude that the relationship between policy rates and government market borrowings is statistically insignificant.

## References

Alesina, A. and L. H. Summers. 1993. 'Central Bank Independence and Macroeconomic Performance: Some Comparative Evidence.' *Journal of Money, Credit, and Banking* 25 (2): 151–62.

Approach Paper. 2012. Financial Sector Legislative Reforms Commission, Ministry of Finance, GOI.

Bank of England. 1995. Report of the Debt Management Review. www.dmo.uk.

Barro, R. J. and D. B. Gordon. 1983a. 'A Positive Theory of Monetary Policy in a Natural Rate Model.' *Journal of Political Economy* 91 (4): 589–610.

Barro, R. J. and D. B. Gordon. 1983b. 'Rules, Discretion and Reputation in Monetary Policy.' *Journal of Monetary Economics* 12: 101–21.

Blejer, I. M. 2013. Central Bank's Outdated Independence, Project Syndicate, 1–2.

Blommestein, H. J. and P. Turner. 2012. *Interactions Between Sovereign Debt Management and Monetary Policy Under Fiscal Dominance and Financial Instability*. OECD Working Papers on Sovereign Borrowing and Public Debt Management, No. 3. OECD Publishing.

Burdekin, R. C. K. and L. O. Laney. 1988. 'Fiscal Policy Making and Central Bank Institutional Constraint.' *Kyklos* 41: 647–62.

Cassard, M. and D. Folkerts-Landau. 1997. *Risk Management of Sovereign Assets and Liabilities*, Working Paper No. 166, IMF.

Committee on the Global Financial System. 2011. Interaction of Sovereign Debt Management with Monetary Conditions and Financial Stability, Lessons and Implications for Central Banks, (Chairman: Paul Fisher), Bank of England.

Currie, E., J.-J. Dethier and E. Togo. 2003. *Institutional Arrangements for Public Debt Management*, Policy Research Working Paper 3021, World Bank.

Dincer, N. N. and B. Eichengreen. 2013. 'Central Bank Transparency and Independence: Updates and New Measures.' *International Journal of Central Bank* BOK WP No 2013–21.

El-Erian, A. M. 2013. The Threat to the Central-Bank Brand, Project Syndicate, 1.

Eschweiler, B. and M. D. Bordo, ed. 1993. *Rules, Discretion, and Central Bank Independence: The German Experience, 1880–1984*, in Pierre Siklos. Varieties of Monetary Reform: Lessons and Experiences on the road to Monetary Union. Kluwer Academic.

Giovannini, A. 1997. 'Government Debt Management.' *Oxford Review of Economic Policy* 13 (4): 43–52.

Goodhart, C. 1989. 'The Conduct of Monetary Policy.' *Economic Journal* 99 (369): 293–346.

——— 2010. *The Changing Role of Central Banks*, BIS Working Paper 326.

——— C. 2012. 'Monetary Policy and Public Debt.' *Financial Stability Review* (16).

Government of India and Reserve Bank of India. 2009. *India's Financial Sector an Assessment, Executive Summary*. Vol. I Committee on Financial Sector Assessment.

Grilli, V., D. Masciandaro and G. Tabellini. 1991a. 'Institutions and Policies.' *Economic Policy* 13: 341–92.

——— 1991b. 'Political and Monetary Institutions and Public Financial Policies in the Industrial Countries.' *Economic Policy* 6: 342–92.

International Monetary Fund and World Bank. 2003. *Guidelines for Public Debt Management – Accompanying Document and Selected Case Studies.* Washington, DC: IMF and WB.

IMF 2010, Stockholm principles: Guiding Principles for Managing Sovereign Risk and High Levels of Public Debt, IMF Forum.

Kalderen, L. 1997. 'Debt Management Functions and Their Location.' In *Coordinating Public Debt and Monetary Management,* edited by V. Sundararajan, P. Dattels and H. J. Blommestein, 57–76. Washington, DC: IMF and WB.

Khan, H. 2012. 'Role of State in Developing Debt Markets.' *RBI Monthly Bulletin.* Speech by Harun R Khan, Deputy Governor of Reserve Bank of India at the Capital Market Conference organised by the Qatar Central Bank & the International Monetary Fund on September 18, 2012, Doha.

Kumar, S and R. Kumar. 2012. *Sovereign Debt Management and Monetary Policy in India: An Empirical Investigation of Conflict of Interest Argument.* Department of Economic Policy Research, RBI.

Kydland, F. E. and E. C. Prescott. 1977. 'Rules Rather Than Discretion: The Inconsistency of Optimal Plans.' *The Journal of Political Economy* 85 (3): 473–92.

Mohan, R. 2003. *Fiscal Issues and Central Banks in Emerging Markets: An Indian Perspective.* BIS Papers No. 20.

OECD. 2002. *Debt Management and Government Securities Markets in the 21st Century.* OECD

Singh, C. 2005. *Public Debt in India: The Need to Separate Debt from Monetary Management.* Working Paper No. 240. Stanford, CA: Stanford Centre for International Development.

Subbarao, D. 2011. *Central Bank Governance Issues Some RBI Perspectives.* Basel, Switzerland: Central Bank Governance Group in BIS.

Taylor, J. B. 1998. 'Monetary policy and the long boom.' *Federal Reserve Bank of St. Louis Review* 80 (November/December): 3–11.

Thorat, U., C. Singh and T. Das. 2003. *Guidelines for Public Debt Management Accompanying Document and Selected Case Studies.* IMF.

Togo, E. 2007. *Coordinating Public Debt Management with Fiscal and Monetary Policies: An Analytical Framework,* pp. 7–9. Washington, DC: The World Bank, Banking and Debt Management Department.

Wagner, H. 1998. *Central Banking in Transition Countries.* IMF Working Paper 98/126. Washington, DC: IMF.

7

# Show Me the Cash

## Direct Benefits Transfer in India

**Rajesh Chakrabarti***

*Two things seem clear. First, if the objective is to alleviate poverty, we should have a program directed at helping the poor. ... Second, so far as possible the program should, while operating through the market, not distort the market or impede its functioning. This is a defect of price supports, minimum-wage laws, tariffs and the like.*

*The arrangement that recommends itself on purely mechanical grounds is a negative income tax. ... The advantages of this arrangement are clear. It is directed specifically at the problem of poverty. It gives help in the form most useful to the individual, namely, cash. It is general and could be substituted for the host of special measures now in effect. It makes explicit the cost borne by society. It operates outside the market. Like any other measures to alleviate poverty, it reduces the incentives of those helped to help themselves, but it does not eliminate that incentive entirely, as a system of supplementing incomes up to some fixed minimum would. An extra dollar earned always means more money available for expenditure.*

–Milton Friedman in *Capitalism and Freedom*, 1962

## Introduction

India, according to the World Bank, accounts for one third of the poor in the world (Olinto and Uematsu, 2013). Delivering benefits to the deserving recipients have been an old and major problem as well as a source of much corruption in India, since decades before former Prime Minister Rajiv Gandhi's famous observation of only 15 per cent of government outlay actually reaching the poor. India is not unique in this respect; most developing countries have

* Executive Vice President, Research and Policy, Wadhwani Foundation. I would like to thank Raj Chandra, Manasa Gopal and Amrita Chakrabarti for research assistance and Dr Kaushiki Sanyal for her comments on earlier drafts. I am particularly thankful to an anonymous referee whose comments have gone a long way in improving this paper as well as to the editor, Dr Supriyo De, for his suggestions.

struggled with such distributional issues. In recent years, direct cash transfer schemes have become a much experimented vehicle of distribution of benefits in much of the developing world, mostly with encouraging results. India has also embarked upon this path with characteristic hesitation and arguments. Both the idea of DBT and the delivery mechanism, essentially a unique ID-based transfer system, have generated much debate and skepticism. This chapter seeks to understand the nature and implications of the direct cash transfer programmes being considered and experimented within India, particularly in light of the experience elsewhere. This chapter is structured in five distinct sections: the issues about direct cash transfers raised in the theoretical literature in the area of public finance; existing subsidy and 'kind transfer' schemes; the experience with direct cash transfers around the world; the political and social impact, and finally the first hesitant steps of India in this direction.

## Does direct benefit transfer work in theory?

The notion of direct benefit transfers (DBTs) is hardly new. Kautilya's Arthashastra, written over two millennia ago, mentions a taxation system where rich were taxed and the amount collected was redistributed among the poor (Sen and Basu, 2006). Under the system of Zakat, Islamic rulers in the Middle Ages provided income transfers to the poor and disabled from state revenue. Nevertheless, Milton Friedman would probably go down as one of the earliest, or at any rate, the most famous and persuasive proponents of a cash transfer scheme in modern economics. The idea and its possible implications for various dimensions of economic policy have been investigated closely by economists over the decades.

However, even before we embark on a systematic study of the DBT or conditional cash transfer (CCT) programmes, it is instructive to take a look at the performance and problems of its main rival, the in-kind transfers. There have often been debates about the *uses and benefits* of subsidizing the cost of goods or distributing them for free. Economists argue that efforts to target goods to poor populations may prove ineffective, with the poor reselling donated goods to the non-poor who value them more highly. Or if these subsidies can backfire – that is usage will be low *because* the price is so low. In *The White Man's Burden* (Easterly, 2006), William Easterly provides examples of subsidized bed nets being used as wedding veils. Others talk about toilets being used as flowerpots or, more graphically, condoms being used as balloons. Currie and Gahvari (2007) present an excellent survey of the literature – both theoretical and empirical – evaluating these programmes and we summarize some of their conclusions here.

Currie and Gahvari (2007) suspect paternalism and externalities as the likely reason behind in-kind transfer programmes. Despite the talk about self-targeting, they find that most in-kind programmes are not self-targeted, and targeting these programmes is quite expensive. In fact, onerous rules aimed possibly at self-targeting often has the undesirable effect of 'screening out the most disadvantaged among the people the transfers are intended to help'. Costs of participation are a huge determinant in the targeting of these programmes.

Similarly, despite the noise about in-kind transfers reducing the labour supply distortions of the tax system, 'the bulk of such transfers are made to individuals who do not supply labor'. The authors are largely persuaded of in-kind benefits often having political motivations though that may not be wholly absent with cash transfers as well.

Moral hazard remains an important problem with in-kind transfers with these programmes possibly ending up with unintended consequences like having more children or splitting families simply to access benefits. Tying programmes to immutable features like race have political costs apart from moral and philosophical issues relating to 'horizontal equity'.

Similarly, Jha, Kotwal and Ramaswami (2013) in their overview of the evolution of food subsidy programmes in Bangladesh, India, Indonesia and Philippines over multiple decades conclude that, the main reasons for consistent failure of targeting are due to elite capture, incorrect identification of the poor, their lack of access, barriers to participation and regional allocation biases.

The principal bone of contention has understandably been the comparison of direct cash transfers with in-kind transfers. A forceful argument of Pareto-superiority of cash transfers over in-kind transfers was made in Aaron and von Furstenberg (1971). Analysing the housing market, he showed that equivalent amount of cash transfers to the household will be more efficient in raising the welfare than the subsidy (or subsidizing the house price). The counter-argument, that one can think of situations where in-kind transfers can Pareto dominate cash transfers, was made in Nichols and Zeckhauser (1982), Guesnerie and Roberts (1984) and Blackorboy and Donaldson (1988). The broad argument here is that while cash transfers are Pareto-superior in a textbook-economy, in-kind transfers can very well Pareto dominate cash transfers under a few far from unrealistic constraints. Typically, the contexts involve multiple consumer types that are difficult to distinguish between and the presence of positive externalities of in-kind transfers, though cases have been made of superiority of in-kind transfers even with homogenous consumers (Gahvari, 1995).

In the presence of quality differentials, universal public provision of private goods can accomplish redistribution of income as well. However, whether the scheme would be 'part of a properly designed redistribution package' would depend upon 'the cost to the government for observing its citizens' incomes'. The debate, therefore, has moved from a right or wrong view to the trade-off between information gathering costs and dead-weight loss from an inefficient policy (Besley and Coate, 1991). Gahvari and Mattos (2007) build on this model to develop a 'conditional' cash transfer scheme by 'linking the provision of the indivisible good to the payment of a lump-sum tax or the receipt of a rebate'. The variation in lump-sum taxes helps achieve the first-best redistribution and improves upon the redistribution outcomes (Besley and Coate, 1991).

In the presence of a linear tax system, in-kind transfer of private goods can be Pareto improving as the revenue generated can be redistributed to improve the welfare (Munro, 1992). Guesnerie and Roberts (1984) showed that in the second best economies, benefits arising out of the redistributive action of in-kind transfer programmes more than offset the cost. Even in case of a non-linear tax system, in-kind transfers can perform well as the programme itself becomes less attractive for the high ability or income households compared to low-income households (Cremer and Gahvari, 1995).

As in much of economics, the theoretical discussion sketched above has helped understand the situations and conditions under which DBT works better than alternative redistribution systems, rather than provide a universal 'yes or no' verdict of the model. Notwithstanding the nuances of this debate, governments around the world have espoused DBT schemes with varying results, some of which we discuss in the next section.

## *International experiences*

CCT programmes have grown enormously and spread wide around the globe in past two decades. Till 1997, these programmes were implemented only in Brazil, Mexico and Bangladesh. Now, it has extended to cover many counties in Asia, Africa, Central Europe, Latin America and Sub Saharan Africa.

Not only has the number of countries implementing such programmes increased, but also has the scale of implementation of the existing programmes. Mexico's PROGRESA, renamed as Oportunidades in 2001, and further rebranded as Prospera started with approximately 300,000 beneficiary households in 1997, and now covers 5 million households. The federal Bolsa Família programme (BFP) of Brazil serves 11 million families which are around a total population of 46 million people. In Colombia, the programme's initial goal was 400,000 households, but it has expanded to cover 1.5 million beneficiary households by 2007 (Fiszbein, Schady and Ferreira, 2009).

The role of these programmes varies from place to place according to the design and the context in which they operate. Most significantly, it varies according to the size of the programme. In terms of relative coverage, these transfer programmes cover 40 per cent of the population in Ecuador, 20 per cent of population in Brazil and Mexico and just 1 per cent of the population in Cambodia. In terms of budget, the costs range from about 0.50 per cent of gross domestic product (GDP) in countries like Brazil, Ecuador and Mexico to 0.08 per cent of GDP (Chile).

The motives behind the transfer programmes also differ across countries. In Chile and Turkey, CCTs are focused more narrowly on extremely poor and socially excluded people, while CCTs in Bangladesh and Cambodia have been used to reduce gender disparities in education. In Sub-Saharan Africa, the CCT programmes have been implemented to alleviate the HIV/AIDS epidemic (Fiszbein, Schady and Ferreira, 2009).

The most conspicuous quality of in-kind programmes is the width of its spread. Gahvari and Mattos (2007) studied the share in GDP of five types of in-kind programme in the Organization for Economic Co-operation and Development (OECD) countries. The health care programmes had the largest share amongst public in-kind programmes, followed by education, childcare, housing and active labour market programmes and school lunch programmes. The key restriction on such programmes is that the recipient cannot resell their allotments without substantial penalty, else in-kind transfers nearly becomes equivalent to cash.

Optimal transfer programmes face a trade-off between 'productive efficiency' and 'target efficiency'. However, there are cases where equity efficiency trade-off will be very low or in some case equity and efficiency might complement each other (Nichols and Zeckhauser, 1982). Mehta and Jha (2012) apply public finance models to food security, to predict that more funds will be stolen in poor communities. They hypothesized that if subsidized food is inferior, the poor will value the increase in deliveries. When India increased food-grain inputs to public distribution system (PDS) from 1.61 to 2.27 kg/(person/month) between the 1999–2000 and 2004–2005, consumption of subsidized food grains improved from 1.01 to 1.03 kg/(person-month), (Jha and Ramaswami, 2013). Food-grain inputs doubled between 1993–1994 and 2004–2005 while output increased by only 2 per cent (Himanshu and Sen, 2013). In almost every nation of the world today, there exist schemes to compensate the costs of the poor through subsidization and free delivery. The aim behind such programmes is to ensure that the poor receive exactly what is necessary and important for survival, as well as to ensure basic living standards.

Jha and Ramaswami (2013) examined the design and performance of safety net programmes through in-kind transfer, cash, nutrition programmes, public work programmes in Bangladesh, India, Indonesia and Philippines to poor, ultra-poor and vulnerable classes. Governments in most of the countries aim to cover poor through safety net benefits. With resource limitations, the safety net programmes will be successful only if it is able to enhance the participation of the poor and lower the programme cost (including fraud). The agenda, therefore, should focus on the targeting design, alternatives to in-kind transfers and the feasibility of cash transfers. Several experiments have been conducted, across the world, to analyse the reactions of the poor towards free and subsidized 'necessary' goods. In one such case, the demand for bed nets was tested. Estimates show that the use of bed nets can reduce malaria infections by nearly half (Lengeler, 2004). However, very few households possessed a bed net. Thus, it would seem to make sense to subsidize prices of bed nets so more households would be able to afford them. Experiments were conducted to test the sensitivity of such target goods to price (Pascaline, 2013). It was found that the purchase of nets was indeed very sensitive to the price. Almost everybody took a free net home but demand rapidly fell with price rise. The experiment was replicated in different regions with slight variations. When people were given time to go home and collect cash (rather than having to buy on the spot), more people bought at a higher price, but demand still went up by several times when the price was brought down to zero. What was troubling was the fact that the demand for bed nets, though very sensitive to price, is not very sensitive to income. Even though a 15 per cent increase in income is far more than the cost of a bed net, people who are 15 per cent richer are only 5 per cent more likely to buy a net than others.

## *Economic impact of transfer programmes in different countries*

Unsurprisingly perhaps, the span and diversity of CCT programmes around the world have only been matched by the heterogeneity of their effectiveness. Impact evaluations of these programmes, a challenging task in itself, have produced evidence of results with significant span. We present some of this evidence below. Box 7.1 summarizes some information about two of the largest CCT programmes in the world and their impact.

**BOX 7.1 overview of two major CCT Programmes**

**Brazil's Bolsa Familia Programme (BFP): Largest conditional transfer programme in developing world**

The BFP created in October 2003, is the merger of four pre-existing cash transfer programmes in Brazil. The programme provides transfers ranging from R$15 to R$95 (US$7–US$45) per month to poor families. Just after the two months of the launch of the programme in December 2003, it covered 3.8 million families and then expanded to 11.1 million beneficiary families (46 million people) as of June 2006. The programme claims to cover 100 per cent of the poor and 25 per cent of the Brazilian population. The annual household survey (PNAD, 2004) result shows that the BFP accounted for a significant reduction in inequality (20–25 per cent) and extreme poverty (16 per cent) (Fiszbein, Schady and Ferreira, 2009).

*Public spending on the programme*

Spending on CCTs has increased from 0.18 per cent of GDP in 2002 (pre-reforms) to 0.36 per cent in 2005. BFP spending in 2005 amounted to R$6.7 billion (US$3.2 billion), and the budgeted figure for 2006 is R$8.3 billion (US$4 billion, or 0.39 per cent of projected GDP).

*Impact of the programme*

*On Education:* Bolsa Família has had a positive impact on school attendance. According to the survey done by IPC, the probability of absence is 3.6 percentage points lower for those children who are enrolled in the programme. Also, their probability of dropping out is 1.6 percentage points lower than that of children in non-treated households (Soares, Ribas and Osório, 2007).

*On Child Labour and School Attendance:* It has been found that the income transfer programmes had no significant effect on child labour but a positive and significant impact on school attendance. These kinds of programmes increase the chance of a poor child going to school but do not reduce his or her labour activity as they prefer doing both.

*On Health:* There has been no impact of the programme on child immunizations, despite conditions attached in obtaining the benefit. According to the report, supply side impediments could be the reason.

*On Labour Force:* The labour market participation rate of treated adults was 2.6 percentage points higher than for non-treated adults. The participation rate of beneficiary women was 4.3 percentage points higher.

**Overview of Mexico PROGRESA (anti-poverty)**

PROGRESA began operations in 1997 covering 300,000 households in more than 5,000 communities and represented 46 per cent of federal government's anti-poverty budget. In 1999, the PROGRESA's budget was approximately US$777 million which was equivalent to 0.2 per cent of Mexico's GDP. In 2002, the programme covered more than four million families, 20 per cent of the Mexican population. The programme's 2002 annual budget was around Mex$18 billion (US$1.8 billion), World Bank Policy Research Paper.

The proportions of first year administrative costs of Mexico's CCT Progresa were 65 per cent on targeting, 8 per cent on monitoring of conditions and 8 per cent on delivery of transfers. Three years later, 11 per cent of administrative costs were spent on targeting, 24 per cent on monitoring conditions and 41 per cent on delivery of transfers (Coady, 2000).

Along similar lines, an IFPRI report found that for every 100 pesos allocated to the programme, 8.2 pesos were administrative or programme costs. That is, the administrative expenses are less than 10 per cent of the total cost. The report claims that the administrative cost incurred is smaller relative to the cost incurred in previous programmes and other programmes in different countries.

*Impact of the programme*

*Poverty:* Programme reduced the number of people with income levels below the poverty level by about 10 per cent. The depth of poverty is reduced by 30 per cent, and the severity index is reduced by 45 per cent. For comparison, an untargeted transfer is found to reduce the depth of poverty by 28 per cent and the severity of poverty by 36 per cent.

(*continued*)

*Education:* Percentage increase in enrolment in secondary education was reported more than 20 per cent for girls and 10 per cent for boys. Effect on enrolment in primary education was very low as more than 95 per cent of children were already enrolled in the rural areas, even before Progresa.

*On Labour Supply and Child Labour:* Labour-force participation for boys shows reductions as large as 15–25 per cent relative to the probability of participating prior to the programme. For girls also there are significant reductions in child labour. The lower incidence of child work due to the PROGRESA programme is found to account for 65 per cent (in November 1999) to 82 per cent (in November 1998) of the increase in the enrolment of boys in school.

Progresa children aged 1–5 years had a 12 per cent lower incidence of illness than non-Progresa children. An increase in 16 per cent in mean growth rate per year was reported for children who received treatment between twelve and thirty-six months of age (Behrman and Hoddinott, 2001). Progresa also had impact on overall expenditure patterns. Overall, median food expenditure was 13 per cent higher in Progresa household than the non-Progresa. Also, 45 per cent reduction in severity in poverty and 15–25 per cent reduction in labour force participation for boys has been reported.

## Effect on education

In Mexico, the impact of *Oportunidades* in rural areas is significant for children making the transition from primary to secondary school (Schultz 2004; Behrman, Sengupta and Todd, 2005). Positive spillover effects were also observed in case of Oportunidades – school enrolment increased for those children also who were not eligible for the transfer. In Nicaragua, the *Red de Protección Social (RPS) programme* targeting the children of age group 7–13 showed large effects on school enrolment – the increase was by almost 13 per cent (Maluccio and Flores, 2005). In Honduras, the *PRAF* also had a positive effect on school enrolment; although the impact was much smaller – increase was only around 3 per cent (Glewwe and Olinto, 2004).

There are, however, certain unexpected consequences as well. A study of CCT in the city of Bogotá, Colombia (Barrera-Osorio et al., 2008), found evidence of the tendency to concentrate resources on one child. The programme offered parents the option to enter any of their age-eligible children into a lottery. Lottery winners would get a monthly transfer as long as the child attended school regularly. It was found that winners were more likely to attend school regularly as well as re-enroll each academic year. However, the fact that in families that entered two or more children and one won, the child who lost the lottery was *less* likely to be enrolled in school than children in families where both lost, was quite disconcerting. It was expected that the increase in family income would help the second child. But, all resources were instead concentrated on only the winner.

## Effect on labour supply

CCT might affect the adult labour supply both through income and price effect. If leisure is a normal good then the income effect associated with the transfers might result in more leisure and less work. And the price effect may make beneficiaries believe that by supplying less labour they will continue to be poor and eligible for the programme. The impacts of CCTs on labour force participation vary across countries. Especially, when leisure is a normal good, impact of in-kind transfers on labour supply is greater than cash transfers that the labour supply will be higher and also goods will be overprovided in that case (Gahvari, 1995).

Critics of Bolsa Família allege that it has a negative impact on labour force participation. However, the evaluation found that the labour market participation rate of treated adults was, in fact, 2.6 per cent higher than for non-treated adults. This impact was different across genders – the participation rate of beneficiary women was 4.3 percentage points higher (Filmer and Schady, 2009).

## Effect on child labour

CCT programmes can reduce child labour through two channels. First, the very conditional nature of the programme requires the enrolment in school and regular attendance. This gives less time to a child to take part in income generating activities. Second is the income effect : households that receive income are less likely to depend on the income of the children and hence child labour reduces. Several CCTs have been successful in reducing child labour.

In Nicaragua, the RPS reduced child work by 3–5 per cent among children aged 7–13 (also, the fraction of children who only studied instead of working, or working and studying both increased significantly from 59 to 84 per cent) (Maluccio and Flores, 2005). PETI of Brazil, which gives stipends directly to the students conditional on participation in school and special training programmes showed significant reduction in the beneficiaries' probability of working. In Cambodia, the CESSP programme, that gives transfers to children in transition from primary to lower secondary school, reduced work for pay by 11 percentage points.

However, Familias en Acción programme in Columbia had no effect on child work (Attanasio et al., 2006) (although the programme does appear to have reduced the amount of time dedicated to domestic chores); and Glewwe and Olinto (2004) find no effects of the PRAF programme on child work in Honduras.

### Effect on health, calorie intake

Jacoby (2002) showed that the calorie intake of children, who were part of the programme, was 80 per cent higher on school days relative to non-school days in Philippines. While comparing, food versus cash in Bangladesh the marginal propensity to consume (MPC) out of wheat transfers in-kind is significantly higher than the MPC out of cash transfers (Del Ninno and Dorosh, 2003).

Further, the children of the beneficiaries of PROGRESA, the Mexican cash transfer programme, have been found to have significantly lower levels of cortisol than comparable children whose mothers did not benefit from the programme (Banerjee and Duflo, 2011). Biologically, there is a strong association between poverty and the level of cortisol produced by the body, an indicator of stress. The cortisol levels seem to go down when households receive some help.

### Effect on inequality

Cash transfers by redistributing the income appear to lead to significant reduction in inequality. An IPC-UNDP working paper shows that there has been 4.7 and 5 per cent reduction in Gini Index for Brazil and Mexico, respectively, for the year 1997–2004. Both the Bolsa Familia in Brazil and Oportunidades in Mexico are believed to have contributed to 21 per cent of reduction in Gini coefficient, while in Chile, the programme has contributed to 15 per cent reduction in inequality. As the programme was implemented at a smaller scale in Chile as compared to Mexico and Brazil, the impact was also smaller. In Brazil and Mexico, the total share of transfer programme was 0.5 per cent of total income whereas in Chile the share was only 0.01 per cent of total income.

It has also been found that the transfer programmes face a trade-off between extending coverage and improving efficiency. The programme in Mexico has more efficient targeting than that in Brazil but at the price of having fewer poor households covered by the programme. Indeed, it is very difficult to expand a targeted programme while keeping the leakage rate from rising. Angelucci and Giorgi (2009) establish how cash transfers to eligible individuals in Mexico go on to affect the consumption of ineligible households living in the same village; operating through insurance and credit markets. They claim ineligible households benefit through gifts, reduced savings and increased loans.

There, however, remains a question whether cash transfers are the *only* possible solution. Lampman and Smeeding (1983) explore the significance of one private alternative to government transfers, namely, direct interfamily giving of cash, food and housing. Fragmentary evidence suggests that such interfamily transfer has decreased in the past few decades as government transfers increased. If current government transfers are conversions of, or substitutes for, interfamily transfers, then it follows that some of the benefits of government transfer 'slide' over to 'secondary beneficiaries', that is, those who would have made the private transfers. Further, it concludes that the effects of government transfers are not much different from those of the private transfers which they replace. Analysis of consumer expenditure data has shown that in-kind transfers can, at times, be an effective way of providing support to the poor. However, the success of the programme also depends on accurate targeting as well as the recipient's valuation of the benefits (Slesnick, 1996).

## *Social and political impact*

Apart from just the possible monetary impact, it is necessary to observe the social, political and long-term effects of cash transfer schemes, as well as compare the impact of 'unconditional' transfers.

A study on the cash transfers in Kenya (Ressler, 2008) noted that participant households appeared to have very weak social networks, an indication of their vulnerability. Cash payments appeared to strengthen their social standing and provided households with capital. Additional resources enabled recipients to participate in community events and share food. They could now borrow when in need because they had a capacity to repay. Thus, families seemed to benefit socially, as well.

A study in Mexico (De La O, 2006) compared the voting results of the 2000 presidential election in villages that had received the social welfare programme PROGRESA. Poor households received cash transfers as long as their children attended school and they visited health care centres. Houses that received transfers for six months were compared against others that had received it for twenty-one months. Both the poll turnout and votes in favour of the party that brought PROGRESA were higher in villages which received benefits for longer.

Because the households that received the benefits longer could see the impact on health and education on their lives, they responded in higher numbers.

The conditionality in PROGRESA is based on the principle that increased income is not enough and that parents need to be monitored. But, do unconditional programmes work the same way? A World Bank study found that conditionality does not seem to matter at all (Baird, McIntosh and Ozler, 2009): The researchers offered the families of school-age girls a transfer ranging between US$5 and US$20 PPP per month. In one group, the transfer was conditional on enrolment. In another, it wasn't. A third group did not receive a transfer. The effects were large – after a year, dropout was 11 per cent in the group that did not receive transfers, and only 6 per cent among those who benefited from the transfer. But, they were the same for those who received the conditional transfer and for those who got the unconditional one, suggesting that parents did not need to be *forced* to send their children to school, they needed to be helped financially.

## DBTs in India

> *The payments that were done through a complex, layered byzantine administrative system that were diminished in value by the time they reached their beneficiaries will now be paid directly*
>
> –P. Chidambaram, 24 November 2012

While the deficiencies of the large and almost perpetual government subsidy distribution – largely in food, fertilizer and fuel – have been recognized for decades, it is fair to say that the move to a DBT regime and the idea of operating it at a national scale began to get serious traction during the UPA rule, particularly in its second term. An essential pre-requisite for making the DBT functional was a national identity system, to address which the Aadhaar card initiative of the Unique Identification Authority of India (UIDAI) was set up in 2006. The stated objective behind the Aadhaar-enabled Cash Transfer Scheme (or DBT) in India is to enhance accessibility, uplift standard of living for majority of the poor and eliminate financial exclusion. For beneficiaries, it aims to reduce dependence on official intermediaries, reducing hassle and widespread corruption, and making funds available on time and in full amount. For the government, it aims at better targeting, removing 'duplicates' and ghosts, reducing the fiscal bill, bringing transparency and accountability, and helping in financial inclusion.

The economic reasoning behind the advantages of DBT over existing systems is, in fact, quite intuitive. As Kotwal, Murugkar and Ramaswami (2011) point out, alternatives to in-kind transfers, like food coupons, provide the seller with economic returns while putting purchasing power in the hands of the recipient, therefore reducing or avoiding incentives for distortions. With appropriate conditionality, like cash incentive for institutional child delivery, self-selection is also likely to far more effective since the incentives for the target group to step up for taking benefits are obvious.

The key element of implementing DBT in India is the Aadhaar card. The exact mechanism of DBT payments using the Aadhaar Payment Bridge is a fairly complex process but one that is necessary to understand in order to get a more complete understanding of the working of the DBT process in India. Box 7.2 attempts to explain the mechanism.

Implementing the Aadhaar card system, a prerequisite for DBT, has its own costs that should be considered in order to get the comprehensive picture of the system, while keeping in mind that the Aadhaar system has several other significant policy implementation benefits as well apart from effective

**BOX 7.2 The DBT delivery process in India**

As DBT gains traction, the primary vehicle of its delivery would be the Aadhaar card. To get most of the benefits under the DBT scheme in India, every resident will need to have an Aadhaar number (based on biometrics) that will be linked to his or her bank account. Entitlements and benefits will be transferred directly to beneficiaries through Aadhaar-linked bank accounts. And ultimately, the disbursements will take place at the doorsteps of the beneficiaries through Business Correspondents (BCs) who will make payments using micro-ATMs. It has been claimed that the Aadhar-enabled DBT system will reduce several layers of intermediaries, points of leakage and delays.

As explained in Figure 7.1, each citizen is awarded an Aadhar number based on her biometric and demographic information, and stored in a central database. The whole process of DBT includes Aadhaar enrollment, opening up of bank account and linking of bank account with the Aadhaar number, digitization and Aadhaar seeding of beneficiary lists, Aadhaar e-KYC (Know Your Customer) services, online authentication and payment to the beneficiaries.

Any area with a population more than 1,000 will be served by BCs. Linking of Aadhaar to the bank account can be done by either BC or bank branches. Those beneficiaries who do not have bank account, instant bank account can be opened by

(*continued*)

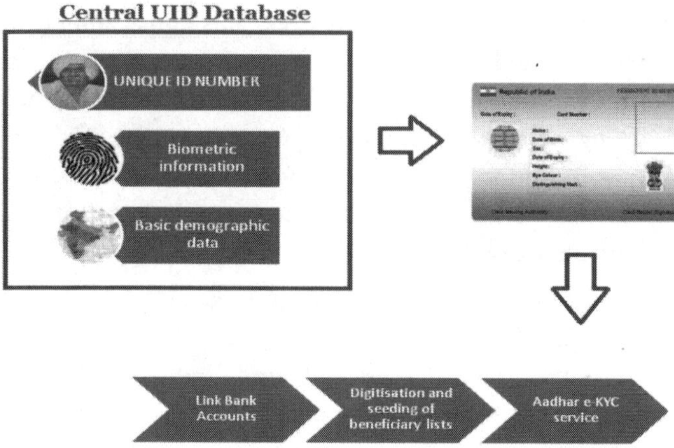


**FIGURE 7.1 The Aadhar process.**

using Aadhaar e-KYC. Aadhaar e-KYC provides data for name, date of birth, gender, address and photograph of the enrolled beneficiary. E-KYC can also be used to avail state government services, banking and insurance services, mobile connection, LPG connections, train travel, and so on. E-KYC can scale up to lakhs of transaction on daily basis.

National Payment Corporation of India has deployed Aadhaar Payment Bridge, which can handle millions of transactions on a daily basis. Payments by the central government, state government, companies or employers will transfer the funds to the sponsored bank or post office and through Aadhaar Payment Bridge those funds will be transferred to the beneficiaries account.

One of the most important components required for smooth operation of Aadhar services is the existence of various interoperable points through which individuals can access their bank accounts – make payments and receive transfers. Though some infrastructure for this is already in place, further growth is required to ensure easy access and no delays. Figure 7.2 highlights these possibilities.

**Financial model for first phase**

Estimates of one time Aadhaar Seeding and Digitization Cost – With an estimated beneficiary base of 250 million and seeding of 1 billion database across all schemes will cost US$ 250 million. According to the report of Task Force on Aadhaar enabled Payment Infrastructure – annually there will be 4,130 million transactions, payment of US$ 48.83 billion and including bank fees, total cost to the government will be US$ 889 million annually.

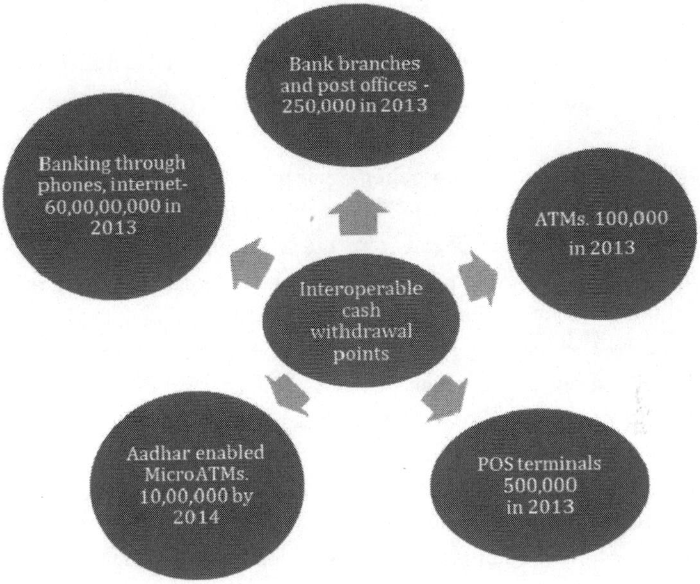


**FIGURE 7.2 Interoperable cash withdrawal points – A component of the DBT system.**

**DBT in its second phase**

Key activities in the second phase will include enrolment and seeding of Aadhaar numbers to the bank account. For that, three Central Public Sector Undertakings (CPSUs) – BEL, ECIL and ITIL – have been assigned the enrolment work. For 33 districts in 11 states, there are 390 Tehsils.[3] Village wise schedule for enrolment will be prepared in consultation District/Tehsil administrator. District magistrates (DMs)/Collectors shall nominate a Nodal Officer for all matters pertaining to DBT.

DC's will be responsible for managing the complete project, providing infrastructure for enrolment-premise, electricity and security, document management, and will ensure quality and timely enrolment. UIDAI will be responsible for appointing registrars, organizing operator training and certification, and providing fund for enrolment.

**DBT through Central Plan Scheme Monitoring System**

To provide solutions for efficient fund management, Central Plan Scheme Monitoring System (CPSMS) is a planning commission scheme implemented by the Controller General of Accounts. It is basically a payment platform for Aadhaar-based payments.

(*continued*)

The main functions of CPSMS will be to keep track of all the releases from central government till last point. It will provide real-time bank balances of implementing agencies and facilitate fund management both at micro as well as macro level.

**Process**

Beneficiaries list along with the amount payable to each beneficiary shall be prepared by the Implementing Agency (IA). They shall also upload digitally signed list on CPSMS. E-sanction for the payment to the beneficiaries shall be made at the Program Division (PD) level in the ministry. PD shall enter the details of sanction order, amount of sanction and other details. PD shall also digitally cross sign the list prepared by the IAs in CPSMS. After receiving the e-sanction, the District Development Officer (DDO) shall generate e-bill and submit it to the Pay and Accounts Officer (PAO). For direct payment through banks, digitally signed electronic payment file shall be created by PAO. PAO will approve the DBT files and any extra payment beyond the limit will require two digital signatories.

(Special thanks to Mr Varad Pandey, Officer on Special Duty (OSD) to Shri Jairam Ramesh, former Minister of Rural Development in UPA-II, for explaining some of the process details.)

cash transfers. The UIDAI has already covered over two thirds of the Indian population. According to an influential study conducted by the National Institute of Public Finance and Policy (NIPFP, 2012), investment in the Aadhaar project would yield a return of 52.85 per cent to the government. The cost of the scheme will double from Rs. 2,265 crore in 2012–2013 to Rs. 4,835 crore by 2020–2021, and the benefits will trickle from Rs. 425 crore in 2012–2013 and to Rs. 25,100 crore by 2021. The study also shows that there will be significant reduction in leakages – 8.3 per cent for the PDS, 5 per cent for the MGNREGA wage disbursement, and 10 per cent of the fertilizer and LPG subsidies.

An internal study conducted by the Prime Minister's Office (PMO) in consultation with various ministries has revealed that, based on the actual money spent by the central government during 2010–2011 under various subsidies totalling Rs. 211,474 crore (approximately $38 billion), the scheme can result in a net saving of Rs. 33,000 crore ($6 billion) by way of plugging leakages the Business India magazine reported.[1] The only major cost for the functioning of the DBT would be the process to obtain an Aadhar number. The Aadhar number, however, can be used for several other purposes. And as calculated in the NIPFP cost benefit analysis, the Aadhar project would yield an internal rate of return in real terms of 52.85 per cent to the government.

However, others (Khera, 2011a; Patnaik, 2012) have questioned the fact that the NIPFP analysis is based on assumptions rather than facts. A Society of Social Audit Accountability and Transparency (Department of Rural Development, Government of Andhra Pradesh) report for July–October 2012 on fraud in pension schemes suggests that the total discrepancies in disbursement of pensions are around 2 per cent while the NIPFP report assumes a 7 per cent discrepancy rate.

## *Implementation challenges and alternatives*

Cash transfers cannot and should not replace the public provision of essential goods and services, but rather complement them. *DBT in India is a new system, not a new scheme.* It aims to make the payments under existing government schemes reach people faster and more efficiently. The success of the DBT also, therefore, depends upon the robustness of other systems and the quality of the payment infrastructure. The new payments banks being formalized by the Reserve Bank of India may address some of these issues.

The literature on the effectiveness of DBT in India is still at a nascent stage given the relative novelty of the programme itself. Nevertheless, empirical studies as well as surveys – several of the journalistic rather than research kind – are already feeding opinions on both sides of the debate, in support as well as in criticism of the new approach. The criticisms of cash transfers have included the standard ones: leaving citizens at the mercy of the vagaries of the grain market price, allowing cash to be spent on non-intended items, and poor self-selection of the needy.

Gangopadhyay, Lensink and Yadav (2012) report the findings of a study in New Delhi to analyse the effects of an unconditional cash transfer in place of the regular food subsidy. Households that were provided cash had the opportunity to invest in non-cereal foods outside the realm of food subsidy. It was noticed that even though the calorie intake in the cereal foods decreased, the consumption on 'bad' goods such as alcohols did not increase significantly. Instead household increased consumption of products such as milk and meat. Further, spillover effects were noticed as PDS shops improved their quality of stock, fearing competition from private shops which individuals now had access to. At the end of the test run, only 4 per cent of households that had opted for the cash transfer wanted to leave while almost 22 per cent of the households that had not initially preferred cash transfers, now preferred cash to kind.

Outcomes of these kinds of transfer programmes are more or less country specific. Transfer programmes in Latin American countries were successful because even before the implementation of the programme, they had highly developed social insurance system with wide coverage. Thus, 'targeting' marginalized groups were easier as the majority of the population was already covered. However, in case of India, majority of population is in need, and also the targeting mechanisms are outdated and not efficient. For instance, in Brazil, health programme is successful because all the basic health care services are universal and more than half of the expenditure on health care is public expenditure. But in case of India, it is barely one quarter. In Brazil and Mexico for instance, CCTs are seen as a complement and not as a substitute for providing the health, education and other basic service (Dreze, 2011). Khera (2014), using quantitative analysis confirmed that in states where the food system works well, respondents are more likely to prefer food over cash. People preferred cash mostly in states where the PDS performed poorly.

A key determinant of the success of targeting of DBT depends on the coverage and functioning of its basic infrastructure, the Aadhaar card. The UIDAI aims at providing a unique identity to each beneficiary and elimination of 'bogus cards' – (1) 'ghost'; (2) 'duplicates' and (3) 'misclassified' cards. UID can, however, aim to eliminate only the first two types of bogus cards. Inclusion error happening due to misclassification cannot be taken care by UID as the classification of BPL families is based on a census which has its own conceptual and implementation challenges (Khera 2011c; Dreze and Khera, 2010a).

On the question of food security, concerns have also been raised about the efficacy of the DBT to reach the desired social goals. Khera (2011c) argues that linking PDS and NREGA with UID may be more disruptive than using cheaper technological innovations to reduce leakages from the existing system in a less disruptive manner. The wage payments under NREGA through bank accounts have become mandatory from 2008, attempting to reduce leakages from the scheme. Again, targeted social welfare schemes are desirable when social welfare expenditure in the country is not adequate to provide universal benefits. Also, as an alternative to the UID providing 'portability of benefits', Khera (2011c) suggests making the existing form of identity authentication, that is, ration cards mobile. Provision of food coupons to households, required to be deposited at the time of purchase of food can also reduce the problem of food grain diversion under the existing PDS system.

There is a counter argument that cash transfer or food coupons are better alternatives as they give more options to the consumers, will be easier to include coarse cereals, and milk-type products and hence broaden the scope of food subsidy and end illegal diversion. Also, it is easier to audit number of food coupons than sacks of grains. For government also, it is more efficient to distribute cash for food rather than incurring a huge cost on procuring, storing and then transporting and distributing, and transporting it to the poor (Ramaswamy, 2007). Some of the key problems with PDS are universal coverage, and exclusion error which is not common with cash transfer. Jha and Ramaswami (2013) estimate the total costs of food subsidy delivered through PDS to include the following: illegal diversion cost 43 per cent, excess costs 28 per cent, income transfer to non-poor 19 per cent and the transfer to poor 10 per cent.

The Targeted Public Distribution System (TPDS) also suffers from both inefficiency and leakage. A Planning Commission study (Planning Commission, 2013) estimates that for every Re.1 worth of benefits delivered, the Government of India (GOI) spends Rs. 3.65. The estimated leakage in Bihar's TPDS for the year 2005 was 75 per cent (PEO, 2005). A pre-pilot study conducted by JPAL in Bihar to check whether consumers prefer cash transfer or TPDS founds that majority of the participants preferred cash transfer over TPDS. The reason given was the poor functioning of FPS. A survey found that the average Fair Price Shop (FPS) remains open only for ten days per month in urban areas and six days per month in rural areas, whereas *kirana* shops open almost every day and for more number of hours than FPS.[2] About 80 per cent of the respondents of the survey reported about adulteration of goods at FPS. Also, the degree of price volatility reported at *kirana* shops (less than 15 per cent) was much less than that at FPS (J-Pal, 2011).

Jha and Srinivasan (2004) point out that the private traders running FPSs manage costs better than the government agencies in the areas of marketing, storage, trade and transport. Control of the excess costs and impact of the programme on the poor can be increased either by increasing participation rate or enhancing the fraction of subsidy granted to the poor or combining both. If the inclusion error could be minimized to zero, the share to poor can rise to 29 per cent in India (Jha, Kotwal and Ramaswami, 2013).

In the case of crucial items like food, direct provision protects consumers from inflation and is also a broader strategy to ensure domestic supply. Also, poor are more likely to prefer provision in kind than those who are better off. An International Food Policy Research Institute (IFPRI) study comparing the impact of cash and in-kind transfer programme in Bangladesh founds that only poorest households prefer food as transfer because as income increases, beneficiaries' preference for food declines. Relatively better-off beneficiaries prefer only cash.

Of course, the DBT is not a silver bullet. Several limitations of cash transfer programmes, particularly when it comes to providing food security, are discussed in Kotwal, Murugkar and Ramaswami (2011) and Khera (2011c). These include the following: under the cash transfer programme, a certain quantity of food per person cannot be maintained in the time of high food inflation; cash may be diverted for purchase of non-food items. An important argument (though based on assumptions rather than empirical analysis) in favour of the existing PDS is that the inconvenience of standing in the line at PDS shops induce the rich to self-select out of the pool of recipients, facilitating universal coverage under the existing system, which is not the case under the cash transfer system.

Khera (2011a) demonstrates a distinct trend in the preference between cash and food, where majority of the household in the Indian states always prefer food to cash transfers where PDS is fully functional. People preferred food only when, they have issues with food security, poor access to banks and post offices (on an average 3.8 km further away from FPS), underdeveloped rural markets and accessibility to staples (rice, especially in Orissa, Chattisgarh). Overall 13 per cent have complained of corruption in PDS, amongst them 47 per cent preferred cash, as it can be spent, however, they liked based on diversification on food of better quality. Food preference is highest in Andhra Pradesh (91.3 per cent) followed by Chhattisgarh (90.3 per cent), Orissa, Jharkhand, Rajasthan and cash preference is highest in Bihar (54.2 per cent), followed by Uttar Pradesh (UP) (34.1 per cent). Khera (2011b) estimated the leakages of wheat and rice through PDS in India, and noted that the situation worsened between 1999–2000 and 2007–2008, 24 per cent of grain was diverted and it got worse in 2004–2005 when 54 per cent of grain leaked.

More recently, Khera (2014) explores the arguments for and against cash and in-kind transfer programmes in the context of food transfer, using qualitative and quantitative data from a survey of over 1,200 rural households in nine Indian states. She finds that two thirds of the respondents expressed a preference for in-kind benefits, that is, food. Unsurprisingly, performance of the PDS system is found to be an important determinant of the reported preferences. The study finds that in places, where PDS performed better at distributing food, respondents are more likely to express preference for food to cash transfer.

Ghatak, Kumar and Mitra (2013) analyse the Bihar government's bicycle distribution scheme and find that almost 97 per cent of the intended beneficiaries received the money for the bicycles and almost 93 per cent of them received the right amount. Further, only 2 per cent of those who received the money did not purchase the bicycle. These show that the project has been performing incredibly well. However, when asked whether the beneficiaries preferred cash or kind, only 45 per cent opted for cash. The reasons behind this were then further analysed. The major issue was that most households had to put in extra cash themselves to buy the cycle, as the money provided by the government was insufficient. Thus, even though the programme was working brilliantly, it wasn't sufficient to convince the recipients. An important lesson to be learnt from this is the fact that careful analysis needs to be done to ensure that cash transfers are sufficient for the benefit of the recipients.

A pilot project launched in December 2011, in Kotkasim village in Rajasthan, proved, by general accounts, to be a failure (see a TERI and IISD report here: https://www.iisd.org/gsi/sites/default/files/ffs_india_kerosene_alwar_final.pdf). Under this scheme, beneficiaries were supposed to receive the subsidy amount in cash into their bank accounts and use that to purchase kerosene from the FPSs at the regular market price. According to the report of District Supply Officer, Alwar, out of 25,843 ration card holders in Kotkasim, bank accounts were opened only for 13,458 card holders which was little over 50 per cent. Villagers' post office accounts were rejected as such accounts do not have online services. A continuous decline in the sale of kerosene was noticed after the launch of the project. It was reported that people who did not buy kerosene received subsidy; others those who bought were deprived of subsidy amount for more than six months. Bank branches were also at a distance of 8–15 km from the village. Even this project, however, has not been bereft of its silver lining: according to supply inspector of Alwar district, the off-take of kerosene was 84 kL a month before the launch of the scheme but after the launch it was barely 100 kL for nine months which led to a savings of worth of Rs. 2 crore (Singh, 2012).

## *A status report of the roll-out of DBT in India*

The first phase of DBT, launched on 1st January 2013 covered 43 districts. It was expected to cover another 78 districts from 1st April 2013 in its second phase. However, because of the slow roll-out in the first phase and inadequate process, government postponed the date for second phase roll-out to 1 July 2013. It will also include LPG subsidy in 20 districts where consumers will get about Rs. 4,000 per annum in cash and will buy the LPG at market price of Rs. 901.50 per 14.2 kg (Business Standard, 2013). In its very first phase, DBT was supposed to be rolled out in 43 districts in 16 states under 26 selected schemes. The selection of districts was done on the basis of coverage of bank accounts and Aadhaar. However, on 1st January, the scheme was rolled only for 7 schemes and covered just 20 out of 43 districts. Out of the rest 23 districts, roll-out in 11 districts were postponed till 1st February 2013 and the other 12 districts till 1st March 2013 (Dhoot and Goswami, 2013). According to the government estimates, about 1.6 million beneficiaries were supposed to be covered under phase 1. Out of these, 1.3 million have been identified by banks but only 5, 50,000 have reported their Aadhaar number (Business Standard, 2013).

The reason for the slow process is mainly because of linking of bank accounts with the Aadhaar number. Seventy eight per cent of the eligible beneficiaries have bank accounts and nearly 32 per cent of them have also been allotted a unique identity number (UID), but just 4 per cent of 16.6 lakh beneficiary's Aadhaar numbers have been linked to their bank accounts. Over one lakh beneficiary who comes under 5 of 26 schemes – 80 per cent of them have bank accounts and 32.2 per cent have UID number and bank account, but only 2.6 per cent of them have their Aadhaar number linked with their bank account (Dhoot and Goswami, 2013). The first phase scheme completed 35 million transactions and transferred only Rs. 45 crore to Aadhaar seeded accounts. Thus, the average transfer for each account was of only Rs. 1,285 since 1 January 2013. According to the officials, major problem is faced in seeding the Aadhaar number to bank accounts (Business Standard, 2013). By mid-October 2013, about Rs. 2.9 billion has been transferred in 121 districts under 28 government schemes in the ten months of 2013. During the same period about Rs. 6.1 billion has been spent on DBT in the LPG scheme, bringing the total to over Rs. 9 billion. The new administration has also been stressing on accelerating DBT.

## Conclusion

While DBT has been a relatively new concept put into effect in India, it has already spurred a spate of studies and opinion wars on its relative benefits vis-à-vis the older system of in-kind transfers. While all agree that the old system is broken, opinion is divided on the extent that DBT is providing the solution. The area of food security seems to be the hottest bed for debates. This debate notwithstanding, the government thrust on DBT seems to be a steady one and DBT appears to be an idea whose time has definitely come in India.

## Abbreviations

BC – Business Correspondent

BEL – Bharat Electronics Limited

BFP – Bolsa Familia Programme

CCT – Conditional Cash Transfer

CPSMS – Central Plan Scheme Monitoring System

CPSU – Central Public Sector Undertaking

DBT – Direct Benefit Transfer

DDO – District Development Officer

ECIL – Electronics Corporation of India Limited

FPS – Fair Price Shop

IA – Implementing Agency

ITIL – Informational Technology Infrastructure Library

KYC – Know Your Customer

LPG – Liquefied Petroleum Gas

MGNREGS – Mahatma Gandhi National Rural Employment Guarantee Scheme

MPC – Marginal Propensity to Consume

PAO – Pay and Accounts Officer

PDS – Public Distribution System

POS – Point of Sale

TPDS – Targeted Public Distribution System

UID – Unique Identity Number

## Notes

1 As discussed in http://knowledge.wharton.upenn.edu/article/can-indias-ambitious-direct-cash-transfer-plan-work/.

2 Fair Price Shops are mandated by government to sell goods subsidized through the TPDS. Kirana shops are small private grocery stores.

3 Tehsils are small regional administration units.

## References


Aaron, Henry J. and George M. Von Furstenberg. 1971. 'The Inefficiency of Transfers in Kind: The Case of Housing Assistance.' *Western Economic Journal* 9: 184–91.

Angelucci, M. and G. De Giorgi. 2009. 'Indirect Effects of an Aid Program: How Do Cash Transfers Affect Non-Eligibles' Consumption?.' *American Economic Review* 99 (1): 486–508.

Attanasio, O., E. Fitzsimons, A. Gomez, D. Lopez, C. Meghir and A. Mesnard. 2006. *Child Education and Work Choices in the Presence of a Conditional Cash Transfer Programme in Rural Colombia*. London: Institute for Fiscal Studies.

Baird, Sarah, Craig McIntosh and Berk Ozler. 2009. *Designing Cost-Effective Cash Transfer Programs to Boost Schooling among Young Women in Sub-Saharan Africa*. World Bank Policy Research Working Paper No. 5090.

Banerjee, Abhijit V. and Ester Duflo. 2011. 'Poor Economics: A Radical Rethinking of the Way to Fight Global Poverty.' *Population and Development Review* 37: 796–97. doi:10.1111/j.1728-4457.2011.00462.x.

Barrera-Osorio, Felipe, Marianne Bertrand, Leigh Linden and Francisco Perez Calle. 2008. *Conditional Cash Transfers in Education: Design Features, Peer and Sibling Effects – Evidence from a Randomized Experiment in Colombia*. NBER Working Paper, W13890.

Behrman, Jere R., Piyali Sengupta and Petra Todd. 2005. 'Progressing through PROGRESA: An Impact Assessment of a School Subsidy Experiment in Rural Mexico.' *Economic Development and Cultural Change* 54 (1): 237–75.

Besley, Timothy and Coate Stephen. 1991. 'Public Provision of Private Goods and Redistribution of Income.' *The American Economic Review* 81: 979–84.

Behrman, Jere R. and Hoddinott, John. 2001. *'An evaluation of the impact of PROGRESA on pre-school child height,' FCND briefs 104*. Washington, DC: International Food Policy Research Institute (IFPRI).

Blackorboy, Charles and David Donaldson. 1998. 'Cash versus Kind, Self-Selection and Efficient Transfers.' *American Economic Review* 78: 691–700.

Business Standard. 2013. *DBT Review Likely Today*, 29 April.

Coady, D. 2000. *The Application of Social Cost-Benefit Analysis to the Evaluation of the Human Capital Impacts of PROGRESA*. Washington, DC: International Food Policy Research Institute.

Cremer, Helmuth and Gahvari Firouz. 1995. 'In-Kind Transfers, Self-Selection and Optimal Tax Policy.' *European Economic Review* 41 (1): 97–114.

Currie, J. and F. Gahvari. 2007. *Transfers in Cash and in Kind: Theory Meets the Data* (No. w13557). Cambridge, MA: National Bureau of Economic Research.

De La O, Ana Lorena. 2006. *Do Poverty Relief Funds Affect Electoral Behavior? Evidence from a Randomized Experiment in Mexico*. New Haven, CT: Yale University.

Del Ninno, Carlo, Paul A. Dorosh. 2003. 'Impact of In-Kind Transfers on Household Food Comsumption: Evidence from Targeted Food Programs in Bangladesh.' *The Journal of Development Studies* 40 (1): 48–71.

Dhoot and Goswami. 2013. 'Direct Benefit Transfer Plan Runs into Red Tape.' *The Economic Times*, April 10.

Dreze, Jean. 2011. 'The Cash Mantra.' *The Indian Express*, May 11.

Dreze, Jean and Reetika Khera. 2010. 'The BPL Census and a Possible Alternative.' *Economic & Political Weekly* 45 (9), February 27.

Easterly, William. 2006. *The White Man's Burden: Why the West's Efforts to Aid the Rest Have Done So Much Ill and So Little Good*. New Delhi: Penguin Group.

Filmer, Deon and Norbert Schady. 2009. Who Benefits? Scholarships, School Enrollment and Work of Recipients and Their Siblings. Washington, DC: Unpublished manuscript, World Bank.

Fiszbein, A., Schady, N. R; Ferreira, F. H. G., Grosh, M., Keleher, N. Olinto and P. Skoufias, E. 2009. *Conditional Cash Transfers: Reducing Present and Future Poverty*. Washington, DC: World Bank Policy Research Report. https://openknowledge.worldbank.org/handle/10986/2597 License: CC BY 3.0 IGO.

Gahvari, Firouz and Mattos Enlinson. 2007. 'Conditional Cash Transfers, Public Provision of Private Goods, and Income Distribution.' *American Economic Association* 97 (1): 491–502.

Gahvari, Firouz. 1995. 'In-Kind Versus Cash Transfers in Presence of Distortionary Taxes.' *Journal of Economic Enquiry* 33 (1): 45.

Gangopadhyay, Shubhashis, Robert Lensink and Bhupesh Yadav. 2012. *Cash or Food Security through the Public Distribution System? Evidence from a Randomized Controlled Trial in Delhi, India.* Accessed October 1, 2012. http://ssrn.com/abstract=2186408 or http://dx.doi.org/10.2139/ssrn.218640.

Ghatak, M., C. Kumar and S. Mitra. 2013. *Cash versus Kind: Understanding the Preferences of the Bicycle-Programme Beneficiaries in Bihar.* International Growth Centre. Working Paper July 2013. http://www.theigc.org/wp-content/uploads/2014/09/Ghatak-Et-Al-2013-Working-Paper.pdf.

Glewwe, P. and P. Olinto. 2004. *Evaluating the Impact of Conditional Cash Transfers on Schooling: An Experimental Analysis of Honduras' PRAF Program.* Minneapolis, MN: Unpublished manuscript, University of Minnesota.

Guesnerie Roger and Kevin Roberts. 1984. 'Effective Policy Tools and Quantity Controls.' *Econometrica* 52 (1): 59–86.

Himanshu and A. Sen. 2013. 'In-Kind Food Transfers – II: Impact on Nutrition and Implications for Food Security and Its Costs.' *Economic and Political Weekly* 48 (47): 60–73.

J-Pal. 2011. *Assessing the Scope for Cash Transfers in Lieu of the TPDS in Rural and Urban Bihar: Pre Pilot Study Summary Report.* South Asia: J-Pal.

Jacoby, H. G. 2002. 'Is There an Intrahousehold 'Flypaper Effect'? Evidence from a School Feeding Programme.' *The Economic Journal* 112 (476): 196–221.

Jha, S., A. Kotwal and B. Ramaswami. 2013. *Safety Nets and Food Programmes in Asia: A Comparative Perspective.* Working Paper Series 371. Manila: Asian Development Bank. http://www.adb.org/sites/default/files/publication/30387/ewp-371.pdf.

Jha, S. and B. Ramaswami. 2013. *How Can Food Subsidies Work Better? Answers from India and the Philippines.* Working Paper Series 221. Manila: Asian Development Bank. http://www.adb.org/sites/default/files/publication/28425/economics-wp221.pdf.

Jha, S. and P. V Srinivasan. 2004. *Achieving Food Security in a Cost Effective Way: Implications of Domestic Deregulation and Reform Under Liberalized Trade.* IFPRI working paper.

Khera, R. 2011a. 'India's Public Distribution System: Utilisation and Impact.' *Journal of Development Studies*: 1–23.

——— 2011b. 'Trends in Diversion of Grain from Public Distribution System.' *Economic and Political Weekly* 46 (21), May.

——— 2011c. 'The UID Projects and Welfare Schemes.' *Economic and Political Weekly* 46 (9), February.

——— 2014. 'Cash vs. In-Kind Transfer: Indian Data Meets Theory.' *Food Policy* 46: 116–28.

Kotwal, A., M. Murugkar and B. Ramaswami. 2011, 'PDS Forever?.' *Economic and Political Weekly* 46 (21).

Lampman, R. J. and T. M. Smeeding. 1983. 'Inter-Family Transfers as Alternatives to Government Transfers to Persons.' *Review of Income and Wealth* 29: 45–66. doi:10.1111/j.1475-4991.1983.tb00631.x.

Lengeler, C. 2004. 'Insecticide-Treated Bed Nets and Curtains for Preventing Malaria.' *Cochrane Database of Systematic Reviews* 2, Art. No. CD000363.

Maluccio, John A. and Rafael Flores. 2005. *Impact Evaluation of a Conditional Cash Transfer Program: The Nicaraguan Red de Protección Social.* Research Report 141. Washington, DC: International Food Policy Research Institute.

Mehta, A. and S. Jha. 2012. 'Corruption, Food Subsidies, and Opacity: Evidence from the Philippines.' *Economic Letters* 117: 708–11.

Munro, Alistiar. 1992. 'Self-Selection and Optimal In-Kind Transfers.' *The Economic Journal* 102 (414): 1184–196.

National Institute of Public Finance and Policy. 2012. *A Cost-Benefit Analysis of Aadhaar.* New Delhi: NIPFP Macrofinance. http://planningcommission.nic.in/reports/genrep/rep_uid_cba_paper.pdf.

Nichols, A. L and R. J. Zeckhauser. 1982. 'Targeting Transfers on Restriction on Recipients.' *The American Economic Review* 72 (2): 372–77.

Olinto, Pedra and Hiroki Uematsu. 2013. *The State of the Poor: Where Are the Poor and Where Are They Poorest?.* Washington, DC: World Bank.

Pascaline, Dupas. 2013. *Short-Run Subsidies and Long-Run Adoption of New Health Products: Evidence from a Field Experiment.* Working Paper. Stanford, CA: Stanford University.

Patnaik, Ila. 2012. 'Identify This.' *The Indian Express,* December 3. http://www.indianexpress.com/news/identify-this/1039542/.

Program Evaluation Organisation. 2005. *Performance Evaluation of Targeted Public Distribution System (TPDS) Planning Commission.* http://planningcommission.nic.in/reports/peoreport/peo/peo_tpds.pdf.

Planning Commission. 2013. *Direct Benefit Transfer on Central Plan Scheme Monitoring System.* Presentation made during conference of district collectors on DBT – 29th April.

PNAD. 2004. *National Survey by Household Sample Survey—2004.* Brazilian Institute of Geography and Statistics. http://www.ibge.gov.br/home/estatistica/populacao/trabalhoerendimento/pnad2004/.

Ramaswamy, Bharat. 2007. 'Food Coupons Are Better Alternatives.' *The Financial Express,* July 30.

Ressler, Phyllis. 2008. *The Social Impact of Cash Transfers*. Regional Network on AIDS, Livelihoods and Food Security, International Food Policy Research Institute.

Schultz, T. Paul. 2004. 'School Subsidies for the Poor: Evaluating the Mexican PROGRESA Poverty Program.' *Journal of Development Economics* 74 (1): 199–250.

Sen, Raj Kumar and Ratan Lal Basu, eds. 2006. *Economics in Arthasastra*. New Delhi: Deep and Deep Publications.

Singh, Mahim Pratap. 2012. 'Let Everyone Suffer Cash Transfer, Say Kotkasim Beneficiaries.' *The Hindu*, December 15.

Slesnick, Daniel T. 1996. 'Consumption and Poverty: How Effective Are In-Kind Transfers?.' *Economic Journal* 106 (439): 1527–545.

Soares Veras, Fábio, Rafael Perez Ribas and Rafael Guerreiro Osório. 2007. 'Evaluating the Impact of Brazil's Bolsa Família: Cash Transfer Programmes in Comparative Perspective.' *IPC Evaluation Note*, Number 1 December 2007.

8

# India's Education Challenges

## Expenditure Effectiveness Issues

**Anu Rammohan and Itismita Mohanty**

## Introduction and overview

Human capital investments through education are widely recognized as being important for economic growth. This phenomenon has led governments in many developing countries to make significant investments in the education sector. Despite this, public expenditure in education remains low in countries such as India, the country which accounts for the largest number of children aged below 15 years. Estimates from the World Bank show that over the last two decades, total public expenditure on education has stagnated in India, and remains below 4 per cent of gross domestic product (GDP). This figure has only increased marginally from 2.8 per cent in 1997 to 3 per cent in 2010, and has declined as percentage of total government expenditure from 12.5 per cent in 1998 to 10.5 per cent in 2010 (World Bank, 2012).

The Indian economy has experienced high levels of economic growth over this period, with the average rate of annual GDP growth in the decade to 2010 slightly above 7 per cent, compared to an annual rate of 4.5 per cent in the previous four decades 1960–2000 (Cagliarini and Baker, 2010). Evidence from Alkire and Santos' (2010) recently developed Multidimensional Poverty Index (MPI) shows that India performs poorly for the education indicators in comparison to other countries where data are available. For example, India is ranked 68th out of 104 countries with data for the indicator 'years of schooling' (which measures if no household member has completed five years of schooling) and is ranked 57th out of 85 countries with data for school enrolment (measured as a school-aged child being out of school in years 1–8). Indeed on July 2013, the Supreme Court of India provided a damning indictment of the education system in India by stating that although literacy rates had increased over the years, the education system in the country has failed to achieve its objective and that it has to be reformed immediately (NDTV, 2013).

India's education sector is at a crossroads. On the one hand, it has a large number of highly skilled individuals. For example, around 1.5 million engineers are trained in India each year, which is more than that of the United States and China combined. Similarly, India controls a large share of the generic drugs markets, with Indian drug makers accounting for 40 per cent of US generic drug imports, based on volume, and 39 per cent of total generic drug approvals by the agency. However, estimates show that a third to a fifth of these newly trained engineers will either remain unemployed or underemployed, due to a decline in employment in the two sectors that traditionally employed them – the information technology and manufacturing sectors (Chaturvedi and Sachitanand, 2013).

Despite these advances in the high-tech sector, India still accounts for just under half of the world's illiterate population (46 per cent), which results in a skewed education system, with public funding of education appearing to largely benefit the richer groups. In particular, the neglect of elementary education has resulted in high levels of out-of-school children, low literacy and numeracy skills.

The aim of this chapter is to explore trends in India's public educational expenditure, its effectiveness and implications. We begin by presenting a snapshot of various public initiatives that were adopted to encourage education in India. Next, using aggregate data, we compare educational attainment in India with the other countries, and we discuss the literacy and numeracy performance of children in different Indian states. However, decisions to educate a child are ultimately made at the household level. Therefore, we discuss the empirical literature on the socio-economic and demographic factors that influence household level decisions on education in India. Finally, we discuss key challenges facing India's education sector.

In the following section, we outline policies that have been initiated by the successive governments to address these shortcomings.

## *Education sector policies in India and their fiscal implications*

The earliest initiatives to improve education in India were undertaken in the post-independence period, with the setting up of the University Education Commission (1948–1949) and the Secondary Education Commission (1952–1953). Irrespective of the fact that several committees and commissions were set up from time to time, the education policy was primarily shaped by the Kothari Commission (1964–1966) and the National Education Policy (1968) (De and Endow, 2008), where the Government of India (GOI) committed to several principles aimed at improving the quality and access to education. These principles included: free and compulsory education, investing in improving the remuneration and quality of teachers, development of regional languages, and addressing regional imbalances in access to educational facilities. All these different committees from time to time had come up with several important recommendations about the structure and the priorities of the education system. Nevertheless, their recommendations regarding the level of education finance were similar. In 1966, the Kothari Commission had recommended an increase in public expenditure on education to reach 6 per cent of gross national product (GNP) by 1986. Subsequently, in 1996, the Saikia Committee's recommendations included making free and compulsory education a fundamental right, with a reiteration for the need for an expenditure of 6 per cent of GNP on education with 50 per cent of it earmarked for primary education (an additional finance of Rs. 400 billion in next five years). In 1999, the Expert Group headed by Tapas Majumdar, made estimates for additional fund requirements for Universal Elementary Education (UEE) – it was in the range of Rs. 1,370 billion over the following ten years (De and Endow, 2008; GOI, 1998). National Common Minimum Programme and CABE Committee also had similar recommendations. However, the actual expenditures in the education sector have fallen far short of these targets (De and Endow, 2008). These recommendations repeatedly emphasize the need for higher investment in education and the importance of different levels of government in its financing.

The Indian Parliament has recently enacted a legislation making free and compulsory education a right of every child in the age group 6–14 years, which has come into force from 1 April 2010. In 2009, the Government of India launched the *Rashtriya Madhyamik Shiksha Abhiyan* (RMSA), with the aim of universalising secondary education. In order to achieve this by 2017, the Working Group on Secondary Education has estimated that 19,946 additional new secondary schools will be required.

An examination of the trends and composition of aggregate public expenditure on education in India, show that although initially education was the primary responsibility of the states, after 1976 it gradually became the joint responsibility of both the central and the state governments. The states still share a greater responsibility for the education expenditure, while their share in the total has reportedly been declining after 2000–2001 (from 87.7 per cent in 2000–2001 to 75.7 per cent in 2005–2006) (budget estimate), and centre's share has increased (from 12.3 to 24 per cent during the same period) (De and Endow, 2008). Transfers mandated by the Finance Commission from the central government to the states to meet any shortfall in state resources for educational expenditures. Following the constitutional amendment of 1993, Panchayat Raj institutions – rural and urban bodies of local self-government also become responsible for elementary education. Though they were funded mostly through the state government, they also spend resources raised at their level.

This system of multi-level funding has consequently resulted in several channels of transfer of funds, greatly complicating the task of monitoring and evaluation of education spending. So, the funds are allocated not only through the Department of Education but through other departments such as ministries/departments of Women and Child Welfare, Ministry of Tribal Affairs, Ministry of Social Justice and Empowerment. In the Department of Education itself, the funding is further allocated under different heads such as general education and technical education.

Further, there is an important distinction between plan and non-plan expenditure in India, while the plan expenditure broadly indicates the direction of changes in the education sector, the non-plan expenditure is the expenditure on operating and maintaining education infrastructure. At the end of the five-year plan period, the recurring part of different programmes or schemes that were introduced through the planning process and part of the plan expenditure become part of non-plan expenditure. Plan expenditure has increased slowly over the period 1996–1997 to 2000–2001, but since then has been increasing rapidly due to the introduction of different schemes in the elementary education sector. Generally, education expenditure as a percentage of GDP in India has been rising since 1951–1952 as shown in Figure 8.1.

In 1951–1952, the education expenditure in India accounted for 0.64 per cent of GDP and 7.92 per cent of total expenditure. By 1989–1990, this had increased to 3.93 per cent of GDP and 13.64 per cent of total expenditure. As shown in Figure 8.1, after 1989–1990 there have been some declines in the education expenditure to GDP ratio. In particular, after increasing rapidly over the period 1998–1999, education expenditure as a proportion of GDP fell sharply in 2000–2001. Since 2004–2005, the trend has generally been positive, with education expenditure accounting for 4.17 per cent of the GDP in 2011–2012.

However, this broad picture does not capture the differential levels of investment made at the state level. In Figure 8.2, we present the state-level share of GDP allocated to education in 2011–2013.

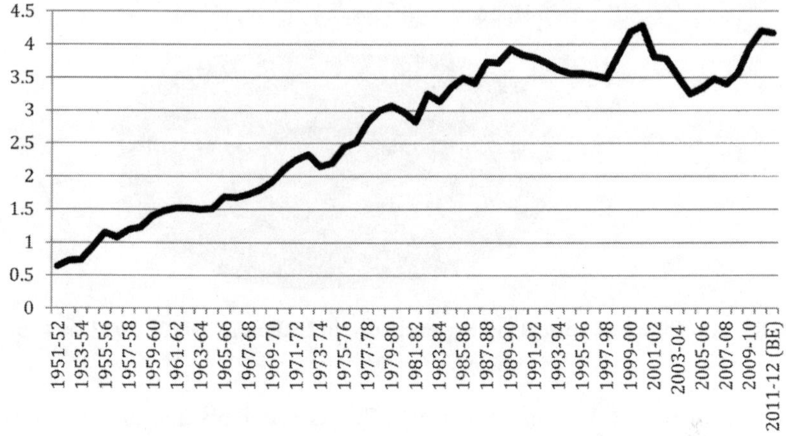


**FIGURE 8.1 Percentage of education expenditure to GDP in India.**

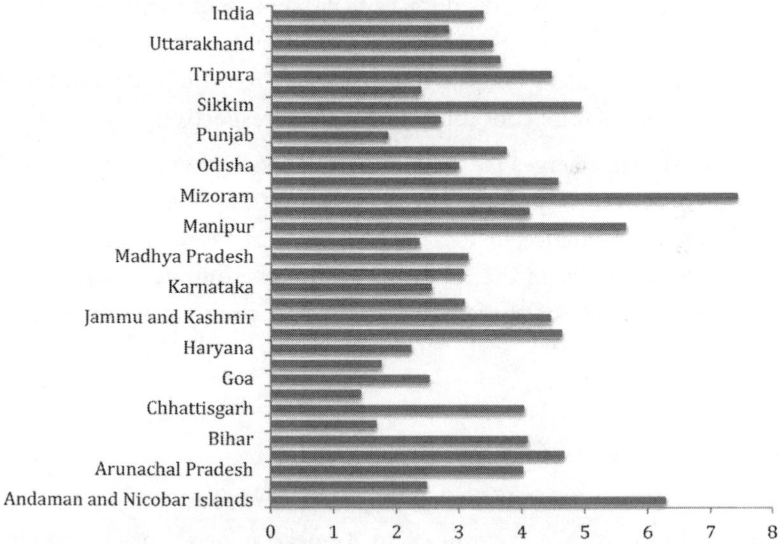


**FIGURE 8.2 Percentage of state education budget to GDP (2011–2012).**

We observe that with the exception of the states of Punjab, Gujarat, Chandigarh and Delhi, across all other Indian states education expenditure as a percentage of GDP was above 2 per cent. Notably, the smaller North-eastern states of Mizoram, Andaman and Nicobar Island, Manipur and Sikkim accounted for the highest investment in education as a proportion of GDP, spending over

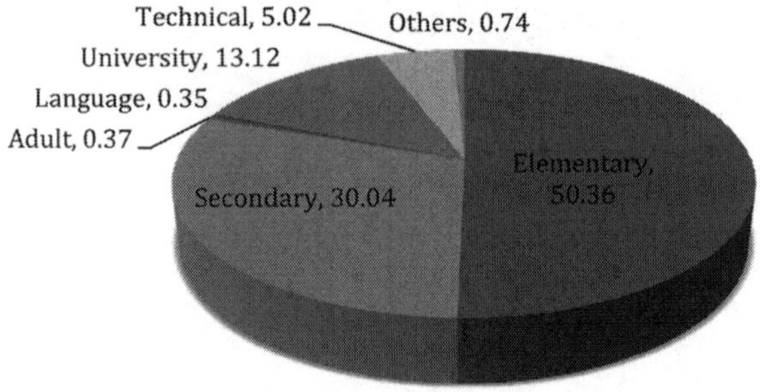


**FIGURE 8.3 Share of education expenditure in Indian in 2012–2013 by type.**

5 per cent of their GDP on education. The national average of the education expenditure to GDP ratio was 3.36 per cent in 2011–2013.

Next in Figure 8.3, we provide figures on the share of education expenditure accruing to different types of education sectors by both the central government and the states in 2012–2013. We observe that over half of the Indian education expenditure (50.36 per cent) is allocated to elementary education. This is followed by the secondary and the university sectors which account for 30.04 and 13.12 per cent of total education expenditure, respectively.

The picture that emerges is one of differing levels of expenditure by states and by type of activity. The question then arises as to what outcomes have been achieved as a consequence of these investments in the education sector. To address these questions, in the following section we outline India's education achievements in terms of student outcomes and compare them to similarly placed countries.

## Education performance

In Table 8.1, we compare India's adult literacy rates with the other Brazil, Russia, India and China (BRIC) countries and its nearest neighbors in South Asia (Pakistan, Sri Lanka and Bangladesh). We observe that in terms of secondary school participation and youth literacy rates, India performs poorly against the BRIC countries (Brazil, Russia, China and South Africa), and its neighbor Sri Lanka. Adult literacy rates in India have increased dramatically in recent years. Over the decade 1985–1994, 48 per cent of the adult population aged over 15 years was literate, and by 2010, this figure had risen to 63 per cent of the adult population. Gender differences are also observed, and while the gender gap in adult literacy has

**TABLE 8.1 Adult literacy rates (15+ year olds)**

| | Total | | Male | | Female | |
|---|---|---|---|---|---|---|
| | **1985–1994** | **2005–2010** | **1985–1994** | **2005–2010** | **1985–1994** | **2005–2010** |
| Bangladesh | 35 | 57 | 44 | 61 | 26 | 52 |
| Brazil | – | 90 | – | 90 | – | 90 |
| China | 78 | 94 | 87 | 97 | 68 | 91 |
| India | 48 | 63 | 62 | 75 | 34 | 51 |
| Pakistan | – | 55 | – | 69 | – | 40 |
| Russian Federation | 98 | 100 | 99 | 100 | 97 | 99 |
| Sri Lanka | – | 91 | – | 93 | – | 90 |
| World | 76 | 84 | 82 | 89 | 69 | 80 |
| Developing countries | 67 | 80 | 76 | 86 | 58 | 74 |
| Sub-Saharan Africa | 53 | 63 | 64 | 71 | 43 | 54 |

*Source*: 2005–2010 data from the Education for All Global Monitoring Report, UNESCO (2012). World Bank (2012) for other years.

narrowed between 1994 and 2010, it is still the case that males have a 24 percent age point higher adult literacy rate compared with females. Overall adult literacy rates in India are similar to the levels observed in Sub-Saharan African countries.

A narrower focus on youth literacy figures also shows that India's performance is poor when compared to China. As Table 8.2 shows, over the period 2005–2010, youth literacy rates in India are 18 percentage points behind China, and 7 percentage points behind the developing countries' average. These figures reflect a significant improvement from 1985 to 1994, when the country was 32 percentage points behind China and 18 percentage points behind the developing countries average.

There has also been a slight narrowing of the gender gap in youth literacy rates, with female literacy rates increasing from 49 to 74 per cent over the period 1985–1994 to 2005–2010. However, the gender gap of 14 percentage points in 2005–2010 still remains unacceptably high. Nevertheless, in the recent decade India succeeds relatively well in terms of access to education such as primary school participation rates and the country has almost come

**TABLE 8.2 Youth literacy rates (15–24 years old)**

| | Total | | Male | | Female | |
|---|---|---|---|---|---|---|
| | 1985–1994 | 2005–2010 | 1985–1994 | 2005–2010 | 1985–1994 | 2005–2010 |
| Bangladesh | 45 | 77 | 52 | 75 | 38 | 78 |
| Brazil | – | 98 | – | 97 | – | 99 |
| China | 94 | 99 | 97 | 99 | 91 | 99 |
| India | 62 | 81 | 74 | 88 | 49 | 74 |
| Pakistan | – | 71 | – | 79 | – | 61 |
| Russian Federation | 100 | 100 | 100 | 100 | 100 | 100 |
| Sri Lanka | – | 98 | – | 98 | – | 99 |
| World | 83 | 90 | 88 | 92 | 79 | 87 |
| Developing countries | 80 | 88 | 85 | 91 | 75 | 85 |
| Sub-Saharan Africa | 66 | 72 | 73 | 76 | 59 | 67 |

*Source*: 2005–2010 data from the Education for All Global Monitoring Report, UNESCO (2012). World Bank (2012) for other years.

close to achieving the much targeted UEE goal. Further, the overall enrolment rates remain very high. Over 96 per cent of all rural children in the age group 6–14 years are enrolled in school for the fourth consecutive year in a row (Pratham, 2012, 2013). The proportion of children in this age group that are not currently enrolled is 3.3 per cent, down from 6.6 per cent in 2006. Girls in the age group of 11 to 14 years are often difficult to bring to school and keep in school, possibly because they perform household chores and contribute to the household production process, which increases their opportunity cost of schooling. However, the retention rates for girls in this age group, continue to increase between 2006 to 2012 (ASER, 2012)

It is noteworthy that substantial progress has been made in the schooling of girls, particularly in rural areas. The figure for out-of-school girls (aged 11–14 years) which was 10.3 per cent in 2006 halved to 5.2 per cent by 2011. In particular, many of the states that in 2006 had a high proportion (over 10 per cent) of 11–14-year-old girls out of school have made significant progress. In 2011, the states of Bihar (4.5 per cent), West Bengal (4.3 per cent) and Chhattisgarh (4.3 per cent) performed relatively well in terms of having a smaller proportion of out-of-school girls relative to the All-India average of 5.2 per cent. However, Uttar Pradesh, India's largest state has shown the least progress with this indicator, with 11.1 per cent girls in this age group out of school in 2006, and compared to 9.7 per cent in 2011.

In addition to female children, there is also evidence of social inequities in access to education and education outcomes on the basis of rural and urban region of residence and social caste structure. The dropout rates for schedule castes (SCs) and schedule tribes (STs) are much higher than the overall average: 27 per cent of all SC primary students dropped out in 2011. Correspondingly, 35.6 per cent of ST students dropped out in 2011.

With regards to secondary school participation and retention rates, there have been significant improvements over the last decade with the gross enrolment rate increasing from 39.4 per cent in 1999 to 63.2 per cent in 2010 (World Bank, 2013, http://data.worldbank.org/indicator/SE.SEC.NENR). However, despite this secondary school retention rates are very low. Additionally, there are serious concerns over the learning achievements of children at both primary and secondary levels. According to a recent survey by the NGO Pratham and reported in the 2012 *Annual Status of Education Report* (ASER), there is evidence of a worsening trend in students' basic reading levels, arithmetic levels and academic levels over the years. More than half of all children in Grade 5 are at least three grade levels behind where they should be. However, for all children in Grade 5, the major decline in reading levels (of 5 percentage points or more) between 2011 and 2012 is seen not just in the poor states of Bihar and Madhya Pradesh, but also in states such as Haryana, Maharashtra and Kerala, where enrolment figures are high. Even private schools in Maharashtra and Kerala, with a large proportion of aided schools, show a decline in reading ability for Grade 5. Likewise between 50 and 60 per cent of children in Grade 3 are at least two grade levels behind their standard (Pratham, 2012).

As with literacy rates, we observe that over a two-year period, there is a worsening trend in Grade 5 students' ability to basic arithmetic such as subtraction and division problem. According to figures from Pratham (2013), with the exception of the three southern states of Andhra Pradesh, Karnataka and Kerala, in nearly every major state there has been a fall in arithmetic learning outcomes, as measured by student ability to do basic subtraction and division. This study finds that in rural India as a whole, in 2010 about two thirds of all children in Grade 5 could not do simple division, but by 2012 this figure had worsened with close to three fourths of all children being unable to do basic arithmetic. This study found that in the states of Himachal Pradesh, Punjab, Haryana, Chhattisgarh, Madhya Pradesh, Gujarat and Maharashtra, the cohort in Grade 5 in 2012 seems to be substantially weaker than the cohort in Grade 5 in 2011. In the southern states, however, the situation is unchanged from 2011 except in the case of Kerala where there is a significant improvement.

Student performance at the secondary school level is similarly found to be poor by international standards. For example, according to figures from The Programme for International Student Assessment (PISA), in 2009, on average 15-year-old students in India perform four years behind the average for the Organization for Economic Cooperation and Development (OECD) countries. In a group of 70 countries, the performance of Indian students aged 15 years was second last with only Kyrgyz Republic being worse than India. Furthermore, a mathematics test of Grade 9 students in the states of Orissa and Rajasthan using questions from the *Trends in International Mathematics and Science Survey* (TIMSS) assessment placed these states 43rd and 47th, respectively, out of 49 countries (GOI, IRR, 2012).

However, progress has been made with gross enrolment ratio (GER) – a measure of the ratio of enrolled students to the total number of people in an eligible age group. Here we observe a doubling of GER over the decade 1999 to 2011, with GER amongst youth aged 18–24 years improving from 9.4 per cent in 1999 to 17.9 per cent in 2011. Despite this, India remains 4.3 percentage points behind the developing countries average and 8 percentage points behind China. Note that in 1999, China was 2.7 percentage points behind India, so India's progress in tertiary education albeit showing some improvement has fallen behind other countries. At 63 per cent, India has a much lower GER at the secondary education stage (Class IX–X) as compared to emerging market economies such as China, Thailand, Brazil and Indonesia.

## Empirical evidence

Decisions on educational investment are typically done at the household level taking into account the private costs and benefits from educating the child, but the question then arises as to whether there is a role for the government to play. Moreover, in the presence of imperfect capital and labour markets, poor households facing financial constraints cannot typically borrow to invest in the education of their children. Under such circumstances, households with more than one child in the schooling-going age group have to make decisions on the optimum allocation of scarce educational resources amongst their children. Hence, in addition to economic factors, a range of child-specific characteristics such as the child's gender, birth order, and the number and sex composition of their siblings, also become important considerations in schooling decisions. These factors are also likely to be exacerbated by rural residence, due to the informal nature of the production process and the possibility of combining schooling with work.

Indeed, this is consistent with the empirical literature which finds evidence of wide heterogeneity across India, with large gaps in the schooling enrolment for children and completed years of schooling for adults between males and females, rural–urban residents and across different states and districts. For example, previous studies from India have consistently found that girls receive lower schooling than boys (see Kingdon, 2002; Kingdon, 2007; Kingdon and Unni, 2001; Sundaram and Vanneman, 2008; Mohanty and Rammohan, 2015). These studies have also pointed to regional variations, with the gender differentials in education greater in the North-western states relative to the South-western states.

The idea is that since decisions on schooling are made at the household level, it is important to consider the household-level constraints faced by resource poor households which may lead to the allocation of scarce education resources being directed towards preferred children, which may be based on factors such as the child's gender and birth order.

Poverty which is widespread and concentrated in India also puts pressure on household resources. In 2010, 32.7 per cent of the Indian population was below the international poverty line of US$1.25 per day (PPP) while 68.7 per cent lived on less than US$2 per day (World Bank, 2013). Therefore, in the absence of well-developed financial and insurance markets, resource-constrained households may rely on children's labour income to supplement their household income. Under such circumstances, despite returns to secondary and higher secondary levels of education being significantly higher than primary and middle levels of education, parents may be unable to access the resources required to educate their children (Agarwal, 2011; Riboud, Savchenko and Tan, 2006; Kingdon and Unni, 2001; Kingdon, 1998). A recent study by Kharbanda (2012) using the 2004–2005 *National Sample Survey* data shows that the returns to education increases at a higher rate after the first seven years of schooling. This study finds that children from households with credit constraints drop out during these first five years and those without any credit constraints continue until tertiary level (which is shown by the positive trend in the estimates from Grades 5 to 12).

Therefore, public intervention in schooling and higher education may be justified on the grounds that the expected public return to schooling investments far outweigh the private return to households, and therefore households may underinvest in child education relative to the social optimum (see Orazem and King, 2008). Public investments in education may take the form of subsidies (where the government may meet some or all of the education costs), vouchers or income transfers (which may be conditional or non-conditional).

## Role of supply side factors

On the other hand, it is quite likely that the secondary school enrolment rates are low owing to the supply side constraints, such as poor infrastructure or lack of access to secondary schools. The Seventh All India Education Survey (NCERT, 2006) found that in 2002, the number of secondary to primary school ratio is 1:5 and the provisional statistics from Eighth All India Education Survey (NCERT, 2013) reveals that between 2002 and 2009, the secondary school growth rate was only 28.9 per cent.

Given the lack of correlation between increased expenditure and learning outcomes within Indian states, the issue of inefficient allocation of resources becomes important, in particular the role of school quality. In a recent study, Ranjan and Prakash (2012) have used data from the District Information System for Education (DISE) to identify some of the school-level quality indicators, which may be impacting on poor schooling outcomes. These include critical factors such as the pupil–teacher ratio, student–classroom ratio, the proportion of schools with toilets for girls, the percentage of schools with drinking water facility and the proportion of classrooms that are in a good condition. Using ASER data for the 20 most populous states, they found pupil–teacher ratio has been on decline since 2003–2004, with the highest being 53 in 2009–2010 with a median of 26. Although there is quite a bit of variation across the Indian states, yet based on Right to Education (RTE) norms,[1] this indicator is showing some improvement. For example, in 2010 nearly 39 per cent of the schools across the country were meeting this norm, and since then this figure has gone up to nearly 43 per cent in 2012 (Pratham, 2012). In 2010, the state of Bihar was the poorest performer both in terms of the pupil–teacher ratio (53) and student–classroom ratio (exceeding 80) (Ranjan and Prakash, 2012).

With regards to the learning outcomes of students, there is hardly any systematic emphasis through policies on student performance outcomes.

Programmes such as RTE, *Sarva Shiksha Abhiyan* (SSA) and RMSA are generally input-focussed rather than being output based. Often, it is found that teachers are not properly trained to handle such systems: interpret the assessments and map student outcomes. Further, there is little uniformity in curricula and standards across states and there is no national-level assessment exists to evaluate the performance in secondary education.

A closer look at the state of schooling infrastructure reveals in 2012, 73 per cent of the ASER sampled schools had drinking water available. Just fewer than 17 per cent of the schools did not have drinking water facility at all and the remaining had a water facility available though not usable. This has remained almost stable since 2010. Whereas in the North-eastern states, the proportion of schools with no water provision varied from 23.8 per cent in Assam to 87.3 per cent in Manipur in 2011 (Pratham, 2012). Kerala has the best record with nearly 94 per cent of schools with a usable drinking water facility.

The PROBE report recognized the availability of a separate girls' toilet is an important determinant of female schooling in India (Ranjan and Prakash, 2012; PROBE, 1999). However, the All-India proportion of schools with working toilets has increased marginally from 47.2 per cent in 2010 to 56.5 per cent in 2012. Approximately 80 per cent of the ASER sampled schools in 2012 had separate provision for girls' toilet. There is significant interstate variation and Bihar is the worst performer in 2010.

## Conclusion

Although education has been recognized as an important component of economic growth, the education outcomes of Indian children continues to lag in basic literacy and numeracy skills, with wide heterogeneity observed across different states.

Clearly, India's expenditure on social sectors such as education suffers from both inadequate allocation of budgetary resources and ineffective implementation on the ground. This chapter has identified four critical issues with regards to child education in India. First, public investment in elementary education remains low, and as a consequence, the proportion of out-of-school and illiterate children is high. Therefore, India compares poorly to other BRIC countries in terms of secondary school participation and youth literacy rates. This is a concern as India accounts for the highest number of youth under 25 years of age, and for the Indian economy to remain competitive, it is imperative that this group receives good education. High levels of skills among this demographic group have the potential for huge dividends in terms of economic prosperity. Second gender gaps in education continue to persist, with retention rates among adolescent girls being a challenge. Although there have been improvements in this measure there continue to be huge challenges, in the larger Northern states. In particular, several studies have found that girls are disadvantaged in the intra-household allocation of resources, with resource constrained households more likely to invest in the schooling of their male children rather than females. Third, there are also wide social inequities with children from the socially disadvantaged groups (SC and ST) particularly disadvantaged, despite nearly seven decades of affirmative action. Finally, although enrollment numbers have improved, concerns remain about the learning outcomes of primary and secondary school educated children.

## Note

1 The Right of Children to Free and Compulsory Education Act, 2009 specifies a series of norms and standards for a school.

## References

Alkire, S. and M. E Santos. 2010. *Acute Multidimensional Poverty: A New Index for Developing Countries.* Oxford Poverty & Human Development Initiative (OPHI), Working Paper No. 38.

Agarwal, T. 2011. *Returns to Education in India: Some Recent Evidence.* Mumbai: Indira Gandhi Institute of Development Research, WP-2011-017, 2011.

Cagliarini, A and M. Baker. 2010. *Economic Change in India,* 19–24. Australia: Reserve Bank Bulletin.

Chaturvedi, A. and R. Sachitanand. 2013. 'A million engineers in India struggling to get placed in an extremely challenging market'. *Economic Times Bureau,* June 18. http://articles.economictimes.indiatimes.com/2013-06 18/news/40049243_1_engineers-iit-bombay-batch-size.

De, A. and T. Endow. 2008. *Public Expenditure on Education in India: Recent Trends and Outcomes.* India: Collaborative Research and Dissemination1 (CORD), WP08/18.

Government of India (1998) 'Report of the Group of Experts on the Financial Resource Requirements for Operationalizing the Proposed Constitutional Amendment Bill Making the Right to Free and Compulsory Education up to 14 years of age a Fundamental Right'. Tapas Majumdar Committee Report, Department of Education. New Delhi: Ministry of Human Resource Development, Government of India.

Kharbanda, Varun. 2012. *Returns to Education in India*. University of Iowa. http://tippie.uiowa.edu/economics/tow/papers/kharbanda-fall2012-revised.pdf.

Kingdon, G. 1998. 'Does the Labour Market Explain Lower Female Schooling in India?.' *Journal of Development Studies* 35: 39–65.

——— 2002. 'The Gender Gap in Educational Attainment in India: How Much Can Be Explained?.' *Journal of Development Studies* 39 (2): 25–53.

——— 2007. 'The Progress of School Education in India.' *Oxford Review of Economic Policy* 23 (2): 168–95.

Kingdon, G. and G. Unni. 2001. 'Education and Women's Labour Market Outcomes in India.' *Education Economics* 9 (2): 173–95.

Mohanty, I. and A. Rammohan. 2015. 'Child Schooling in India: The Role of Gender.' *Indian Growth and Development Review* 8 (1): 93–107.

N.C.E.R.T. 2006. *Seventh All India Education Survey:* 2002–03. New Delhi: National Council of Educational Research and Training. http://gov.ua.nic.in/NScheduleData/main3.aspx.

——— 2013, *Eighth All India Education Survey:* 2002–09. New Delhi: National Council of Educational Research and Training. http://gov.ua.nic.in/NScheduleData/main3.aspx.

NDTV. 2013. http://www.ndtv.com/article/india/india-s-education-system-failed-to-achieve-objective-needs-reform-supreme-court-388000.

Orazem, P and E. King. 2008. 'Schooling in Developing Countries: The Roles of Supply, Demand and Government Policy.' *Handbook of Development Economics* 4: 3476–559.

Pratham. 2012. *Annual Status of Education Report*. Pratham, New Delhi, January 2011.

——— 2013. *Annual Status of Education Report*. Pratham, New Delhi, February 2013.

PROBE Team. 1999. *Public Report on Basic Education in India*. New Delhi: Oxford University Press.

Ranjan, P and Prakas, N 2012 'Education Policies and Practices: What Have We Learnt and the Road Ahead for Bihar, *IZA* Discussion Paper No. 661, Institute for the Study of labour.

Riboud, M., Y. Savchenko and H. Tan. 2006. *The Knowledge Economy and Education and Training in South Asia: A Mapping Exercise of Available Survey Data*. Washington, DC: mimeo, World Bank.

Sundaram, A and R. Vanneman. 2008. 'Gender Differentials in Literacy in India: The Intriguing Relationship with Women's Labor Force Participation.' *World Development* 36 (1): 128–43.

UNESCO. 2012. *Education for All: Global Monitoring Report.* Accessed August 31. http://unesdoc.unesco.org/images/0021/002180/218003e.pdf.

World Bank. 2012. *World Development Indicators.* Washington, DC: World Bank.

——— 2013. *India–New Global Poverty Estimates.* Available at http://povertydata.worldbank.org/poverty/country/IND.

# List of Contributors

**Amitendu Palit** is a Senior Research Fellow and Research Lead (Trade and Economic Policy) at Institute of South Asian Studies, Singapore. He is an economist specializing in comparative economic studies, international trade and investment, political economy, and public policies.

**Anu Rammohan** is a Professor in the Economics Discipline at the University of Western Australia, Australia. Her research has focused on intra-household distribution of health and education in developing countries, and the labour force participation decisions of Australian mothers.

**Charan Singh** is Reserve Bank of India Chair Professor at IIM Bangalore, India. He has worked as Senior Economist at the IEO of the IMF and Director of Research at the Reserve Bank of India.

**Itismita Mohanty** is a Research Fellow at Centre for Research and Action in Public Health, University of Canberra, Australia. She has extensive experience in research on child health, education, poverty and inequality in developing countries and child social exclusion and health in Australia. Her research focuses on applied microeconomic research involving quantitative modelling of economic, social and health related issues using applied data analysis, microsimulation modelling, econometric analysis and policy evaluation methods.

**N. R. Bhanumurthy** is a Professor at the National Institute of Public Finance and Policy, New Delhi, India. He has worked as a Macroeconomist at UNESCAP, Bangkok, Thailand and UNDP Regional Centre for Asia-Pacific region, Colombo, Sri Lanka.

**Raghbendra Jha** is Head, Arndt-Corden Department of Economics, Professor of Economics and Executive Director Australia South Asia Research Centre at the Australian National University, Australia.

**Rajesh Chakrabarti** is Executive Vice President, Research and Policy at Wadhwani Foundation, New Delhi, India. He has been a faculty at the Indian School of Business (ISB), Georgia Tech, Atlanta, GA, USA and University of Alberta, Canada, and also served as the founding Executive Director of the Bharti Institute of Public Policy at ISB.

**Ruth Kattumuri** is Co-Director of the India Observatory at the London School of Economics (LSE), London, UK. Her research interests are in population and development issues including growth, inclusion and climate change policy.

**S. Narayan** is Head of Research and Visiting Senior Research Fellow at Institute of South Asian Studies, National University of Singapore, Singapore. He had a long and fruitful carrier in the Indian Administrative Service and was Economic Adviser to the Prime Minister of India from 2003 to 2004.

**Supriyo De** is a Senior Economist with the Development Economics Vice-Presidency of the World Bank, Washington, DC, USA. Prior to this, he was an Officer on Special Duty to the Chief Economic Adviser, Ministry of Finance, India. He belongs to the Indian Revenue Service.

# Index


Aadhaar card, 194, 195, 200
above-poverty-line (APL), 114, 132, 146
acyclical, 8
Ad valorem taxes, 53
administered pricing mechanism (APM), 92–94
adult literacy rate, 216–217
Antodaya Anna Yojana (AAY), 114, 124, 126, 146
auction of telecom spectrum, 25

backward areas, 19, 29
balance of payments (BoP) crisis, 1–3, 11, 17, 19, 31
Bank of England, 157, 160, 163
below-poverty-line (BPL), 114, 124, 128, 132, 146, 147, 200
Bolsa Família, 122, 188, 191, 192
Budget, 4, 5, 9–11, 14, 20, 22, 24–30, 33, 50, 62, 77–79, 87, 89–95, 100, 101, 103, 105–107, 113–115, 130, 132, 133, 168, 170, 177, 178, 186, 188, 189, 213–215, 223
business cycle, 7, 8, 24
calorie intake, 117, 118, 192, 199
capital expenditure, 3, 4, 15, 18, 29, 75, 87, 90, 100, 122
capital gain (or loss), 11, 12
capital goods, 13, 21, 53, 54
capital receipt, 3, 4, 62
capital subsidies, 107, 108
cascading effect, 13, 53
Central Sales Tax (CST), 53, 55, 59, 60
Central Value Added Tax (CENVAT), 20, 28, 29, 53–55, 58
Centrally Sponsored Schemes (CSS), 11, 36, 37, 63, 76–79, 83, 135
child labor, 189–192
Coal India Limited, 100
Committee on the Global Financial System, 162
Committee to Review National Small Savings Fund, 181
Concurrent List, 36, 76
Conditional Cash Transfer (CCT), 125, 183, 185, 186, 188–191, 200
consumer subsidies, 91, 114
corporate income tax, 11, 13, 18–19, 24, 26
Corruption, 130, 182, 194, 202
cost of compliance, 55
cost plus pricing, 91, 92
counter-cyclical, 7, 8, 24
counter-cyclical measures, 3, 31
crowding out, 2, 7
current account balance (CAB), 5, 6
current account deficit (CAD), 6, 27, 108
customs duty, 10, 11, 13, 20, 28, 29, 53, 54, 60, 91, 96, 97
cyclical component, 7–8, 18, 25
cyclical stance, 7, 24

debt management, 155–177
Debt Management Office (DMO), 155–177
debt/GDP ratios, 12, 21, 26, 44, 155, 173, 214, 216
deductions, 19, 28, 29, 55, 104
defence expenditures, 17, 26
deficit, 1, 2, 4–6, 11, 15, 16, 21–31, 33, 44, 47–49, 52, 54, 55, 60, 82, 87–93, 101, 103, 108, 115, 141, 152, 161, 172, 173, 176, 177
Department of Education, 214
depreciation, 1, 7, 13, 29, 100, 105–107
destination-based tax, 53, 56
devaluation of currency, 7
diesel subsidy, 27, 30, 32, 90
Direct Benefits Transfer (DBT), 134, 135, 182–205
direct cash transfers, 144, 183, 184
Direct Tax Code, 26, 29
Direct taxes, 2, 11–14, 19, 21, 26, 30, 56, 59
disinvestment, 1, 3
divisible pool, 10, 79, 80
domestic debt, 164–165

economic growth, 12, 35, 44, 54, 82, 87, 141, 142, 147, 177, 211, 223
effective tax rates, 8, 13
Electricity Act, 2003, 104, 149
eminent domain, 140–142, 144
exchange rate, 7, 23, 160
exchange rate depreciation, 1
excise tax, 53, 57
Exemptions, 14, 19, 26, 28, 55, 58, 60
expenditure policy, 1
Export Processing Zone (EPZ), 140
export promotion, 15, 19–20
exports, 5–7, 15, 19, 23, 24, 31, 53, 59, 114, 133, 141, 152,

federal transfers, 63, 64, 68, 75, 83
Federalism, 10, 35–83
Fertilizer subsidies, 87, 114
Finance Act, 9, 26
Finance Bill, 9
Finance Commission (FC), 9–11, 24–26, 30, 32, 37, 47–69, 72, 74, 75, 78–80, 83, 114, 115, 135, 168–170, 214
financial inclusion, 3, 29, 32, 194
fiscal consolidation, 2, 3, 19–32, 115, 141, 149, 172
fiscal discipline, 2, 11, 21–23, 30, 69, 139, 179
Fiscal federalism, 35–83
Fiscal Responsibility and Budget Management Act (FRBMA), 11, 22, 25–26, 30, 89, 114, 141, 168
fiscal sustainability, 4
fiscal transfer, 32, 44, 68, 69, 75
fixed exchange rates, 7
**Foreign borrowing**, 5–7, 15
Foreign Direct Investment (FDI), 6, 43, 44–46
foreign exchange reserves, 1, 5–7, 24, 27
**Foreign exchange reserves**, 7
freight equalization subsidy, 100
fringe benefit tax (FBT), 20
fuel pricing, 87

Gadgil-Mukherjee formula, 69, 70, 72
Gini coefficient, 192
global financial crisis (GFC), 2, 3, 22–24, 30, 31, 88, 114
Goods and Services Tax (GST), 11, 21, 26, 30, 37, 47–63, 82, 83
government bonds, 172, 174
government consumption, 5
Government guaranteed bonds, 93
government securities, 155, 156, 160–162, 166, 168, 174

Green revolution, 87
Gross Domestic Product, 5, 7–9, 12, 15, 16, 18, 19, 21–27, 29, 47, 48, 58, 63, 65, 66, 88, 89, 98, 114, 115, 119, 130–132, 134, 141, 155, 163, 164, 173, 176, 186, 188, 189, 211, 214–216
Gross Enrolment Ratio (GER), 220
gross fiscal deficit (GFD), 15, 21–23, 170

harmful tax competition, 54
heads of income, 11
horizontal imbalances, 57, 58

import parity, 91–92
import substitution, 87
income effect, 163, 191
Indian fiscal year, 3, 8, 12–19, 23–31
Indirect Tax Enquiry Report, 13
Indirect taxes, 2, 11–14, 19–21, 26, 28, 35–83
Inequality, 12, 42–44, 64, 188, 192–193
inflation, 1, 3, 6, 7, 23, 29, 31, 114, 122, 123, 159–160, 168, 202
in-kind transfers, 130, 183–187, 191, 193, 195, 202–203, 205
input tax credit, 13, 20, 30, 53–55
interest, 1, 4, 5, 6, 11, 15, 17, 18, 21, 24, 26–28, 33, 59, 74, 93, 100, 123, 147, 148, 157, 159, 161–163, 166–168, 172–174, 175, 177, 178, 181
investment, 1, 2, 5–7, 12, 15, 19, 27, 31, 43–44, 75, 88, 90, 101, 104, 106, 114, 115, 123, 131, 141, 148, 149, 172, 181, 198, 211, 213–216, 220, 222, 223

Kelkar committee, 27, 57
Kisan Vikas Patra, 181
Kothari Commission, 213

labour supply, 184, 190, 191
labour force participation, 190, 191
Land Acquisition Act (LAA) of 1894, 139–145
Land Acquisition Act, 2013, 139, 144
Liquefied Petroleum Gas (LPG), 27, 92–94, 96, 98–100, 134, 196, 198, 204
Lok Sabha, 138
Long-Term Fiscal Policy, 14

Mahatma Gandhi National Rural Employment Guarantee Act (MNREGA), 23, 76, 125, 144
manufacturing value added tax (MANVAT), 13
marginal rate, 13
Minimum Alternative Tax (MAT), 20, 26
Ministry for Renewable Energy, 105, 107
Ministry of Coal, 100
Ministry of Power, 103
Ministry of Social Justice and Empowerment, 214
Ministry of Tribal Affairs, 214
modified value added tax (MODVAT), 13, 20
Monetary policy, 1, 114, 155, 156, 159–163, 166, 172–174, 177, 180, 181
Multidimensional Poverty Index (MPI), 211
multinational oil companies, 92

National Advisory Council (NAC), 128, 129, 142
National Education Policy, 213
National Food Security Act, 2013, 145
National Hydro Power Corporation (NHPC), 103

National Saving Certificates, 181
National Thermal Power Corporation (NTPC), 103, 107
Nationalization, 100, 103
Natural gas, 55, 93, 99, 100, 108
NDA Government, National Democratic Alliance (NDA), 3, 28, 29, 32, 100, 108, 139, 142, 148–150
net exports, 5, 6
Neyveli Lignite Corporation, 103
Nicholas Kaldor, 12
NITI Aayog, 10, 75, 83, 86, 135
non-conventional and renewable energy, 89
North Eastern Electric Power Corporation, 103
Nuclear Power Corporation, 103

Oil and Natural Gas Commission (ONGC), 93
Oil Co-ordination Committee, 92
oil price shock, 87, 92
oil-marketing companies (OMCs), 27, 92–94, 96, 98, 100, 103, 108
Oportunidades, 186, 190, 192
origin-based tax, 53
over recoveries, 92

*Panchayati Raj*, 36
Pareto-efficiency, 140
Pareto-superiority, 184
peak rate, 20
personal income tax, 13, 18, 19, 24–26, 28, 29, 34, 59
Planning Commission (PC), 10, 12, 37, 63, 69–75, 76, 79, 83, 86, 104, 117, 142, 197, 201,
portfolio managers, 159
primary and secondary market for government securities, 156
primary balance, 5, 8, 9, 18, 25
primary deficit, 5, 33, 47
private consumption, 5
private sector, 1, 2, 7, 12, 19, 27, 92, 104, 131, 140, 141, 160
pro-cyclical, 8, 9, 18, 19, 24, 30
producer subsidies, 91, 109
PROGRESA, 186, 189–190, 192–194
provident funds, 164, 165
public debt, 2, 7, 17, 30, 31, 155, 156, 160, 164–167, 171, 172
Public Debt Management Agency (PDMA), 29, 170, 173, 181
public distribution systems (PDS), 90, 113, 146, 187
public goods, 64, 75, 79, 140, 141, 151
Public Provident Fund (PPF), 166, 176, 181
public purpose, 140, 141, 144, 152
public sector, 3, 12, 27, 29, 31, 87, 90, 93, 173, 174, 177, 178, 181

railway budget, 100
*Rashtriya Madhyamik Shiksha Abhiyan* (RMSA), 213, 223
real interest rates, 1
reserve funds, 164, 165, 167
revenue expenditures, 3–4, 10, 15, 17, 18, 21, 25–27, 69, 72, 74, 87
revenue receipts, 4, 33, 61, 67, 69, 87
Right to Information (RTI) Act, 142, 144
rights-based economic approach, 139
risk assessment, 157
rural electrification, 90, 101

Saikia Committee, 213
Sales tax, 11, 13, 20, 47, 57, 85
Schedule Castes (SC), 145, 147, 219, 224
Schedule Tribes (ST), 145, 147, 219, 224
Secondary Education Commission, 212
securities transaction tax (STT), 11, 20

seigniorage, 4–7, 33
service tax, 11, 20, 24, 26, 28–30, 53–55, 60
Sixth Pay Commission, 24
small savings, 164–166, 167, 176, 181
solar power, 106, 107
sovereign wealth funds, 33
spatial inequality, 44
Special Category states, 63, 69, 70, 72, 86
Special Economic Zone (SEZ) Act, 140–141
Specific duties, 13, 34
State Electricity Boards (SEBs), 101, 103
State List, 36
State power utilities, 99, 101, 103–106
stimulus packages, 24
subsidies, 4, 17, 18, 21, 24–27, 30–32, 87–110, 114, 115, 131, 132, 134, 135, 139, 144, 183, 198, 222
subvention, 104
surplus management, 1

tariff structure, 14
tax administration, 19, 21, 30, 34, 55, 57–59
tax brackets, 13, 19
tax deduction at source (TDS), 34
tax evasion, 13, 20, 31, 59
tax incentives, 19, 20, 30,
tax policy, 1, 12, 18, 19, 26, 30
tax rate, 7–9, 12, 13, 18, 19, 29, 31, 34, 56, 59
tax reforms, 3, 19–21, 31, 32, 35–83
Tax Reforms Committee, 19
tax revenue to GDP, 12
technology development, 20

under recoveries, 92–96, 98, 100, 115, 134,
Union List, 36
Unique Identification Authority of India (UIDAI), 194, 197, 198, 200
Universal Elementary Education (UEE), 213, 218
University Education Commission, 212
UPA government, United Progressive Alliance (UPA), 138–150, 153, 194
US Treasury borrowing advisory committee, 162

Value Added Tax (VAT), 11, 13, 19,20, 30, 31, 47, 53–55, 57, 58, 60,85, 86
vertical imbalance, 57, 58

wind power, 106
Working Group on Secondary Education, 213

youth literacy rate, 216, 217, 218, 223

zero-rated, 53
zero-tax companies, 20